Border Patrols

To Jenshan,
With much love,

Richard
20.9.04

The Politics of Sexuality Group
Cultural Studies, Birmingham

David Abdi
Louise Curry
Debbie Epstein
Marion Hamm
Vasilis Ikonomides
Richard Johnson
Adrian Kear
Mary Kehily
Libby Kerr
Máirtín Mac an Ghaill
Anoop Nayak
Peter Redman
Deborah Lynn Steinberg
Shruti Tanna

This book arises out of four years of discussion
and writing by the Politics of Sexuality Group.
All the people listed have made
significant contributions to this project.

Border Patrols

Policing the Boundaries of Heterosexuality

Edited by

Deborah Lynn Steinberg,

Debbie Epstein

and Richard Johnson

CASSELL

For a catalogue of related titles
in our Sexual Politics/Global Issues list
please write to us at the address below:

Cassell
Wellington House
125 Strand
London WC2R 0BB

PO Box 605
Herndon
VA 20172

First published 1997

British Library Cataloguing-in-Publication Data
A catalogue record for this book is available from the British Library.

ISBN 0-304-33478-2 (hardback)
     0-304-33479-0 (paperback)

Typeset by Ben Cracknell Studios
Printed and bound in Great Britain by Biddles Ltd, Guildford and
King's Lynn

Contents

for Jill

*and in acknowledgement of the tradition
of group work from the
Centre for Contemporary Cultural Studies,
Birmingham, of which this project is a part*

Contested Borders, Contingent Lives:
An Introduction[1]

Richard Johnson

The Politics of Sexuality Group

The Politics of Sexuality Group – the complicated collective author of this book – started meeting in October 1991. At the beginning it consisted of people who were connected with the Department of Cultural Studies, at the University of Birmingham, as teachers, students or ex-students. Patterns of membership and involvement shifted over the five years. People ended their periods of study in Birmingham, got jobs or moved back to Germany or Greece or London. Although the first reason for convening the group was to support a collective project on schooling and sexuality organized by Debbie Epstein and myself, members were conscious from the beginning of the tradition of sub-group work in and around the Centre for Contemporary Cultural Studies (as it then was). These groups had usually begun as reading and support groups but had often gone on to collective research and publication. Of course, the group soon acquired a momentum and programme of its own only loosely related to the schooling and sexuality project. Its work went through three main phases.

In the first phase we were preoccupied with autobiographical memory work on questions of sexual identity. We borrowed and developed the method of 'memory work' from a previous CCCS Group, the Popular Memory Group of the early to mid-1980s.[2] Memory work consisted of the writing of short autobiographical fragments around the active remembering of particular episodes, chosen for their relevance to a group theme. Other conventions were to seek to recall details rather than generalities, and to try to convey the emotions of the time. In the discussion and analysis that followed authors were asked to talk about the significance of the episode and its telling for their identities today.[3]

During the academic year 1991–92 we worked on two story sequences. The first concerned our relationships to lesbian and gay identities. It was chosen in part because of the importance of the homo/hetero division in contemporary sexual discourse, not least in positioning members of the group. This particular boundary remained central to the 'borderlands' we explored. The theme for the second sequence was formative moments in our own sexual identities. This allowed us to explore questions of the composition and recomposition, and the relative stability and fluidity of sexual categories at the level of our own 'contingent lives'.

Throughout the history of the group, though with differing intensities, we also read and discussed key texts in the explosion of political-theoretical work on sexuality and identity, especially the different variants of 'queer theory' (Butler, 1990, 1993; Bristow, 1989; Dollimore, 1991; Dyer, 1989; Fletcher, 1989; Foucault, 1988; Gough, 1989; Modelski, 1991; Rich, 1983; Wittig, 1992). In retrospect, it was this double programme – autobiographical writing, with its critical reflection and cross-border dialogues, and reading in the theories of sexuality – which was so excitingly generative in the early and middle phases of the project.

The second phase of the work was dominated by discussions that followed the decision to do a book together. We took an early decision not to produce a unified text with a single authorial voice, but to produce individual, joint or group articles which shared a frame of reference and engaged in dialogue with each other. This was symptomatic of the way we were handling differences within the group itself. Dialogues were particularly intense in this second phase. They crystallized a shared language and conceptual framework, including the central metaphor of 'border patrols'.

My own notes of meetings suggest that a book was first discussed in May 1992. The book was the main item on the agenda at the beginning of the academic year in October 1992. At around this time, several members had to leave and we sought out new members. By November we were organizing sessions around meetings of authorial sub-groups within the larger group and around progress reports and first ideas. There was much excited and sometimes wild discussion about forms of representation and some conscious experimentation with different ways of writing. Some of our more daring ideas did not unfortunately survive the vicissitudes of authorship or group process – a commitment for example to utopian fiction writing as a way of opening out possibilities towards the end of the volume or to a sequence of 'Letters I did not send' as a way of dealing with 'unfinished business'. Nor was the memory work we produced in the first phase used directly in the volume – though its traces are often present. What did survive was a commitment to a variety of ways of writing – a certain crossing of generic borders (which are also policed) as well.

It is important to insist that this is not a book of academic essays with some poetry and autobiography tacked on. In fact the academic/other distinction isn't at all helpful in describing the book. It contains a wide range of genre including critical media analysis (Chapters 2 and 4), the ethnography of school (Chapter 6), the deconstruction of public discourses and professional practices (Chapters 3 and 4), psycho-analytic readings (of film in Chapter 10 and of public discourse in Chapter 4), reflexive auto/biography (Chapters 7 and 9) and poetry in more or less autobiographical modes (Chapters 5 and 9). Auto-biography (including autobiographical poetry) was central to the generation of our categories and some shared political sensitivities in phase two of the work. These then informed the different writing projects.

Though the two poem sequences in this volume are very different, both aim to be analytical, explanatory and 'intellectual' as well as about feelings, personal experiences, metaphor and image. We would also argue that the modes of reflective autobiography and of ethnography-with-the-ethnographer-left-in are best thought of as adjacent or even continuous genres, so that it is often hard to say where the analysis of the Self ends and the encounter with Others' worlds begins. Certainly, autobiography may be as analytical and theoretically organized as a competent ethnographic account. Our chapters are placed in an order that encourages such comparisons and we hope our readers will make up their own minds about these claims.

By the spring and early summer of 1993 a fairly stable list of contributions – including some from people not involved in group discussions – had emerged. After we had secured the contract with Cassell, a third phase in the history of the group began. This was the most difficult phase for a number of reasons. In any writing project, there is a moment when pragmatic closure has to take over from dialogue, the product from the process. This moment coincided with the unavoidable geographical dispersion of the group which made it impossible to meet on a regular basis. (The earlier routine had been weekly or fortnightly.) Some of the chapters planned for the book were, for different reasons, not completed.[4] There was, for a period, a distinct loss of group identity which we had to struggle to recapture. The appointment of three of us as 'editors', something we had previously assumed would be done by the whole group, was part of this necessary pragmatism.

While the group retained a strong collective identity, especially in the first and second phases, discussion, sometimes on key theoretical texts, sometimes on members' stories, sometimes on chapter drafts or ideas, was a dynamic in the work. Dialogues were always wide-ranging and sometimes unfocused, but two themes tended to recur. Since these became the themes which dominate this book, I discuss them in turn below.

Key themes I : the critique of heterosexuality

The first theme was the critique of heterosexuality, with particular emphasis on its hegemonic or 'compulsory' character. From my own point of view, as a man with strong past and present investment in heterosexual relations, I experienced the questioning here as hard and sometimes difficult to take. I understand well now that this was to do with my own reading of the group's dialogues. The questions we posed intersected very powerfully with events in my own life. I think this was so, in different ways, for us all. Actually, the questions were put carefully, as much out of pain as hatred or anger.

Is heterosexuality by definition oppressive? Do heterosexual relations necessarily subordinate women, privilege straight men and oppress lesbians and gay men? If we can imagine a world where there was no gender power, no gender as a major social difference, would 'heterosexuality' exist, or indeed, 'lesbian' or 'gay'? How, in the here and now, do forms of power within heterosexuality work? In what ways is heterosexuality oppressive? Why are men misogynistic? Why are they violent towards women? Why are men sexually abusive? What is the relation between heterosexuality and gender inequalities? How far are relations of possession/dispossession in the sexual sphere central to gender and to other inequalities more generally?

Public debates about heterosexuality today often seem to be polarized around opposed tendencies. There is a strong and fully justified impetus to render heterosexuality visible to critical scrutiny and, to make it, in some sense, politically accountable. This agenda often (not always) comes from people who identify as lesbian, gay or 'queer' and understand very well the often horrific consequences of the presumption of heterosexual 'normality'. The critique of heterosexuality is also pursued as a deepening or extension of a feminist politics of gender. There is some continuity with earlier feminist critiques of patriarchy, but also some significant differences. The newer critiques of heterosexuality are attentive to differences and conflicts between women, and to the force of other forms of oppression. There is a strong interest indeed in the social, cultural and psychic relays and reinforcements between the heterosexual matrix and other forms of power. Some of the key theoretical developments here have been around the (non-reductive) connection between heterosexuality and 'gender trouble', and the radical instabilities and gender-laden policing of the hetero/homo distinction itself (Butler, 1990).

At the same time there has been a strong tendency to seek positives in heterosexual relations, especially from the point of view of women (and some men) who identify as heterosexual and feminist. In particular there is an attempt to construct a positive version of heterosexual sexuality or heterosexual sex. There are different versions of this current, more or less consciously political and more or less radical in their implications. It is possible to seek improvements in heterosexual relationships, while leaving the larger structural inequalities of gender and sexuality in place. Reconstructing heterosexual relations is indeed a revolutionary project: it involves a decentring of mainstream sexualities and a giving up of privileges by straight men and by heterosexual people.

While it is men who are most often found defending heterosexual institutions, one not uncommon defence of heterosexuality is conducted by some feminists. These writers see a direct relation between earlier feminist identifications of sexuality as a key domain of male power and the need to assert the positives of heterosexuality for women. This riposte to so-called 'radical feminism' is based on a revaluation of critiques of power in sexual relations, sometimes explicitly drawing on an earlier debate around sado-masochism within lesbian relationships (e.g. Segal, 1995). Here, it is argued, erotic domination and abandonment can be re-evaluated as a form of consensual play. Other writers explore the erotic consequences of strategies of gender equalization, including the re-working of psychic relations of recognition, to make them more 'mutual', less ordered around possession and dispossession (e.g. Hollway, 1995). These debates, on either side and neither, are strongly influenced by psychoanalytic theory and a contemporary interest in dialogic or dialectical views of identity. Notions of recognition, mutual or otherwise, are central here. In feminist debates an important starting point has been Jessica Benjamin's work on the dialectics of erotic domination, and especially her account of recognition and its failure in sado-masochistic relations.[5]

Often, in the public sphere (at conferences, for example)[6] this 'debate' seems locked into a bitter and intransigent replaying of older conflicts. Powerfully remembered past struggles acquire strongly imaginary contents when judged against political alignments in the present. A similar dynamic was sometimes present within the Politics of Sexuality Group, though articulated from different points of view, not primarily as a conflict between feminists. Quite often, for example, I found myself defending the project of transformed, equalized and 'non-compulsory' heterosexual relations against a project which I imagined to be critical of heterosexual desire as such, privileging a gay or lesbian sensitivity. On these occasions I could be angry, defensive, even paranoid. On one occasion, after a discussion of child sexual abuse and heterosexuality, I wrote in my diary:

> My overwhelming feeling at the end of the Sexuality Group meeting was that I would never entrust this group with accounts of my own actual abusiveness . . . After all, if they will blame me for abuses I'm not personally responsible for, what will they do to me/think of me for my actual abuses? (16 November 1992)

What is interesting in retrospect is how I ascribed powerful imaginary positions to the women in the group and also distanced myself from the men who rushed, it seemed to me, to disown their own more or less ambiguous heterosexual orientations, leaving me exposed. Yet venturing into the discussion of personal sexual abuse within the context of a mixed group (in gender and sexual terms) was a most courageous, painful and creative bid for recognition and at the same time an important move for the politics of the group. We were indeed being asked: So why does this thing happen? And what are you going to do about it?

It seems that what often happens in such exchanges is a curious changing of places or inversion. In the minds of those who are challenged, the dominant positions – here heterosexuality and masculinity – seem threatened with annihilation. The fact that they are overwhelmingly dominant in public discourse and institutional arrangements is lost sight of. The usual relations of power are turned, it seems, upside down. This temporary and subjective re-experiencing of relations of power may have very different outcomes. It can lead to the negation of the original critique of the dominant categories. This forgetting and its inversion can then be woven into the personal and political strategies of those who have most to lose from change. The problem shifts: not *my* power and oppressiveness but that of the Other who is then typically named in public discourses as 'radical feminist', 'strident aggressive lesbian' or 'militantly gay'.

At the same time, risk-taking stories of the kind told in the Politics of Sexuality Group open up the possibility of change in both dominant and subordinated categories and, indeed, in the terms in which sexual identities and dichotomies are defined and lived. Of course the paranoid defences and other closures never disappear and have to be handled, but I do think that the second dynamic, that opens up the possibility of dialogue and of personal and social change, became the *main* way of relating across these issues in the group. The particular conflict over child sexual abuse, for example, was in fact worked through in subsequent group meetings where the theme was revisited several times, and by meetings between individuals, including myself and Debbie Epstein who had written the original 'Unsent Letter to Jonathan'.

This avoidance of the disastrous deadlocks observable in other forums of debate was, possibly, the most important achievement of the group. The critique of heterosexuality as an institution need not evoke an overwhelming sense of personal threat and subsequent closure. The justice of the case is clear enough after all. Once this, rather than the common inversion, is focused on, it may reinforce the search for better ways. 'Better ways' was understood unevenly within the group of course. Often there was uncertainty about what it meant. For some it involved bringing to an end the heterosexual/gender matrix, not by punishing those who currently identify as heterosexual, but by working to make these and other sexual distinctions irrelevant. Sometimes this position was met by, or converged with, a commitment to change the relations of force within heterosexuality to benefit women (and ultimately men?) and change its compulsory status. To what ultimate social destinations such a politics will lead is often unclear. The most important immediate consequence, however, was that our different positions, or the ways we held them, allowed the dialogues to continue. No one was forced to go away. Consequently group discussion fed powerfully into our writing: certainly it fed powerfully into mine.

Of course such challenges and the critical frameworks from which they arise aren't just intellectual constructs. They may also aid the reinvestments of desire and pleasure which are a necessary (though not sufficient) condition if sexual relationships are to change and not just, in Debbie Epstein's and Deborah Lynn Steinberg's phrase, be 'fixed quickly'. Challenges to oppressive or abusive forms of heterosexuality and the search for transformations in sexual relations are key axes in this book, no doubt with all their contradictions and problems. As Peter Redman puts it:

> There is an inherent ambivalence in heterosexual men writing even 'critically' about heterosexual masculinities. On the one hand, such writing may open up possibilities for change; on the other, it may also expose contradictions, vulnerabilities and previously 'naturalized' processes of subordination simply to recoup these for reconfigured but still hegemonic relations of gender and sexuality. There is probably no way out of such double-binds, either at a personal or a public level.

Key themes II: reproducing / deconstructing sexual categories

The second major theme in discussions was the relative stability or fluidity of sexual categories. This theme reverberates through the published literatures on sexual theory, through the rival strategies of movements and through everyday life dilemmas. In the broader culture, indeed, there is a heightened clash of frameworks. As stressed in Chapter 3, there is a revival of frameworks in scientific and everyday discourses which fix and naturalize sexual categories. On the other hand, the continued drive of much gay, lesbian, feminist, 'cultural' and generally 'critical' theory is to stress the radical social constructedness and contingency of sexual categories – the multiplicity of sexual identities, their contradictoriness, their instability, the importance of circumstances and processes in determining outcomes, the sense in which identity is always deferred and 'impossible'. These tendencies are most fully expressed in variants of 'queer theory'. Queer theory is linked to forms of politics which deliberately seek to break down the fixed boundaries between the hetero/homo, gender and other binaries, to multiply sexual categories and ultimately dissolve them, insisting that 'queer' itself is not some bounded community, or not only so, but is 'everywhere'.[7]

This theoretical difference is not related to liberal, conservative or radical positions on the politics of sex and gender in any simple way. Lesbian and gay activists, for example, are divided on issues around the ontology of sexual identity – whether gay identities are inborn or acquired. There are important differences too around the strategic value – both as resistance and as control – of the arguments from nature and from culture.[8] There are differences of emphasis too within socio-cultural theories of sexual identity. In particular, the 'queering' of political frameworks is often in conflict with forms of feminist and lesbian and gay politics. One strand of this is inherited from the 1970s. It constructed women, gay men and lesbians as political identities and 'communities', with relatively homogeneous cultures of resistance and identification and relatively stable interests in common. Other strands are critical of 'queer', while espousing a similar sustained critique of binary oppositions and of universalizing and homogenizing categories.

Tensions around the relative stability/fluidity of sexual categories were clearly present in the group. We were all attracted to much in contemporary academic writing about sexuality, including the informing frameworks of (variants of) poststructuralist and psychoanalytic theory. But there was also a self-definingly 'materialist' impulse in the group that resisted what were seen as premature strategies of 'deconstruction'. It is all very well, this argument went, to deconstruct the key binaries of sex and gender, but what if major asymmetries remain in place? These inequalities cannot be reduced to cultural forms, discourses or even to 'performativity'. If inequalities remain, aren't subordinated groups robbed of necessary defences and forms of resistance? Deconstructive moves may disorganize the project of organizing alternative gay lifestyles – forms of commemoration and grieving for instance, necessary as alternative sources of social recognition. Informing this argument is the belief that it is never easy to slip across the borderline, nor is individual transgression all that significant in the overall relations of power. Sexual and gender inequalities are not just matters of 'identity'. They are inscribed in regularly repeated institutional practices, and patterns of work and domestic life. It is one thing to transgress in terms of self-image or lifestyle; another to construct sustainable ways of living for large numbers of people.

There was polarization on these issues in the group, especially when radically deconstructive theses were proposed or starkly pessimistic scenarios implied! Typically, I think we held these theoretical poles – in shorthand the 'materialist' and the 'postmodern' – together and in tension, working across them. On the whole, theoretical positions did not coincide in any simple way with social positionings. Most of us moved between different positions, or came to see new points of view. There was some tendency towards an alignment of gender differences with the materialist/poststructuralist opposition, though generation or age was also important here. Significantly, the men in the group were more likely to understand their own experience in terms of some version of the postmodern themes. For several men this included personal ambivalences around the hetero/homo divide. This was expressed through stories of homoerotic desire, but also through other identifications with gay or queer – close friendships, alignments of style and performance, intellectual borrowings, political alliances. This involved taking a distance from 'straight' heterosexual masculinities, even where the question, as in Chapter 7, was why/how/in what sense did I become heterosexual?

Minimally this meant that the men in the group were less likely to respond in defensive ways to the critique of heterosexuality than if their sex-gender identities had been unqualified in these ways. This distancing from hegemonic masculinities and their political forms was an indication, at the personal level, of broader political positions. It is also worth pointing out another absence in the group – the politics of the 'men's movement'. We were all interested in masculinity as a problem. Some of us made a point of researching and writing in critical, feminist-influenced modes, with other men (see, for example, Chapter 7). Some of us have also worked intellectually with or in relation to 'men's studies'. We agree with R. W. Connell's argument, however, that you cannot build an anti-oppressive politics around the interests of men as Men (Connell, 1995: especially Chapter 10). This implies the need, as in this project, to make cross-gender and other alliances. This was possible because the men in the group, while differing in frameworks, choices and life circumstances, did share a critical, feminist-influenced orientation towards masculinities, including our own. It is doubtful, indeed, whether the group would have been sustainable if we had organized 'as men' in relation to it.

On the other, 'materialist' side of this dialogue there was also room for manoeuvre. Aside from the interest which we all shared in contemporary sexual theory, the preferred version of materialist or social analysis was itself of a complex and qualified kind. We shared the project of developing an 'anti-oppressive politics' or a 'complex anti-oppressive politics' as the political foundation for our work. This meant a commitment to feminist and lesbian and gay struggles, but within the context of other forms of oppression, especially those of class and 'race'. Again, for reasons I do not altogether understand, another familiar blocked path, the playing off of one oppression against another, the cancelling out of sexual struggles by issues of race for example, was avoided. Debbie Epstein's study of the politics of education, race and sexuality in Hackney (Chapter 8) illustrates how disastrous (for both causes) such competition can be. Our shared position is that all sources of oppression are important and that they are interwoven in ways that only close empirical study can show. Both the Jane Brown study and Deborah Lynn Steinberg's analysis of the eugenic heterosexism of *in vitro* fertilization (IVF) (Chapter 3) are particularly concerned with this interweaving.

'Border patrols' as metaphor and framework

The outcome of these discussions was a theoretical model which was agreed as the book's framework. It was our attempt to combine in some syncretic outcome the differences within the group. At first, we thought we would write this framework into the structure of the book itself as a three-part division. In the meantime it became a kind of 'charter' which enabled us to work together.

Our starting point is that sexual categories and divisions – 'borders' in terms of our central metaphor – are multiply oppressive constructions. They are oppressive because they are invested with power and involve unequal conditions on either side of the borderline. Some of these oppressions are directly related to the domain of sexuality and gender. They hinge on the privileging of those who live and benefit so to speak in male-gender-land or on heterosexual territory, or function most confidently on these sides of the borderline. Sex/gender relations, however, also operate as nodes of power which attract or condense other power relations.

Once we have grasped how power invests borders of this kind (we intend both the military and the capitalist connotations), and creates oppressive relations, we can stress that borders – or fixed and exclusive identities – are also themselves a problem. They carve up the spaces of identity in ways that are unlivable without high personal and social costs. In gender relations it is not only the relations of power between men and women that are a problem; it is also the way in which masculinities and femininities are constructed as separated categories that describe and circumscribe individual persons. Against this the main critical tendency of contemporary identity theory is to stress the relational character of identities, including interrelations which operate in an inner or psychic space. Opposed identities like men/women and hetero/homo are not only constructed in relation to each other, they always carry, in their inner configurations, some version (fantasy, image, imago) of the Other. The Other which is inside the Self, which partially constitutes it indeed, is a focus of much psychic energy, feelings both of disgust and desire, which, of course, have major consequences for actual persons 'outside' who become the targets of these feelings. Nor are these processes only inter-subjective or individual. Paranoia, phobia, panic, Othering, powerful desires to possess and to be like can all be identified in the forms of public culture – in scientific discourses (Chapters 3 and 4), in forms of 'news' (Chapter 4), in film (Chapter 10) and in other popular cultural representations. These theorizations of identity, which draw strongly on schools of psychoanalytic theory, are further elaborated and applied in several chapters in the book (see especially Chapters 4, 6, 7, 9 and 10).

There are many contemporary sexual practices which signal the unlivability of the conventional divisions of gender and sex. These include transgender, bi-sexuality and some forms of cross-dressing. More telling because of their ubiquity are the everyday ambivalences and half-articulated desires that show the limits of rigid sex/gender identities. One version of sexual politics is the deliberate pushing of such ambivalences into overt transgression, designed in part to shock. Where espoused in the group such strategies tended to produce strong reactions. Difficulties certainly arise when the radical stress on difference as contingent and constructed (and therefore de-constructable) boldly leaps over the first key thesis on difference as power. Transgressive or deconstructive performances often have unpredictable effects on the relations of power, especially since there are many such fronts at any one scene of battle. There is a constant play between the rigidity of sexual boundaries and the powers invested, unequally, on either side of them. Thus, for example, the fixed hetero/homo division is acted out, again and again, to create hierarchies between young men, as more or less conforming to the hegemonic norms of manliness. As Anoop Nayak and Mary Jane Kehily show in this volume (Chapter 6), the accusation of being gay carries more than the charge of the monster homosexuality itself – it also signifies any way of being a young man that is insufficiently masculine or laddish, or too close to the adjacent boundary of the feminine. As Nayak and Kehily put it: 'homophobic performances are . . . closely interconnected with the struggle for masculinities'.

It follows that to shift borders, to challenge the conventional lines, is indeed to disturb (and potentially to re-order) the forms of subjectivity and the social powers invested on either side. Maginot Lines and Berlin Walls do not crumble at a single deconstructive performance. But we should not ignore the accumulating power of individuals and groups, who, dispersed but acting on similar lines, start to live their lives in ways that transgress the existing divisions. Mass migrations from the 'East' did play a major part in a hugely significant boundary change.

In these first two steps of our argument, then, key tensions in our own dialogues were rendered into resources we could use for the shared project. The stress on the regulation and forcible reproduction of sexual identities and on their instabilities can be read as two sides of the same argument, ultimately of the same contemporary historical conjuncture. It is because the categories are so unstable that the policing is so intense. It is here that the whole spatial metaphor of border seemed (after much disagreement) so apt to our case. Borders are heavily defended lines drawn between territories, categories or identities. But they are closely watched and well-defended precisely because they are points of danger for one or other or both of the territories or identities involved. The metaphor suggests that both of the typical moves in contemporary theorization of identity are indispensable – the materialist insistence on matrices of power and their ability to reproduce themselves in relatively stable but complex ways and the postmodern, poststructuralist and psychoanalytic stress on instabilities and change, most radically on 'the necessary error of identity' as Judith Butler puts it (Butler, 1993, citing Spivak, p. 229). In particular cases – the border between lesbian and gay, and straight identities for example – the intensity of policing can be shown to be related to the levels of incursion or subversion. The heightening of homophobia in Britain today – on the streets, in the press, within the Conservative policy-making élites, in the military, the Anglican church and Parliament – is directly related to lesbian, gay and queer assertions in pressure groups, street styles, some forms of media and in popular culture more generally.

Any adequate account of sexual categories and gender oppressions has therefore to grasp both sides of this process: the work involved in drawing and redrawing sexual boundaries, but also the contradictions and instabilities that make this work of power so necessary in the first place. If we attend closely to the processes of policing themselves, we can also see instabilities inscribed there too, as though the borders themselves are shaking under the patrolling tread. In relatively more open forms of policing that frame a popular or personal voice by forms of expertise – like chat shows for instance (see Chapter 2) – the instabilities are glaring and the contradictions gross.

If the borderlands between categories are, potentially at least, especially creative spaces, it is important to stress that old problems may be reproduced there in new forms. Variants of the dominant identities may set up enclaves of their own. Peter Redman and Máirtín Mac an Ghaill's account of the genesis of 'mental masculinity' (Chapter 7) is a good example here, especially poignant and telling for a group of academic women and men. Though experienced as a protest and defence against macho or laddish masculinities, investment in mental competencies is a by no means rare form of masculine competition and domination. In any case as R. W. Connell argues, not all forms of masculinity are hegemonic, but many more are 'complicit', or benefit, without really trying, from a patriarchal dividend (Connell, 1985, pp. 79–80). As Debbie Epstein puts it, 'Challenges to normative versions of heterosexuality are frequently incorporated within changing versions of what it means to be heterosexual' (Chapter 8). Even where there is a desire to be different or oppositional, it is not easy to find a genuinely transformative space.

This discussion of conservative or reproductive defences and more transformative strategies is the third stage in our argument. It is not easy to separate out conservative and transformative strategies. Indeed there are many instances in which the reproduction of boundaries is an absolutely necessary defence for the most subordinated categories and where some spectacular transgression is simply unwise and self-defeating. The difficulty and danger of coming out as a lesbian or gay teacher or student in a school is a case in point. Even so, often in the face of our own pessimism, we kept a space for the search for transformative strategies, not as a way of standing free from the everyday entrapments, but as a way of working through them to hope, energy, solidarity and equalization. Judith Butler, developing her theory of the 'performativity' of sex–gender categories and differences, puts it like this:

> Performativity describes this relation of being implicated in that which one opposes, this turning of power against itself to produce alternative modalities of power, to establish a kind of political contestation that is not a 'pure' opposition, a 'transcendence' of contemporary relations of power, but a difficult labour of forging a future from resources inevitably impure. (Butler, 1993, p. 241).

Although, on the whole, we do not explore this 'difficult labour' in this book, the movement of our argument – from power-invested differences, to their instabilities and policing, to defensive, recuperative or transformative strategies – does strongly suggest that the more dispersed or spontaneous models of political action are not enough, even in so decentralized an area as this. It is important, for example, to start to construct and campaign around new forms of 'family'. By 'family' we mean networks and nodes of support, solidarity, friendship, intimacy and nurturing that can better survive (and maybe check) the larger social and environmental disintegrations of the day. One condition of success is that such forms must not seal individuals into narrowed and prescribed roles as 'proper' men or women, nor draw that heavily policed procreative line between queer and straight ways of desiring and of living. Similarly, if there are to be collective agencies that will nurture such alternatives, they will have to cross over the borderlines. To do this will require at least as strenuous, protracted and determined a process of negotiation as has formed the modest project of this volume.

Policing boundaries?

We have not grouped our studies according to the model I have just outlined, mainly because the moments of the model are hard to separate. If there is a logic in the order of our chapters, it is a movement from forms of public representation to 'contingent lives', from the analysis of key regulatory discourses to the ways in which sexual categories are formed and lived out at an everyday level. Not all the studies, however, were easily ordered in this sequence. The poems selected and collected as *Impedimenta,* for example, carry a strong sense of structural determinations and a painful sense of personal strategies of struggle. Similarly, the study of the Jane Brown case, though clearly about media policing, does come back to an individual – Jane Brown herself – and to the vile everyday realities of 'queerbashing'.

Where individual articles proved difficult to place, a desire to juxtapose in revealing ways took over. We wanted the last three chapters to be read in sequence: a study in 'compulsory heterosexuality' (Chapter 8), a study of a crisis in heterosexual masculinity (Chapter 9) and an account of some of the psychic processes involved in 'possessing' the Other (Chapter 10) . Similarly, the juxtaposition of Chapters 6 and 7 allows for comparisons of method (ethnography and auto/biography), and a double look at the sexual dynamics of schools. Generally, however, the earlier chapters discuss public discourses – media forms, professional codes and practices, scientific knowledges – and focus on 'policing', while the later chapters concentrate on individual lives, inner spaces and the ways in which sexual identities are formed, recognized and punished.

The particular interest of 'Love's Labours: Playing it Straight on the *Oprah Winfrey Show*' (Chapter 2) is, as its authors say, that this most popular of the chat shows 'both problematizes and normalizes the boundaries of heterosexuality'. It therefore represents, in the one essay, the double movement of our argument. The essay reviews the typical discourses of the programme, especially the discourse of therapy, and provides a close and critical reading of a particular episode. On the one hand, the programme and Oprah's own presence and performance have a strongly educational character, 'with a very explicit agenda of social responsibility and justice'. The programme regularly explores problematic areas in heterosexual relations including child sexual abuse and violence against women. On the other hand, Epstein and Steinberg show how, in its dominant discourses, especially those of an individualized therapy, the programme serves to reproduce the taken-for-granted legitimacy of heterosexual relations and of marriage as its dominant form.

Their reading of one particular episode shows how this works through interpersonal interaction in the studio. Some of the more abusive sides of masculine 'mental' behaviour towards women are on display here. At the same time, because there is no analysis, within the framework of the show, in terms of gender power and the compulsory nature of heterosexuality, the therapeutic expert and the show as a whole reproduce or worsen the contradictory situations they address. The analysis also shows how the preferred versions of heterosexual relations, particular forms of marriage and coupledom, have a specific class, racialized and national character – here middle-class, white and American. On the whole, then, the emphasis in this study is on the closing down of the possibilities for transformation that arise when the contradictions of heterosexuality are articulated and publicly aired in the absence of an analysis of power. Love's labours really are lost.

'Technologies of Heterosexuality: Eugenic Reproductions Under Glass' (Chapter 3) explores the ways in which the selective rationality central to *in vitro* fertilisation (IVF), other new reproductive technologies and genetic medicine generally constitutes a eugenic praxis that operates as a medico–moral (Mort, 1987) patrol of sexual boundaries. In tracing the grounds for the selection of IVF patients and of genetic screening in this context, Deborah Lynn Steinberg makes several key arguments. She suggests that the reproduction of hetero-sexuality constitutes both a eugenic objective in itself and a matrix through which ableist, classist and racist selections (more convention-ally associated with eugenics) are organized. Her research shows that selection on grounds of 'proper' heterosexuality and 'fit' heterosexual family is overt and rarely questioned by IVF practitioners. In contrast, these practitioners were clearly sensitive to and defensive about any suggestion that selections might be being made on overt racial grounds. Practitioners, then, made a clear distinction between acceptable and unacceptable selection, justifying the one, condemning the other, seemingly conscious of a discredited discourse of racial hygiene. Yet, as Steinberg demonstrates, an investment in 'fit families' on heterosexist grounds reinvests in a discourse which is implicitly and intrinsically racialized and classed. Indeed, as Steinberg argues, regardless of practitioner intentions, the selection of patients on overt heterosexist grounds recuperates the very miscegenation discourses historically (and explicitly) configured around ableist, classist and racist lines.

In the context of the book as a whole this chapter is our most intensive scrutiny of one particular way of patrolling the boundaries of heterosexuality. It is interesting to compare it with the other main study of scientific and medical discourse in the book (if we exclude therapy here), that is the discourse of venereology discussed in Chapter 4. Both studies show how sciences operate as forms of power/knowledge in ways that are particularly difficult to challenge from outside a scientific community. At the same time both studies show how sciences incorporate in their knowledges and in their practical operations quite profane, even commonsensical, popular beliefs, themselves often the product of past political hegemonies and ideologies. Nowhere is this more true than in matters to do with sexuality and gender. In these connections with popular knowledges the boundaries of the sciences themselves, despite much fierce self-disciplining, are most permeable. One difference between venereology and embryology, however, is that while the former is connected with public health practices, the latter (in the cases explored) are closely linked to clinical practice. This both provides further professional exemptions and responsibilities, but also involves a different construction of 'the natural'. One feature of technologies like *in vitro* fertilization is that they actively intervene in the bodies of women, changing and manipulating the nature and location of biological processes. At first sight, it seems very contradictory that such practices, which clearly reconstruct the 'biological' or 'natural', are accompanied by such deeply naturalized conceptions of gender and sexual relations. Or is conservative conformity to heterosexist criteria more or less consciously offered as legitimation for the radicalism of the intervention in female bodies? In any case it is often this combination of technological ambition and social conservatism that is so disturbing to critics of contemporary science, and should be to us all.

In another context the practice of producing human bodies under glass and through definite social relationships of power echoes the forms of possession (here by a largely male profession or, where women practitioners are involved, through an androcentric ethos) of women's persons and bodies, discussed elsewhere in this book: notably in Deborah Lynn Steinberg's poems and in the themes of incorporation and introjection (including physical ingestion) analysed by Adrian Kear in Chapter 10.

'Invasion of the Monstrous Others: Heterosexual Masculinities, the "AIDS Carrier" and the Horror Genre' (Chapter 4) takes a close look at the discourses and narratives which framed moral panics about the AIDS epidemic in the 1980s. It is one of two essays in this book which centre on the role of scientific (specifically medical) discourse in the policing of sexual boundaries. (See also the comparisons and similarities drawn with Chapter 5 later in this Introduction.) A central question here is why one set of scientific and medical discourses (those that focused on 'the AIDS carrier' as a threat to mainstream heterosexual society) predominated over others – discourses of viruses and 'safer sex' for instance.

There are three main explanatory moves. The first is to draw attention to the history of the venereological study of epidemics of sexually transmitted diseases. The figure of the 'AIDS carrier' as a promiscuous gay man found a familiar place in public-health discourse in the 1980s, a place at different times occupied by the prostitute, black immigrants or young single women. The second move in the argument is to draw attention to the convergences between scientific and political discourses – between venereology, as one relevant medical approach, and the sexual politics of the New Right and the Conservative press. The third and most complex move starts with noting the relation between venereological accounts, press narratives and the horror genre. The 'AIDS carrier' mobilizes many of the emotions and psychic processes which are set in train by the fantasy figure of the monster – of the vampire for instance, a sexually and psychically powerful figure also discussed in Chapter 10. The monster is the Other whose existence and predatory activity threatens all social and sexual boundaries, and indeed, seems to threaten the dissolution of identity itself. In particular, the monster in the shape of the actively sexual gay man is a powerful Other in the psychic dynamics of heterosexual masculinity. One of the chief conclusions of the study, in the context of this book, concerns the instability of heterosexual masculinity as a form of invested social identity, depending as it does on the repeated expulsion of homoerotic desire as threatening, disgusting but also as a source of fascination. The essay ends with some careful reflections on the possibilities of change in heterosexual masculinities and the importance of making visible both the constructedness and the anxieties and instabilities which popular representations both show and hide.

In the poem sequence 'Impedimenta: Dramaturgy of the Divine Offspring' each poem tells a story and there are significant differences between the poems, and especially between clusters of poems. At the same time, any selection of this kind from a larger body of writing is a construction, which produces its own meanings, and may change the sense of individual poems quite radically. These poems are not directly autobiographical. Indeed the use of mythical figures gives a strongly archetypal character to the stories told. The ancient Greek and modern Jewish references resonate also with the psychoanalytic narratives which are told more explicitly in other parts of this book and staged in a brief but cutting parody in the poem 'Theatrics and Melodrama'. There are stories of swallowing and ingesting the (female) Other, of recognition and especially misrecognition, of the Father's power, word and law, and of graphically misogynistic forms of introjection and incorporation (Chapter 10). There are stories of birth, death, resurrection and transmutation.

At the same time, most of the poems can be read as handling a similar pattern of experiences: of possession and dispossession; and of resisting both. The relations between possessor and possessed are strongly gendered, in regimes (like the myths themselves) which are clearly patriarchal. Viewed as 'theory' indeed, the poems consist of an extended analysis of the forms and experiences of gendered dispossession, in close up, and with the benefit of a tight and concrete emotional focus. This is often very painful (for this reader at least): the possessed is full of pain, on the one hand, in despair, but also filled with implacable wrath. The poems themselves seem to hit back, strike back, bite back, especially in their last lines. If this is doing theory, it is theory with the feelings left in, with a concentrated emotional focus indeed, so that we can read these poems, as having dominant or preferred *feelings* as well as structures of meaning.

Analytically, then, possession does take different forms here, often referencing sexuality but not limited to it. Possession is ownership or slavery. It is the subordination of the child. It is sexual violence. It is being used. It is being stopped or stilled. It is becoming a thing. And, especially, it is, or it involves, deep misrecognitions of the self by Others. The self is faced with the choice of conforming to the pattern of recognition or acceptance that is offered, cutting itself to fit a very self-denying or humiliating image or rebelling or running away and so losing this source of recognition entirely. In the poem 'Fear', it even seems that one's dreams can be possessed by another: does she dream someone else's inspiration? In the long central poem 'Still Life', a particular scene of misrecognition is revisited in a horrified and fearful remembrance. This stillness at the horror of cruelty or betrayal or at remembrance or anticipation of these things is a theme of other poems too.

There are, however, threads through the poems which are in tension with the dynamics of dispossession. There is a strong thread around the preservation of the self. The 'possessed' surprises and disturbs the 'possessor': of course, because the s/he does not really know her. There are unintended consequences: the birth of Athena does not turn out so well for the monstrous Father–God Zeus (Umbilicus, Creation Myth I). The refrain of the two linked 'Father Lamentations' expresses the double movement of oppression and its limitation in a single phrase – 'Do not mis/take her'. It also condenses a sexual imposition and the non-recognition or misrecognition which accompanies it. Similarly in other dreams she who is misrecognized, blamed or possessed dreams of being strong and really living ('Dreaming'), spits in the eye of her guardian

('Theatrics and Melodrama'), can name herself and her misrecognizer as cruel ('Still Life'), can write and write of freedom ('Possession'), can be born again and fall into her mother's hands ('Miriam's Letter') and in the final poem, most movingly of all, and in the shadow of horrific remembrances, 'tell you my body is myself' ('Work'). This complex and ambiguous poem with its powerful repeated negatives, manages both to put aside and to re-invoke each past horror with even its title making a holocaust reference 'Arbeit Mach Frei'. Is the final line a comment on strategies of resistance and their dominant emotional economies that can now be left behind? Is this what Impedimenta means?

Contingent lives?

There is a shift of emphasis in the passage from Chapters 2, 3 and 4 to Chapter 6. Although professional, political and media discourses do very powerfully police sexual boundaries, they are also activated at a popular, everyday level too. So far as sexual categories are concerned, it won't do to see professional knowledges as simply an imposition on the fluidities of the everyday. Some of the most unremitting and destructive forms of homophobia and misogyny are acted out in the street, in families and in schools.

'Masculinities and Schooling: Why Are Young men so Homophobic?' (Chapter 6) poses its key question through ethnographic work in two secondary schools. Here method shifts from the use of ('qualitative') questionnaires and the analysis of discourse (compare Chapter 3) to observation and interviews. The form of ethnographic analysis used by the authors. however, is distinctively concerned with cultural forms, especially with dramatic performance and with storytelling, so that any very clear distinction between 'textual' and other forms of analysis breaks down. It is by listening to, recording and analysing the accounts of girls and boys of homophobic episodes and performances that Anoop Nayak and Mary Jane Kehily show the ubiquity and ritual character, social consequences and subjective significance of school homophobias.

Like other studies, the chapter stresses the pervasiveness of homophobia in schoolboy cultures. It reveals a whole landscape of boundaries in which speaking or walking wrongly, or getting too interested in a sex education video, or admitting it, or being too academic or 'going [too] near him' is *ipso facto* evidence of gay identity, and a disqualification from manhood. Homophobia is understood here, however, not as a gratuitous or ignorant discrimination, easily remedied by school policies, but as a central aspect of the production of heterosexual identities and of forms of masculinity. Homophobic performances are 'self-convincing rituals', defences against the labels of peers to be sure, but also ways of handling the anxieties and the splittings produced by growing up a proper man. It is only by understanding such investments and the discriminatory behaviours they produce that students, teachers and others can intervene intelligently in these processes.

Chapter 7 'Educating Peter: The Making of a History Man' is also, among other things, a study of the hetero/homo boundary which takes schooling seriously as a site of identity. It shares some theoretical roots with Chapter 6, including a version of cultural studies which is thoroughly 'social' and empirical, but influenced by psychoanalytic traditions and, we might add, by analytically literate ways of reading.

There is, however, an important shift of methods here. The 'ethnographic' look or gaze, based on observation and reported observation, is quite an 'external' one, though it is possible (as in Chapter 6) to move to the 'inside' of observations to seek explanations of behaviour, which can then be reinterpreted. Writers of autobiography, including autobiographical poetry, however, are faced with the possibility and challenge of speaking more directly 'from the inside' (Redman and Mac an Ghaill, Chapter 7, quoting Dawson, 1994). They work with remembered thoughts and feelings. In this way, it is possible to make available the processes through which we produce ourselves as subjective agents, constrained and limited in the world but also creatively productive. This project of a self-reflexive auto/biography is pursued in Chapter 7. The fact that auto/biography was undertaken here with the help of a discussant and co-author, who also wrote his own stories, is a reminder that, methodologically, auto/biography need not be quite so 'auto'. The researching and writing of this essay indeed was closer to the model of 'memory work' – as a collaborative group-based process of remembering, writing, analysing and writing again – than autobiography as classically practised or understood.[10] The presence of an Other or Others in the process of research and writing must modify (and may also imperil) autobiographical reflection. At best, it may strengthen the reflexive self-analytical side of the process by inserting another point (or points) of view. This may be disturbing, but also very productive.

In this essay the critical reading of an auto/biographical story yields an account of investment in a particular form of masculinity which the authors call 'muscular intellectualness'. Muscular intellectualness appears in the story told, in the form of a teacher who was also an intellectual, but the analysis places 'John Lefevre' within the play of different masculinities in an all-boys school. The teacher was attractively different from the local masculine repertoire: the macho lads, the sportsmen, the scientists and indeed, Peter's 'high camp' friends. For particular reasons, these competing forms of masculinity did not offer an easy route to proper boyhood. The attraction to Peter of 'muscular intellectualness' can partly be understood in social or sub-cultural terms: it was the best route available to the future identity of 'student', a route which also asserted a form of heterosexual masculinity which in the sixth form at least, won some recognition. Such an analysis misses, however, the elements of anxiety, fear and desire which unconsciously motivate such identity work. As Peter Redman and Máirtín Mac an Ghaill argue a psychoanalytic perspective is important in grasping the force of homophobias in the school as one aspect of the dynamic psychic relations at work. In this account, as in Chapter 6 , school homophobia is understood as a sign of the instability of heterosexual masculine identities. In Chapter 7, the argument is taken further. Auto/biography allows the authors to consider the empirical potential of Lacanian theory which stresses the importance of identification with and desire for phallic power as an element in masculinities. From this point of view, Peter's identification with (and desire for) his teacher were moments in the reconfiguration of his masculinity which included a turn towards heterosexuality. This was not the culmination of a fixed developmental sequence, nor a wobble in indefinite change and flux, but the result of a particular contingent combination of social and psychic determinations.

This approach to heterosexual masculinities suggests a range of wider questions which the authors pose with caution. What are the relationships between psychic dynamics of heterosexual masculinities and the ways and conditions under which lesbianism, gay masculinities and heterosexual femininities are lived? How does class and race intersect with these processes? What are the political implications of an analysis which stresses the social–psychic contingency of the ways hegemonic masculinities are formed, and the fact that they continue to be lived and reformed in deep inner contradiction?

Most of the essays in this volume are concerned either with the policing of sexual boundaries, or with the ambivalent dynamics of heterosexual identities. The oppressive implications of the heterosexual presumption, of 'compulsory heterosexuality' in the more familiar phrase, informs all our analyses. Chapter 8, however, is the only chapter in this final version of the book which centres on a case of direct homophobic persecution. 'What's in A Ban? The Popular Media, *Romeo and Juliet* and Compulsory Heterosexuality' explores the ways in which the media, especially the national press, managed to construct a *cause célèbre* around the actions of a primary-school headmistress in turning down an offer from a charitable foundation for tickets for children to see the ballet *Romeo and Juliet*. It was alleged that the offer was declined on the grounds that the ballet was 'blatantly heterosexual'. This story was taken up by the *Evening Standard* some months after the event occurred and was then connected up with a mélange of conservative mythologies in a flurry of press attacks – attacks on 'political correctness', on the school teacher's lesbianism, on the alleged role of her partner in her appointment, and, more generally, on what was presented as a resurgence of 1980s' 'loony leftism' in schools.

Analysis of this episode centres on the different socio-cultural boundaries activated and policed in the press coverage of the case. In each case the press found ways to defend 'proper culture', hegemonic culture or simply 'Culture' by presenting Jane Brown's decision as an attack or threat. In a familiar reversal, the aggression which was actually visited on Jane and is visited on lesbians and gay men more generally, was presented as a necessary defence of Culture. High culture with its strong connections to ideas of Englishness ('Shakespeare' no less) and its civilizing address to working-class children was allegedly threatened by another example of 'political correctness' and 'trendy teaching'. Schools and innocent children were mythically threatened by lesbian and gay teachers and in particular by a lesbian who had conspired with others to become a headmistress. Later, as the local popularity of Jane Brown became clear, together with her excellence as a school head, a new story emerged: proper control in the schools was threatened by obstreperous and misguided parents who dared to do more than 'choose'.

Debbie Epstein explains the intensity of the attack in terms of the wider political context: the preoccupation of the Conservative press with anti-gay campaigning on the eve of the debate on the age of consent for gay men, and the multiple contradictions (over sexual behaviour and corruption in and around the Government and the Conservative Party) in the wake John Major's call to return to moral 'basics'. She also explores the complex and disorganizing interaction between issues of 'race' and sexuality in the conflict between Gus John, the Director of Education in Hackney and supporters of Kingsmead School. She concludes that the affair is significant as an example of the way moral panics of this kind both keep heterosexuality in place and constitute a form of 'queerbashing'. Like other forms of queerbashing the practice served as a kind of policing. The extreme punishment of Jane Brown for being a lesbian and a school teacher gave warnings to other lesbian and gay teachers who wish to be out of the closet in school. Partly because the actual 'threat' in this case was trivial or non-existent, there is no better illustration of the ways in which defending the privileges of heterosexualities, on an exclusive or 'compulsory' basis, must involve the marginalization and oppression of other ways of living and loving, even or especially, where their agents are doing work of social value.

Chapter 9, 'Grievous Recognitions' is in two parts. The first, subtitled 'Poems of Love, Loss and Reparation' is a series of poems I wrote in the process of grieving for my wife Jill, who died suddenly in January 1992. The second part, subtitled 'The Grieving Process and Sexual Boundaries' is a commentary, not on the poems themselves but on the circumstances in which they were written. This includes, very centrally, the accentuation of inequalities which has been involved in Jill's death and in my survival, including the problems of my voice and Jill's silence in the writing and publishing of the poems. This problem is discussed more fully in the commentary itself. It is also suggested that poems and commentary might be read in the order in which they are printed and as relatively independent reflections, using different means, on the same events and feelings.

The poems are not presented in the chronological order in which they were written, though dates are provided for readers interested in the progress of grieving or who are grieving themselves. The help I received from other people's accounts made me want to write in ways that would help other grievers – though much of this is not, I am afraid, comforting. There is an order in the poems, however. The first poem, 'Your Self Not Mine' was a source poem, much discussed and revised, in ways I explain in the commentary. The next two poems are about the process of grieving itself. The 'dated' poems ('Portraits of 1959', and 'Wedding Album: Chapter and Verse (1963)') are preoccupied with the unanswered questions of memory. The next two poems were hard to write: they expose cruel contradictions and angry feelings. The last poem is a kind of (non-religious) blessing, and also (contradictorily perhaps) an attempt at a 'nature poem'. It is based on walks in the Wyre forest.

I cannot face writing a commentary on the 'commentary'. Anyway perhaps that would take self-reflection too far! But both poems and commentary are a form of reflexive and self-critical auto/biography, very much in the spirit described by Peter Redman and Máirtín Mac an Ghaill in this volume and by many other writers involved in the auto/biographical turn in cultural and social studies.[11] Both poems and commentary reflect, in different registers, on power and inequality in heterosexual relations, and, in a less sustained way on the possibility of equalizing alternatives and transformations.

'Eating the Other: Imaging the Fantasy of Incorporation' (Chapter 10) takes as its starting point the conflation of the verbs 'to consume' and 'to consummate'. It explores the complex psychic and discursive interactions of eating and of sex. Such common conflations as 'good enough to eat' are a clue to the ways in which the child's early oral pleasures are repressed from conscious memory in favour of genitally organized desire and pleasure in the Oedipal narrative. However, Adrian Kear argues that they 'return *within* the dominant structures of heterosexuality'. Important for this book is his argument that oral relations, especially with the Mother, are a means by which the borders between self and other are created – 'precisely through transgressing them'. Incorporation (the actual or symbolic ingestion of the other) remains active as a fantasy in adult life. It is in turn related to the operation and the abuse of power in heterosexual (and other?) forms of sexuality. Does this help to explain, for instance, why male fantasies of self aggrandizement so often involve the annihilation or subordination of a female Other? This chapter invites us re-read earlier discussions in this volume – of abuse, of possession, of misrecognition – in the light of contemporary fantasy narratives of this kind (see particularly Chapters 2, 3, 5 and 9).

Kear's argument unravels a complex matrix which is physical (involving the body), psychic (involving unconscious processes) and social (involving power relations of sexuality). A central distinction is Maria Torok's between internalization which occurs literally through objects and things (here termed 'incorporation') and the internalization of the Other through language and images (here termed 'introjection'). Introjection is a psychic process by which the ego enlarges itself by imitating and possessing the Other. Incorporation may be understood as a failed introjection where, as a result of loss, the Other is not transformed into the self, but becomes incarcerated within the self as though in an internal 'crypt' or tomb. In incorporative modes, grieving is silent or expressed in somatic symptoms.

The argument moves closer to issues of power, sexuality and gender through a reading of Judith Butler's account of the melancholic structures of heterosexuality. Here the identification and introjection of sexual objects and dispositions are accompanied by the incorporation and fantastic encrypting of identifications and desires which are forbidden. This work is repeated (policed?) by discursive practices and institutional formations. This is how Butler can describe gender identification as a kind of melancholia, underscored by grieving for what is lost yet still preserved. Similarly in this article, Kear notes how the fantasy of incorporation is 'literalized' in oral forms of sex and in the multiple crossovers or conflations of sex and eating.

The rest of the essay consists of close readings and comparisons of particular filmic and literary narratives, including the films *Tampopo*, *9½ Weeks, Like Water for Chocolate, Babette's Feast*, George Bataille's novella *Story of the Eye*, and versions of the vampire myth. These illustrate different variants of fantasies of incorporation always of a very startling kind. At the same time, the politics of the analysis is sharpened. These films represent different versions of the fantasy of incorporation as they are played out within adult heterosexual relations and gendered relations of power. For the most part images and narratives enact very oppressive relations of sexuality and gender. Sometimes they seem to reverse or play with the dynamics of power. Rarely, they seem to offer, magically and not without recuperation, images of mutuality.

The political force of Kear's readings rests on the fact that looking and its attendant pleasures are themselves a form of incorporation. The watching of films like these is itself a ground of struggles over relations of gender and sexuality. Fantasies are narrativized, conventional desires are transgressed and familiar forms of power are challenged and recuperated.

One purpose of this chapter, which has also been an introduction, has been to mark in bolder script the crisscross of relations, the products of dialogue, which connect and sometimes differentiate our chapters. I hope the book will be read in the same spirit, with the readers' own experiences and identifications also in the dialogue.

Notes

1. Although we had earlier plans to write a collective introduction and then a jointly authored one, I eventually wrote the first draft on my own. Inevitably the final version represents my perspective on the work of the group and on the significance of what we have produced. A draft of the introduction was read and commented on in detail. Considerable changes were made by my co-editors. All authors were asked to comment on the paragraphs about their own contributions. I am especially grateful to Debbie Epstein and Deborah Lynn Steinberg for their suggestions for revisions of this chapter as a whole and for their help and encouragement, to Deborah Lynn Steinberg for revisions to the paragraphs on Chapter 3, and to Adrian Kear for discussions that extended and clarified the introduction to Chapter 10.

2. The Popular Memory Group was influenced by the work of a group of women around the Berlin left journal *Das Argument*. For a description of the method see Haug (1987) and Clare and Johnson (forthcoming).

3. From the later 1980s, memory work became a regular resource in my own teaching in the Department of Cultural Studies especially in courses I taught on the Masters programme around questions of identity. Experimentation was accompanied by an interest, shared by other members of the Politics of Sexuality Group, in the subsequent broader turn to auto/biography in cultural studies, sociology, and, more generally in feminist theory and research.

4. The (working) titles of uncompleted contributions were 'Speaking out loud: the experiences of young lesbians and gay men in school'; 'Loving blackness: Asian lesbian sexualities'; 'Knowing your place: cartographies of the subject'; 'Trials and transgressions: homophobic prosecutions from Oscar Wilde to Operation Spanner'. These losses were bound to affect the overall character of the volume and the extent of our engagement with key areas. Disproportionately, the volume lost studies of the intersection of racism and sexual identities and with

lesbian and gay experiences. Lesbian and gay experiences (and theories written from these points of view) were, however, integral to all our discussions and have influenced all the published studies. The loss of two out of our three black group members' contributions is more serious and, though several essays engage with questions of racism, this loss is not remedied in this volume.

5. See especially Benjamin 1990.

6. This seemed especially apparent at the Conference on Sexuality at Middlesex University, 14–15 July 1995.

7. Criticisms of queer politics – the argument, for instance, that it represents yet another form of masculine pre-emption – were touched on but not fully discussed in the group. It is clear that writers whose work is often named as 'queer theory', especially Judith Butler and Eve Kofosky Sedgwick, were a major influence on the work of some members of the group. These readings produced some reservations too, notably about the strongly 'literary' character of queer theory and the difficulty of some of the writing.

8. See for example Jackie Stacey's argument about 'the terms of resistance' (Stacey, 1991) and Sedgwick's important argument that the naturalizing of sexual difference is by no means a guarantee against 'manipulative fantasy in the technological institutions of the culture' (Sedgwick, 1994, p. 164). Compare Deborah Lynn Steinberg's argument in Chapter 3.

9. I am grateful to Deborah Lynn Steinberg and Debbie Epstein for suggesting additions and revisions to an earlier discussion of queer politics and theory.

10. For a fuller discussion of this difference see Clare and Johnson (forthcoming).

11. The literature of the 'auto/biographical turn' in cultural studies, women's studies and sociology is now vey large. For a sample of different approaches – and useful reviews of issues – see Stanley (1993) and Probyn (1993).

References

Benjamin, J. (1990) *The Bonds of Love: Psychoanalysis, Feminism and the Problems of Domination*. London: Virago.

Butler, J. (1990) *Gender Trouble: Feminism and the Subversion of Identity*. London: Routledge.

Butler, J. (1993) *Bodies that Matter*. London: Routledge.

Bristow, J. (1989) Homophobia/misogyny: sexual fears, sexual definitions, in Shepherd, S. and Wallis, M. (eds), *Coming on Strong: Gay Politics and Culture* . London: Unwin Hyman.

Clare, M. and Johnson, R. (forthcoming) Memory work as process and method, in Radstone, S. (ed.) *Memory and Method*. London: Dent.

Connell, R.W. (1985) *Masculinities*. Cambridge: Polity.

Dollimore, J. (1991) *Sexual Dissidence: Augustine to Wilde, Freud to Foucault*. Oxford: Clarendon Press.

Dyer, R. (1989) A conversation about pornography, in Shepherd, S. and Wallis, M. (eds), *Coming on Strong: Gay Politics and Culture*. London: Unwin Hyman.

Fletcher, J. (1989) Freud and his uses: psychoanalysis and gay theory, in Shepherd, S. and Wallis, M., (eds) *Coming on Strong: Gay Politics and Culture*. London: Unwin Hyman.

Foucault, M. (1988) *Technologies of the Self: A Seminar with Michel Foucault* (eds Luther H. Martin, Huck Gutman and Patrick Hutton). Amherst: University of Massachusetts Press.

Gough, J. (1989) Theories of sexual identity and the masculinization of the gay man, in Shepherd S. and Wallis, M. (eds) *Coming on Strong: Gay Politics and Culture*. London: Unwin Hyman.

Haug, F. (ed.) (1987) *Female Sexualisation: A Collective Work of Memory*. London: Verso.

Hollway, W. (1995) Paper presented at the Sexuality Conference, University of Middlesex, July.

Modleski, T. (1991) *Feminism Without Women: Culture and Criticism in a 'Post-feminist' Age*. London: Routledge.

Mort, F. (1987). *Dangerous Sexualities: Medico-moral Politics in England since 1830*. New York: RKP.

Probyn, E. (1993) *Sexing the Self: Gendered Positions in Cultural Studies*. London: Routledge.

Rich, A. (1983) Compulsory heterosexuality and lesbian existence, in Snitow, A., Stansell, C. and Thompson, S. (eds) *Powers of Desire: The Politics of Sexuality*. New York: Monthly Review Press.

Sedgwick, E. K. (1994) *Tendencies*. London: Routledge.

Segal, L. (1995) Paper presented at the Sexuality Conference, Middlesex University, July.

Stacey, J. (1991) Promoting normality: Section 28 and the regulation of sexuality, in Franklin, S., Lury, C. and Stacey, J. (eds) *Off-Centre: Feminism and Cultural Studies*. London: Harper Collins.

Stanley, L. (1993) On auto/biography in sociology, *Sociology* 27 (1) 41–52.

Wittig, M. (1992) *The Straight Mind and Other Essays*. Brighton: Harvester.

2

Love's Labours:
Playing it Straight on
the *Oprah Winfrey Show*

Debbie Epstein and Deborah Lynn Steinberg

Prologue

The *Oprah Winfrey Show* is commonly regarded as the iconographic chat show, the jewel in the crown of daytime television both in her domestic and international markets. The *Oprah Winfrey Show* began network broadcasting in the United States in 1986. There, it is a daily daytime television broadcast across the United States. Oprah, herself, owns the production company, Harpo Productions, and is one of the wealthiest and most powerful people working in television. Indeed, as has been frequently pointed out, the extent to which she has been able to direct, own and determine the conditions of production of her show (among her many other projects) stands as contrast to the more usual positions of women and African–Americans in the media. The show appears in a number of different countries on national networks, cable and satellite television. In Britain, the *Oprah Winfrey Show* has been broadcast twice or three times a week in the late afternoon, with occasional 'mini-series' of late night 'Adult Oprah'. Some of the programmes are current, going out almost as soon as they have appeared on American television (such as, for example, 'Waco and Other Cults' and 'Home Alone Kids'), while others have been culled from the show's archive. It is a testament to the contradictory sexual politics of British television that some issues have been deemed 'adult' and broadcast late at night (around 11.00 p.m.) some of the time, while very similar issues have been broadcast at the regular 5.00 p.m. slot.[1]

The staggering success of the *Oprah Winfrey Show* has incited a veritable deluge of female-headed chat shows, the most competitive of which is another American import, the *Ricki Lake Show*. It is interesting to consider the appeal of the chat-show genre, and in particular, why American versions seem to have a considerable edge, in Britain, on home-grown productions. Chat shows have a complex appeal. Not only are they a site for gossip, controversy and light entertainment, but they also provide an opportunity and frame for the pleasurable voyeurism of 'real lives'. Significantly, it is this very voyeurism which enables the show to breach the boundaries of public and private in ways which may approximate the cruel exploitation of the side-show or may serve as a forum for collective education and consciousness raising. What is particularly interesting is the way in which both processes can simultaneously constitute the text of any particular programme.

The interest of American versions of the genre also rests on the ways in which they seem to provide a window on America. They are at once: a fetishistic spectacle of American weirdness, that willingness to 'let it all hang out'; a flash of American Dreaming, of rags to riches, of self transformation, of 15 minutes of fame; an encapsulated moment of 'American democracy' in which it appears that 'we, the people' have an equal voice with the great and the good, the potential to shape and change 'ourselves' and 'our' society, to make a better America, a happier life, and even a world safe for democracy. The American domination of the genre, not only in Britain but worldwide, is a testament to the cultural imperialism underpinning processes of globalization. Indeed, even the objectification of the American 'Other' often seems less a subversion than a reconfirmation (and reconstitution) of the pervasive currency of American cultural common sense.

The frequency of transmission demands that the presenter becomes familiar (or is at least briefed in order to appear familiar) very quickly with an enormous range of topics and materials. The format enables presenters, including Oprah, to do this and to produce more or less tidy packages, lasting not more than an hour, in which complex issues are, almost inevitably, reduced to simplistic explanations and 'quick fixes'.

Thus there is a virtual certainty that one's expectations as a viewer will be met. Personal pain will be recognized. Your power to transform yourself, your life, your circumstances will be promised. These constitute no small part of the ability of such programmes to inter-pellate a range of viewers from the oppositional to the mainstream, from the critical to the voyeuristic.

The tensions that characterize the chat-show genre are, perhaps, most interestingly configured on the *Oprah Winfrey Show*. There is something special about the *Oprah Winfrey Show*. Oprah's charisma and warmth captivate the viewer. She demonstrates a feeling of kinship with her studio audience, even when she clearly disagrees with them. In almost every programme, Oprah either literally or verbally embraces members of her audience. This, combined with her presence as a powerful black woman with a very explicit agenda of social responsibility and social justice and a commitment to educate herself and her audience, captures something of the spirit of the Civil Rights movement in the United States and of feminism.[2] It is this which creates a potentially radical foundation for her regular airing of subjects commonly seen as taboo, such as child sexual abuse, violence against women and other issues of social inequality.

At the same time, there are aspects of the *Oprah Winfrey Show* which contradict its strengths. The show regularly takes a liberal point of view which ignores issues of power, allowing equivalences to be made between people who do not have the same social power and situations which are not equal. Consequently, although the *Oprah Winfrey Show*, regularly addresses issues of gender and sexuality, it does so without an analysis of gender politics and compulsory heterosexuality. This absence permits and, indeed, fosters forms of audience participation which are decidedly abusive, particularly towards women. Furthermore, it also sets up a basis for audiences to be smug, self-righteous and judgmental, rather than critically interrogative and self-reflective. The 'us/them' thinking which underpins the complacency of so many of her studio audience and guests is frequently expressed in terms of a form of Christian charity which hearkens back to the Victorian Lady Bountiful giving only to the 'deserving poor'. The show also addresses other issues of oppression, such as racism, poverty and homophobia as special-issue programmes, but again most often without political analysis which goes beyond the liberal agenda. As a consequence, the links that can be made between different forms of oppression and the ways they are mutually reinforcing are generally left unexplored.

At the heart of these problematics, is a presumption and, indeed, a pursuit of normalized heterosexuality. This is most obviously expressed through the extensive kinship work which the show undertakes. From matchmaking to family reunions and resolving problems in relationships, heterosexuality is construed as the ultimate object of desire, despite the consistent airing of problems which are the result of heterosexual gender relations. Indeed, it is these problems of heterosexuality which constitute the central fodder and focus of the show.

The attractiveness of Oprah herself, and the potential for a conscientized,[3] radical politics which we see in her show, have drawn us to be regular viewers. It is, however, the contradictions of the show and our deep disappointment when it does not fulfil that potential which have led us to write about it here and elsewhere.[4] In this chapter, we are interested in the ways in which the contradictions displayed in the *Oprah Winfrey Show* are played out in the arena of sexuality. Central to our analysis will be how the presumption of heterosexuality as 'normal' forms the matrix through which the show investigates issues.

The *Oprah Winfrey Show* can be seen as a stage for the playing out of the negotiation and mediation of sexuality. The show provides an interesting set of contradictions. On the one hand, it appears to challenge common sense assumptions about relationships, specifically heterosexual relationships (for example, by consistently raising issues of sexual violence within a heterosexual context). Yet, at the same time, Oprah's presentation often works to reinforce precisely the norms she seeks to challenge. Through a close analysis of a selection of clips from one particular programme among many about relationships, sexuality and families, this chapter will consider the ways in which the *Oprah Winfrey Show* both problematizes and yet normalizes the boundaries of heterosexuality. Here we shall discuss both the resolute exposure and exploration of what could be termed the casualties of normative (and compulsory) heterosexuality and, paradoxically, its recuperation as a 'rational' ideal.

In exploring the ways in which this recuperation takes place, we shall begin with a brief consideration of the discursive frameworks of the show.[5] Here we shall focus on two discourses: that of therapy and that of kinship.[6] Our analysis of the sexual politics of the *Oprah Winfrey Show* in these terms will focus on the programme, 'How to Make Love

Last' (18 January 1993). This programme is characteristic of the show both in the prominence it gives to therapeutic and kinship discourses and in the way it illustrates not only a presumption of universal hetero-sexuality but an active reinscription of its institutionalized borders. Like so many other programmes, 'How to Make Love Last' intends to highlight and deal with problems within heterosexual relationships as distressing but solvable (through the medium of therapeutic self-help). At another level, however, the programme also (unwittingly) reveals a different order of problems which, ironically, can only be reinforced by the mode of rescue proposed and staged. We have chosen to examine this programme, in part because of the prosaic character of problems experienced by each couple. That is to say, the programme 'treats' the daily grind of unequal heterosexual relationships, rather than presenting overt or dramatic instances of abuse or violence. In this way, it represents one end of the continuum of problems which the show addresses in relationships between women and men. Indeed, as we shall see, within the programme itself connections are overtly as well as implicitly made (though not necessarily critically) between the 'mundane' and the 'extreme'.

It is important to note that in examining dominant discourses which shape and are reproduced in the *Oprah Winfrey Show*, we are not suggesting that audiences necessarily receive the show in straight-forward terms. Indeed, the fact that we ourselves have been able to read against the grain of the show is evidence that this is not the case. However, we suggest that the presumption of heterosexuality, hetero-sexual kinship and discourses of therapy are strongly encoded into the *Oprah Winfrey Show* in ways which provide contradictory, but nevertheless preferred, readings. This article provides, then, a detailed deconstruction of the text of one *Oprah Winfrey Show* in relation to several specific but typical discourses in play within it.

All the world's a stage and all the players are in therapy

Therapy is a central discourse on the *Oprah Winfrey Show*. It is manifested in the format of the show and is a key lens through which issues are understood. Characteristic of the show are a number of therapeutic signifiers: for example, the ubiquitous 'expert' (usually a psychologist with a PhD); the mediating of a kind of group therapy encounter involving audience and guests under the direction of the 'expert' and Oprah; and the staging of 'therapy sessions' for guests (and sometimes for Oprah herself), which are witnessed by the audience (both studio and televisual).[7] Furthermore, the show frequently functions as an advertisement for the self-help books which have almost invariably been written by the invited 'experts'. These books are often used to provide the source for the structure and framing of particular programmes.

There is a certain appeal beyond the solely voyeuristic in the therapeutic format of the show. Firstly, it provides a space within which personal experience can be aired and validated. The importance of this should not underestimated, particularly in the context of a show aimed, as Oprah herself has frequently stated, at empowering people who generally do not have social power (for example, African Americans and other 'ethnic minorities' and women). Secondly, the *Oprah Winfrey Show*, along with the efforts of other feminist activists, has contributed substantially to making issues of violence and abuse by men against women and children publicly speakable.[8] Finally, there is a relationship between the kind of testimony offered by Oprah's guests and the role testifying has played in fuelling the organized pursuit of social justice in both the civil rights and women's liberation movements.

Despite this appeal, there are a number of tensions produced when a therapeutic discourse is used as a medium through which to understand personal and social issues. We would suggest that these tensions accrue to therapy as a framework in general as well as to the particular brand of therapy which is characteristic of the *Oprah Winfrey Show*. Elsewhere, we have explored problems with the discourse of therapy with respect to the show in more detail (see Epstein and Steinberg, 1995a; 1995b). It is beyond the scope of this chapter to reproduce these discussions. Nevertheless it is important to outline some of the key issues raised by the therapy dimension of the *Oprah Winfrey Show* in order to put our analysis of the negotiation of heterosexuality in the programme 'How to Make Love Last' into context.

The particular mode of therapy employed on the show is one which derives from the popular end of the self-help movement. This is typified in the 'How to . . .' books which are often used to frame the programme. A common element of both self-help and therapy in general is that it tends to be very individualistic. Even within schools of psychoanalysis which attempt to locate the individual psyche within the social (e.g. R.D Laing and existentialist approaches; Nancy Chodorow and other feminist approaches), there are tensions between the overall propensity of treatment towards individualism and the attempt to theorize behaviours, emotions, experience etc. in relation to the social. It is particularly evident within the self-help paradigm that problems are posed as individual pathologies subject to individual solutions.

Moreover, within this context, the self and family are seen as world and this has the effect of eclipsing both power relations and social context. As will be seen below, for example, issues around abuse are predominantly constructed as 'negative patterns we repeat' rather than as indictments of unequal social relations. This kind of formulation locates responsibility for suffering, and indeed for abuse, primarily, if not only, within the 'victim' and sets up terms of inquiry which do not (and, perhaps, cannot) interrogate perpetrators.

A second and related assumption underpinning the therapy mode of the *Oprah Winfrey Show* is the notion that 'we can help ourselves' (and, indeed, that only we can help ourselves). Thus, we set up our own destructive patterns to repeat them and, conversely, we can break these cycles by 'working on ourselves'. Again, in this context, the emphasis is on personal healing rather than social change, on individual rather than collective action. Personal healing is clearly a key issue for 'survivors'[9] of abuse. But a limited focus on the personal can beg the question of how personal healing can be possible without an analysis of the power relations and social contexts within which sexual, physical or emotional abuses take place. Furthermore, we would hold that even where 'negative patterns' do not involve obvious forms of abuse, all relationships are implicated in and bespeak a range of social inequalities.

In this context there is an implication that the route to self-healing can be accomplished centrally, if not totally, through a set programme of therapeutic exercises or steps (whether twelve or not). The reliance on this kind of programmatic 'therapy' is, inevitably, reductionist and mechanistic. To make a healing process programmatic, in itself implies that all problems can be dealt with in the same way. It mitigates against making necessary distinctions, for example, between different forms or levels of abuse and miscommunication and making necessary connections between the personal and the social/political. Moreover, it implicitly suggests that things can be 'fixed' quickly, if not in the space of a fifty-minute television programme, then in the space of a popular book, or, as Oprah wishfully suggests on 'How to Make Love Last', seven hours of Harville (the invited expert) and Helen Hendrix talking about their 'conscious marriage' on video.

A little more than kin and less than kind?

Kinship work, that is mediating the making, breaking and negotiating of familial and romantic relationships, is another staple of the *Oprah Winfrey Show*. As with therapy, kinship work too is specifically staged. Countless programmes feature reunions of estranged family members, meetings of blood relations who have never met ('Fathers and the Sons they Never Knew', 31 October 1990; 'Baby Selling', 26 May 1993), introductions of potential (heterosexual) partners (e.g. 'Desperate Women Meet Alaskan Men', 17 February 1989) and issues around sexual, romantic and family relationships (e.g. 'Obnoxious Husbands' 11 January 1989, 'Raising a Child with Family Values' 6 April 1993).

Therapy often provides the conceptual foundations for the evaluation of kinship relations. For example, there seems to be a general assumption that almost all family relationships are, in the language of the show itself, 'dysfunctional' (until you work on yourself). It seems to us that when people on the show say things like 'I come from a dysfunctional family', what they are trying to describe is an experience of unhappiness, abuse and/or betrayal in relation to their own families. The term 'dysfunction' clearly makes speakable this unhappiness and simultaneously invokes the possibility of change. This, in our view, is an obvious reason for the currency which has been gained by the term 'dysfunctional family' on and beyond the show.[10] Yet, whatever particular participants in the show might mean when they use it, to invoke the term 'dysfunction' nevertheless also calls into play the specifically medical, pathological connotations of the word. Furthermore, 'dysfunction' implies 'function'. Because of this, the investment of participants in escaping their unhappiness becomes inextricably entwined with an investment in the fantasy of the 'functional family', that discourse which has been racialized white, classed middle class, sexualized heterosexual.[11]

Thus, within the dominant kinship discourse of the *Oprah Winfrey Show*, the white, middle-class family is constructed as both object of desire and project of therapy.[12] In this context, a range of familial relationships are made Other. This is illustrated in programmes such as 'Lesbian and Gay Baby Boom' (10 May 1993), in which Oprah places lesbian and gay parents in a defensive position by stating at the very start of the programme that, '[t]he big question that a lot of people want to ask, I know, is will their kids also grow up to be gay or will they be emotionally damaged?' (p. 2). Although the grammar of this sentence may suggest that the children will be emotionally damaged if they are not gay, the meaning of the sentence, in context, is clearly that being gay bespeaks emotional damage and that having a gay parent is, axiomatically, emotionally damaging to children. It is this accusation against which her lesbian and gay guests were required to defend themselves. Much of the show was devoted to disproving the accusation. In addition, this programme clearly assumed a heterosexual audience; it was not lesbians and gays who constituted the 'many people who want[ed] to know'.

The Othering process is also illustrated in the ways in which working-class parents often come in for audience abuse, being blamed for the oppressions and deprivations that they experience which may be damaging to their children. This was poignantly and disquietingly evidenced in the programme 'Would You Leave Your Kid Home Alone' (11 January 1993). In this programme, a working-class woman was subjected to highly emotional verbal castigation by the audience for leaving her children on their own for 20 minutes. In stark contrast, a middle-class woman, whose children spent much longer periods on their own, and one of whom was seriously injured during such a period, was able to garner audience approval. One reason for the discrepancy was the use of shocking footage about gross child neglect to frame the story of the first woman, almost ensuring the bloodlust of the audience. The second woman, whose story followed the break, was also able to draw on her cultural capital to distance herself from the mis/association between gross child abuse and leaving children to mind themselves for short periods. Thus she was applauded for her work in preparing them to look after themselves.

We would suggest that such processes of Othering result, in part, from an underestimation of the power of common-sense discourses. Oprah frequently frames a programme by posing a question which she clearly wishes to have nullified, for example, 'Won't children be damaged by having gay parents?'; or uses extreme and provocative material in order to initiate discussion of a serious issue, for example, footage of graphic and gross child abuse to discuss leaving children on their own. Effectively, this means she is positioning her audience, herself and her guests inside the common-sense discourse. At the same time she lays the responsibility for the overthrow of the discourse at the feet of the very people who are disempowered by it, thus, ironically, locking any particular programme into the very common sense she may be trying to challenge.

Furthermore, there is a racialization of Oprah's kinship work which takes place in a number of different ways. Firstly, it is very rare to see any but white/Anglo families presented as the ideal. In the four months during which we taped every programme transmitted in the UK, there was not one occasion on which a family of colour was held out as a positive example. Indeed, most of Oprah's guests are white (although the studio audience is normally very mixed). Moreover, the con-figuration of ideal family is itself exclusive. As shown in the programme 'Raising a Child with Family Values' (6 April 1993), these values are implicitly linked with wealth, particular assumptions underpinning white middle-class culture and quite conventional heterosexual divisions of labour. Secondly, Oprah's invited experts are virtually all white, and where they have been black that has largely been in the context of programmes about racism. So, in effect, much of Oprah's work involves the mediation of white expertise and white kinship relations. The combination of expertise and selection of guests, thus provides a white heterosexual and middle-class backdrop against which all kinship relations are to be measured.[13]

So far then, we have noted that the *Oprah Winfrey Show* makes the link between kinship and work at two levels. Firstly there is the work, performed by Oprah and her invited experts, of mediating the relationships of guests and various audience members. Secondly, kinship is, in itself, posited *as* work, specifically (and ideally) as therapeutic work on oneself. As numerous feminists have argued, kinship work is generally done by women. Moreover, not only is it gendered (Rubin, 1975; Chodorow, 1978, 1989), it is also racialized and classed within a broader 'heterosexual matrix'.[14] For example, the maintenance of white families has often been done by black women both under slavery and after its abolition (hooks, 1982; Collins, 1990). Furthermore, the modes of kinship work and conditions under which it takes place are class and culture specific (Barrett and MacIntosh, 1982; Anthias and Yuval-Davis, 1993; Delphy and Leonard, 1993). As we shall see on 'How to Make Love Last', these dimensions of the politics of kinship work are reflected and reproduced on the *Oprah Winfrey Show*.

The therapeutic kinship work which is done (and promoted) on the show often takes the form of an attempt to retrieve what is seen as 'dysfunctional' in order to make it desirable, ideal and in every way 'functional'. In other words, the underpinning framework is one which identifies much that is 'wrong' in normative heterosexuality, but draws back from using this as a basis of critique of the institutions of heterosexuality. Rather, building on the therapy mode, the *Oprah Winfrey Show* typically locates these problems centrally in the individual and the work, on the self. In the process, the show maintains the heterosexual family and heterosexual relationships as ideal.

In this context, the show could be said to provide a window on 'the long grey stream of heterosexual misery' (Duncker, 1993, p. 142).[15] The show displays a continuum of gendered abuse in relationships – from men who don't listen to women to those who are violent to their female partners and their children.[16] However, within the therapeutic/kinship framework of the show, a gendered analysis of power seems to be resolutely resisted. Thus while child abuse and domestic violence, for example, are regularly interrogated and condemned, they are generally not examined in relation to gendered social inequalities. This is typically manifested in the ways in which female 'survivors' of domestic violence are invariably subjected to interrogation by expert guests, Oprah and audience while male perpetrators are taken for granted. In this context, women survivors are typically asked to defend themselves against the accusatory question 'Why didn't you leave him?', a question which implicitly constructs the woman as 'passive aggressor' and as responsible for the commission of (male) violence against her. Indeed we have only viewed two occasions in which a man is asked to explain and defend *his* choice to injure and violate a woman or a child. Instead, as noted above, concerns are raised about 'patterns *we* set up and repeat', about misunderstandings and miscommunications, all of which may be remedied by a combination of therapy and 'rational' dialogue. Precisely because it does not consider the issues of power and inequality, the currency of the notion of 'patterns we repeat' makes comprehensible why women are interrogated for not leaving situations of domestic violence. Leaving could be construed both as 'breaking the pattern' and as a 'rational' response to the situation. This begs the question of how the experience of abuse can destroy the emotional and psychological belief in the possibility of freedom and the material obstacles to making the 'rational choice' to leave. Thus kinship is located not within a matrix of power relations, but rather within one of presumed equality where relationship problems derive only from unresolved and irrational patterns which we (sic) set up in childhood.

Love's labours: 'How to Make Love Last'

'How to Make Love Last' (broadcast in the UK as 'Unsuccessful in Love') invites us, the audience, to observe the mediation of two heterosexual relationships which are 'having problems': Cari and Dale are seeking a divorce and Jay and Madelene, a relatively 'new' couple, are beginning to run into problems. In the expert seat is Harville Hendrix PhD, therapist and author of two self-help books: *Getting the Love You Want* and *Keeping the Love You Find* and, as Oprah informs us, 'he also has this great new series of home videos for couples that [we are] going to be seeing . . . throughout this programme' (p. 1).[17] The programme stages each couple undertaking a potted therapy session following the format which we are given to understand is proposed in Harville's second book. Harville and Oprah put each couple through a series of paces on stage. It is made clear that these are intended to provide a model for us, the audience, to work on ourselves as a way of working on our relationships and ultimately to make love last, or failing that, to dissolve our relationships in a 'rational' fashion.

Staging heterosexuality

Oprah   OK. So you're smart and you're strong. And you're successful in every area of your life but love. What *is* it that keeps you from having a happy love life? This show today is going to help you unlock a lot of those fears, 'cause that's really what it is. And the beauty of this show is, is that it applies to everybody, whether you're married, whether you're divorced, whether you're single, whether

you're looking, whether you're looking and single, looking
to get rid of the man you already have, the woman you
already have – everybody! *(audience laughter)* (p. 1)

From the start, Oprah invokes a universal 'you'. This 'you', in fact
locates the programme squarely within a terrain of heterosexual kinship
on at least two levels. Firstly, Oprah's litany of 'whethers' has some
obvious omissions. While there are explicit referents for heterosexual
partnering (e.g. 'married', 'divorced') such referents are lacking, for
example, for lesbian and gay relationships. It could be argued that this
omission is not deliberately exclusive.[18] And, indeed, 'getting rid of the
man you already have . . . etc.' could conceivably refer to same sex
partners. However, we would suggest that such a reading would
necessarily be against the grain of the flow of the list of relational
possibilities which purportedly includes 'everybody'. We would suggest
that Oprah's list assumes heterosexual guests, audience and a
heterosexual issue, all of which are taken as universal.

Secondly, there seems to be a related assumption that people whose
relationships *are* excluded from the list can (and should), nevertheless,
relate to and through the parameters of heterosexuality. Thus the
lesbian or gay viewer, for example, is offered a straight subject position
through which to understand her or his own relationships and to
participate in the ostensible global village of Oprah's educative
democracy. In this context, what is offered at best is a kind of 'liberal
equivalence'[19] drawn between (rather conventional) straight relationships and non-straight relationships. To draw this kind of equivalence,
which is characteristic of the *Oprah Winfrey Show* more generally (and
in relation to a range of issues), has the effect of erasing social context
and material relations of social inequality. It denies that the character of
sexual/intimate/familial/ friendship relationships (amongst others) are
shaped through the social positions of the people involved in them.
These kinds of relationships are typically, within liberal thought,
understood as 'private' and therefore not political or beyond politics. It
is an interesting dimension of the *Oprah Winfrey Show* that it both
challenges the public/private distinction of liberal politics (for example
by putting relationships on a public stage) and at the same time
reinscribes it by examining relationships in terms which effectively
exclude a consideration of power relations. Furthermore, the

presumption of heterosexuality set up in Oprah's opening speech is reinforced and further narrowed as we are introduced to Oprah's guests, the ubiquitous white professional expert and the two white couples whose visual presentation is clearly affluent as well as conventionally attractive.[20]

Staging therapy

After opening the programme in this way, Oprah's introduction of her expert guest, Harville Hendrix, initiates an interchange which locates it firmly within the therapy discourse. Here, we see the key assumptions of the therapeutic discourse of the show exemplified in strikingly stark terms. Right from the start, Oprah tells us that Harville is going to help us 'examine the patterns *we* set up in our childhood' (p. 1) [our emphasis].

Oprah   there are a lot of things that I like about this [Harville's work] is that there are a whole lot of cause and effects that you set up.

Harville   Yes.

Oprah   One that concerns me is if you were abused as a child, you may pick an abusive partner or be an abuser yourself.

Harville   Yes. That – that's always the case. Whatever happens in childhood, whether its mild or intense, there is something that's going to replicate itself in adulthood in an intimate partnership. Because the early childhood experience where there's a wound has to be repaired. And it always has to be repaired in adulthood with somebody similar to your parents.

Oprah   Now, doesn't – can't you get over that, though? Because, see, I believe that – that all of my relationships in my twenties and early thirties were – were – I continued the abusive pattern that I set up in my childhood.

Harville   Yes.

Oprah   Stedman is not an abusive person. So I think I've gotten over that.

Harville Yeah. And that's the clue, when you're saying that in the twenties and thirties, you began to work on some things in yourself. (p. 2)

Here we see a painful example of the theory of the 'cycle of abuse' and the way in which it shifts responsibility from the abuser to the abused. Indeed, it is excruciating to see Oprah talking about her experience of being abused as a child in terms of 'the abusive pattern that *I* set up in my childhood'. In other programmes Oprah has been clear that abuse is not the fault of the child and it seems likely that she would extend that to herself. It is a testament to the seductiveness of the cycle of abuse framework that she could make such a reversal in this context. This shifting of responsibility is reinforced twice more. Not only are those who have been abused effectively held, within this formulation, to be responsible for the original abuse, but they are also held to be responsible for any repetition of these abusive dynamics in their adult relationships. Moreover, it seems as if they are seen as ultimately able to challenge these dynamics only by changing ('working on') themselves rather than, for example, calling upon abusers to change (or indeed calling the police).

This construction is all the more disquieting for its refusal to acknowledge or consider the gendered character of child abuse (particularly of child sexual abuse) and of abuse within adult relationships. At the very least, if we take into consideration the skewed gender profile of abusers and abused, to posit those who are abused as responsible for 'setting up the patterns' implicitly posits girls/women as responsible for what is largely male perpetrated abuse.[21] Thus the call to 'work on ourselves' means, in effect, a call primarily for women to be the ones who change. As we shall see below, this responsibility is also located with the women (i.e. Cari and Madelene) in the particular relationships under scrutiny in this programme. Moreover, within this paradigm, there seems to be an extraordinary implication that men have no agency or responsibility in relationships!

A second point which emerges from this interchange is the mechanistic and uni-dimensional construction of cause and effect in the formulation of repeated patterns. It seems, from what Harville says, that the future life of the 'wounded' child is pre-, indeed over-, determined. This point is driven home through a subsequent exchange in which Oprah asks Harville to explain the outcome of a range of childhood 'wounds' (e.g. having a jealous parent, a critical parent, a parent who abandons you and so on). Harville's response is to explain that all these patterns are invariably repeated by the child-as-adult. More specifically, he posits that:

Harville You either pick 'em, provoke 'em or project on to them. But if you had – if you had a problem in childhood, you're going to pick somebody to help you redo it. If they don't, then you'll project on to them that they are. And if they aren't, you'll provoke them into doing it. Because we have to resolve that issue . . .

It's like in – in an adult relationship, you'll either act like the child that you did with your parents or you'll behave like the parents behaved toward you as a child.

Oprah Isn't that fascinating?

Harville It's really fascinating and it's so predictable (pp. 5–6).

In addition to the stark and mechanistic determinism of this posited pattern, we see here a case-in-point of the construction of parents as world-entire for the child. Moreover, Harville seems to consider two parents as a single entity. If this were not the case, it would not be possible to choose *a* partner like 'your parents'.[22]

And bring them hither straight

What Harville is saying then, is that children are invariably wounded in and through their relationships with their parents and that they are then trapped into repeating those wounding patterns in their adult relationships (and implicitly with their own children). If this is true,[23] it could be read that Harville is making a considerable indictment of normative heterosexual paradigms of 'the family'. However, it is clear in the context of the programme that this is far from Harville's (or Oprah's) intention. This is demonstrated by the way that, having defined 'the problem' in these terms, Harville then goes on (with Oprah) to recuperate conventional modes of family and marriage. This recuperation is achieved in two ways. First there is the display of Harville and Helen Hendrix as living the ideal (or as Helen puts it 'conscious') marriage. Here a short extract of Harville's seven hours of instructive self-help video is screened showing Harville and Helen talking rather mawkishly about their relationship. Oprah shows us how we are meant to respond to this spectacle when she comments:

Oprah   So that clip we just saw . . . that was Harville and his wife. And I was saying that is really – that's – I mean I got a little goosebump looking at it because that's what marriage should feel like. You should feel like you're – it should be like unconditional love. You should feel like you're totally supported and loved just because of who you are (p. 11).

The notion of 'conscious marriage' seems a rather odd, if not invidious proposition. At one level it seems to posit that the problem with most marriages is that they are in some basic way 'irrational' (if not under-taken under anaesthesia!). A 'conscious' marriage is constructed as an act of rational agency. Together with Oprah's understanding of this as a state of (implicitly egalitarian) 'unconditional' love and acceptance, there is the implication that we can determine the fundamental character of our relationships abstracted from the conditions in which they occur, that we can, as male and female individuals, for example, simply choose to be equal. Indeed, this would posit that individual 'consciousness' can supersede or cancel out the social/legal/economic meanings of marriage as a contract historically premised upon sexual/gender inequality. In sum, the notion of 'conscious' marriage either presumes a gendered social equality that does not exist and/or it promises that individualized 'consciousness' is a route to an interpersonal equality which in itself, implicitly overrides social inequalities. We are not suggesting that heterosexual couples have no agency in their relationships. However, we would argue that all choices are constrained by and through social conditions and the complex social positions of the actors.

In addition to the romanticization of the very relationships which were earlier problematized by Harville (and Oprah), a second way that conventional heterosexuality is recuperated is through the notion of self-help. The idea of self-help, as we noted earlier in this chapter, is based upon those therapies adopting programmatic approaches to individual change.[24] Harville's books (and videos) are seen to provide a rational route to the realization of this ideal of heterosexual love. Underlying the process is the assumption of equality within heterosexual relationships and, presumably, it is necessary that both men and women undertake this work. However, as we shall see, the primary responsibility for the work of self-help is clearly laid at the feet of the women in the relationships shown on the programme.[25]

The pleasing punishment that women bear (Scene 1)

The next phase of the programme begins with Oprah introducing Dale and Cari Reporto who are about to get a divorce. As noted above, what will follow is that Dale and Cari will undertake a brief therapy session, mediated by Harville, for the dissolution of their marriage. It is therefore necessary for Oprah and Harville first to locate Dale and Cari's relationship problems within Harville's framework. Thus, Oprah's opening sentence to Dale and Cari is: 'Did any of this sound familiar to you?' (p. 14). Cari responds by saying that she recognized the pattern of herself being criticized by Dale, a pattern which she had experienced from her parents. Dale agrees:

Dale   Yeah. Well, I know I'm very critical of her.

Oprah   Uh huh.

Dale   So that's exactly what you're talking about.

Oprah   And you were criticized a lot as a child? (p. 15)

At this point, one might have expected Dale to answer Oprah's question ('And you were criticized a lot as a child?') since it was his comment that provoked it (and since within Harville's framework either/both being criticized or/and being a critic would be the result of having critical parents). In other words, it would have been logical for the 'you' in Oprah's question to have referred to Dale. Yet what actually happens is that it is Cari who responds by saying:

Cari   In a lot of ways, it was for the betterment . . . (p. 15).

So, within the space of a moment, the emphasis on the problems of the couple shifted to an emphasis on Cari's problematic patterns. That is, the 'you', as object of inquiry, became female.[26]

After being introduced in this way, there follows a 'good-bye process'. Harville explains the purpose of the exercise:

Harville   The – the whole point is that you need – in preparation for marriage, you need to finish what you didn't finish or

what's left over from another relationship. And this good-
bye process is, in a sense, an essential ingredient in getting
ready to go on to your next relationship or to go on with
your life if you decide not to go on to another relationship,
but to finish that. (p. 18)

This suggests that although a marriage may have been negative and
therefore in need of dissolution, the desirable outcome is the repetition of
the pattern of getting married. This is despite Harville's disclaimer which,
as one view's the programme, clearly comes through as an afterthought. In
other words, while marriage is understood at one level to be constituted
out of negative patterns by the individuals involved in it, at another level,
the institution of marriage is seen as being a positive pattern and
(re)marriage is set up again as an unquestioned object of desire.[27]

The staged therapy that follows illustrates the implicit assumption that
problematic patterns are located in the woman. The actual exercise
consists of each partner in turn going through a set sequence of 'saying
good-bye', first to the 'bad parts' of the marriage, then to the 'good
parts', then to the dream of what might have been and finally to the
marriage as a whole. The other partner is asked to 'mirror' back what has
just been said (i.e. 'if I'm hearing you right, you are saying good-bye
to. . .). In this process, there is an appearance and, indeed, an ostensible
assumption of equality between the two partners. With Dale and Cari,
this is visually reinforced by the way they are seated (i.e. the scene is set):
each sits facing the other (squared off) and in profile to the audience with
Harville, facing front, between them. There are two particular inter-
changes in which the gender bias of the process becomes poignantly clear.

In the first exchange, Cari has just been asked to begin the 'good-bye'
to the 'bad things' in the marriage:

Cari I'd like to say good-bye to being critiqued as often as I
was. To always having to prove that I'm better than what
you thought I was. And I'd like to say good-bye to some of
the frugality that existed between us. And I'll be happy to
say good-bye to the struggling with who I am on the one
hand to make you happy and on the other hand to make
me happy.

Harville OK. So just – just briefly, can you paraphrase back the part
         – the bad part she's saying good-bye to in the relationship?

Dale   Sure. As to the critiquing, she's right I. . .

Harville Yeah. And don't explain it. Just say, so I'm hearing you say
         – you're saying good-bye to the critiquing.

Dale   Right.

Harville Just mirror it back and paraphrase it back.

Dale   To the living up to my standards instead of yours and
         doing what I want you to do. And I really don't feel any of
         that's true.

Harville No. I don't want you to comment. *(audience laughter)* (pp.
         18-19)

In a later exchange, Dale is 'saying good-bye' to the 'good stuff' about
the marriage:

Harville OK. Now shift to the good stuff that won't ever be again
         with the end of this marriage.

Oprah   *(whispering off camera)* Oh, this is so sad.

Dale   OK. The good stuff . . .

Harville Say good-bye to that.

Dale   *(looking at Harville)* With a lot of fun, a lot of good
         conversations.

Harville And tell it to *her.*

Dale   Your enthusiasm about everything you did from who you
         came in to *(sic)* work and who you talked to. And that I
         never really had to carry a conversation, that you could
         carry the whole conversation; that you're always smiling;
         you're always up. You were never depressed. That when
         you were depressed, it was over minor things, like – oh,
         just nonsense things. I can't even think of them. And
         that we could go places and do things and I never had to
         be embarrassed of you or that you would never be, you
         know . . . (p. 25)

It is interesting to note that Dale finds it very difficult either to listen to Cari or to address her. Not only does he need repeated reminders to paraphrase what Cari has said, he also often fails to talk *to* her when he is saying his good-byes. By contrast, Cari addresses Dale throughout and, when it comes to her turn to paraphrase, does so with great articulacy and accuracy.[28] This would suggest that what we are seeing here, ironically, is a pattern in the relationship, but one which is not commented upon by Harville, Oprah or, indeed, by Dale or Cari: that is, a pattern of relating in which the listening is mostly one way (i.e. Cari listens to Dale but not vice versa). We would argue that in a performance (such as appearing on television or in front of an audience) it is difficult to do that which you have not rehearsed. It seemed to us that the reason that Cari was able to perform the exercise easily and Dale was not, was because she was practised in listening to and engaging with someone else and he was not. Indeed, this seems precisely what Dale means when he tells us that he 'never had to really carry a conversation, that [Cari] could carry the whole conversation'. Not only does this seem to be a pattern in Dale and Cari's particular relationship, it is well documented that active listening is gendered.[29]

Secondly, it is striking that Dale describes, as one of the good things about the marriage, that Cari was depressed only over minor things which he was unable to remember. In the context of everything they had both said about the relationship, this seems to represent a trivialization of Cari's feelings. It seems likely that Cari's experiences of depression were not 'trivial' to her (and indeed, it is likely that the experience of being married to someone who has difficulty listening to you and who criticizes you constantly would be profoundly depressing). It is also possible that Cari had been depressed over 'serious things' (like being constantly criticized/put down) and Dale did not register it. Cari's body language and facial expression (shown in reaction shots) during this speech seemed to emanate considerable frustration and anger, suggesting that her experience was quite different from Dale's version of it. This seems another pattern of gendered inequality between Dale and Cari which escapes comment in the programme.

Finally, and most importantly, what is made clear here is that Dale's problem in the marriage is the sort of person that Cari is. Cari's problem, on the other hand, is Dale's problem with her, as she indicates in her comment about 'always having to prove that I'm better than what you thought I was'. In other words, Cari is, in herself, the territory of dispute here. This is clear even when Dale is saying good-bye to the good parts of the marriage. The blatant arrogance of the statement that one of the good things was 'never [having] to be embarrassed of [her]' is a clear indication that she was expected to live out his fantasies of what marriage should be and of what a wife should be. Her inevitable 'failure' to do so is obviously the subject of his constant criticism of her. Moreover, it is reinforced throughout the rest of the exercise that Dale also has a problem with Cari having a life and relationships outside of her relationship with him.[30]

The pleasing punishment that women bear (Scene 2)

The final segment of the programme involves what Harville terms 'a process called changing our frustration into a positive communication – a behaviour-change request' (p. 31) in relation to the second (recently formed) couple, Jay and Madelene. As with Dale and Cari, the segment begins with an identification of the couple's 'problem' within Harville's therapeutic framework. The exercise then follows the same pattern as the good-bye exercise in two ways: firstly, what they are asked to do is programmatic in the same terms (i.e. involving the mirroring process); and secondly, the terrain of the problem is located in the woman.

Oprah Joining us are Jay and Madelene. They've been going out now for about a year, but they already have minor conflicts. She's shy and he's the life of the party. And how's that bringing about conflict, guys?

Madelene When we go out – before we go out, I usually ask him who will be there. And if there's anyone I know that will be there. And he gets mad at me that I ask him that. And I'm the type – well, he'll go to a party, he'll walk in. And he'll just – he won't know anyone, but he'll just talk to anyone. And I'm the type where I'll walk in, I'll talk to people, but it takes me a while to warm up.

Oprah And isn't that what attracted you to him?

Madelene Yes. *(audience laughter)*

Oprah So why is there now conflict?

Madelene He – 'cause he gets mad at me.

Oprah For not being . . .

Madelene For – well, he gets mad at me when I ask him about – when
I ask him questions, 'well, who's going to be there?' (p. 28)

What we see here is that Madelene is describing a dynamic similar to the
one between Dale and Cari. That is, as Madelene puts it, Jay has a
problem with her shyness and Madelene has a problem with Jay's
problem with her. The subject of the whole interchange was supposedly
Madelene's frustration with Jay. However, this is quickly turned into an
inquiry into Madelene herself when Oprah asks 'Isn't that what
attracted you to him?', a question which is not at any time asked of Jay.
The shift of scrutiny is reinforced when Harville then explains that:

Harville You always are attracted to somebody who has a strength
you don't have. Then, when you get involved in the
relationship, that strength becomes a problem to you and
then you criticize them and ask them to give that strength
away (p. 30).

Clearly, Harville's comment cannot be ascribed to Jay. It can only be
Jay's ability to 'get on with people', not Madelene's shyness, which is
construed as the strength the other partner does not have. Nor, within
these parameters, can we know what 'strength' (if any) Jay is attracted
to in Madelene since only her 'weakness' (shyness) is mentioned. We
would argue, furthermore, that there is a mis-ascription here. Harville
seems to be saying that Madelene is both attracted to (if not envious of)
and critical of Jay's outgoingness and ability to mix. However, it seems
to us that while she is indeed attracted to his outgoingness, what angers
her is his insensitivity to her feelings. Harville conflates extroversion
and insensitivity – two quite different qualities. Furthermore, according
to Harville's analysis, *Madelene* seems to have constructed (or projected) her own frustration with herself on to Jay. In other words,
Madelene only *has* a problem because she *is* the problem. Jay, on the
other hand, has a problem because Madelene is a problem.

Given this reversal, it is hardly surprising that the exercise which
ensues becomes a parody of itself:

Harville Madelene is going to communicate a frustration to Jay.

Madelene Jay, it gets me really mad when we are going out that you jump down on me and say, 'Why do you get that way?' I want to – it gets me mad that you know how I am but you yell at me for how I – I am.

Harville So then, the next process is to mirror that back so you're sure you've got it, Jay. So, if I got it right. . .

Jay If I got it right, I – I understand that I shouldn't be getting all over you for, you know, not being more aggressive or – or not being as loud as I am.

Harville Did I get it?

Jay Did I get that right?

Madelene Yes.

Harville OK. Now, we want you to change that frustration into what you would want instead, which if you had it, you wouldn't be frustrated. We call that 'the desire hidden in the frustration'.

Madelene Jay, when we go out, I wish that when we're at a party or somewhere where I don't know a lot of people, that you would come up to me and put your arm around me and say 'How're you doing?' (pp. 31–2).

At this point, it seems clear that what Madelene is asking for is for Jay to be aware of how she is feeling, to notice her when they are in company and, in fact, to be *with* her. It is significant that she describes her feeling about Jay's behaviour as anger ('it makes me mad') while Harville again mis-ascribes to her a very different emotion. 'Frustration' is defined as 'having a sense of discouragement and dissatisfaction' which may indeed lead to anger but is not the same thing. In attributing to Madelene frustration rather than anger, Harville effectively trivializes what she actually says. It is also important to note that, while Harville seems to construct Madelene as 'criticiz[ing Jay's strength]', Jay by contrast, seems to understand that Madelene is criticizing his insensitivity in expecting her to be 'aggressive or . . . as loud as [he is]'. However, in the exchange which follows, Harville and Oprah, between them, subvert Jay's understanding by requiring, from Madelene, a mechanistic, behaviour modification type of demand. Harville says:

Harville   OK. Now I want you to refine it a little more. And say how many – usually we give a timeframe to it, which is the practice, the training period. Like for the next month, each time we're at a party, I'd like you to come up to me once or twice or three times or whatever . . .

This forces Madelene into the rather absurd position of saying:

Madelene Jay, for the next month, I'd like – when we do go to a party, I'd like you to come up to me and introduce me to people and to . . .

Oprah   How – how many times?

Harville   Once – once or twice or three times?

Madelene Three times.

Harville   Three times *(audience laughter)* All right.

Jay   OK. If I – Madelene, if I got it right, you want me to, in the course of the next month, when we go to these parties, I'll come up to you at least three times and tell you that I'm thinking of you and that I know you're there. Do I have this right?

Madelene You got it right.

Harville   OK. And now . . .

Oprah   Can I just stop you here and say – and make note of how important this is? The reason why this struck me – I don't know if it struck you guys, too, and you guys watching at home – is because so many times – like when she said that at first . . .

Harville   Yes.

Oprah   Like, 'I'd like you to come up to me at a party'. You have in your own mind about how many times it would make you comfortable.

Harville   That's right.

Oprah   But he doesn't know what those times are unless you say it. But you assume that because you've now said, 'I want

56

you to come up to me at the party,' that he knows how many times. That's why the how many times, although it sounded a little corny, really was really effective and essential (p. 33).

Once more, Jay seems, despite the mention of frequency, to understand the gist of what Madelene was really saying. But Harville and Oprah's insistence on putting a number on Madelene's request again makes light of what is a far from trivial problem. It misconstrues as quantitative a problem which is, in fact, qualitative. As with Dale and Cari, what seems at issue here is a pattern of male expectations of ideal wife/girlfriend imposed on his partner through critique of her person. The audience's laughter during this exchange seems to indicate an awareness of how inappropriate the quantification of the request is. Possibly this is why Oprah seems to feel impelled to justify it in order to re-place the audience with the flow of the programme. Furthermore, it is disquieting to note that the misconstruction of what Madelene wants, places her in an invidious position. Although clearly this is not their intention, Oprah and Harville nevertheless set up conditions for the further disempowerment of Madelene within the relationship. If Jay and Madelene follow through with the exercise for the next month, Madelene will not get the kind consideration she (quite reasonably) wants and yet Jay will have done exactly what he was supposed to do (to the number). In other words, she will have no comeback if she is still angry or unhappy; it will be even more her problem (and her fault) than it was before. Rather than a recipe for improved relations, as intended, it seems to us that the couple have been given a recipe for disaster.

All's well that ends well?

We are not trying to argue here that the ideas put forward by Harville and Oprah have nothing of value to offer. It makes sense to us to recognize that good relationships require work, that people carry their previous experiences with them and that these experiences affect how they behave in the present. It is also clear that active listening is important and needs to be demonstrated in the course of dialogue, particularly where people are struggling with problems in their relationships. However, for both couples, we can see that the exercises they are asked to undertake are, at best, problematic and, at worst, damaging. Just how dubious they can be as ways of 'solving' problems or 'saying good-bye' can be seen if we apply them to situations involving violence and abuse. Imagine, for example, the good-bye process re-deployed:

Her   I'm saying good-bye to the times you came home drunk, to the beatings, to the rapes, to the terror you inflicted on me and the children . . .

Harville Now say good-bye to the good stuff that won't ever be again . . .

Any attempt to rewrite either of these exercises, or indeed Harville's self-help approach as a whole, to apply to patterns of severe abuse would inevitably emerge, at the very least, as inappropriate. This is because there is no framework which recognizes inequality as a central problem in heterosexual relationships.[31]

As we have seen, 'How to Make Love Last' is characterized by a repeated pattern of mis-ascription, mis-recognition and mis-understanding. Power relations are understood only in terms of individual unresolved patterns from childhood; problems between couples are construed as the problems of the woman; problems within marriage are dissected without reference to the institutional character of marriage. In similar vein, choice and responsibility are invoked in ways which assume equality of position between men and women but inequality of responsibility. Women are seen to be responsible both for the origin and solution of problems within heterosexual relationships. Indeed, women are effectively seen to be the problem and to be the site for and agent of remedial work.[32] Moreover, heterosexuality is assumed to be a site for dysfunction and the 'repetition of [women's] bad patterns' on the one hand, and yet on the other hand the universal ideal. Furthermore, because of the lack of a critical framework which considers power relations, it is possible at one and the same time both to invoke and to deny the continuities between 'extreme' forms of abuse and 'mundane' misunderstandings. Clearly, then, the model of self-help therapy underpinning the programme is not capable of resolving the issues raised within it precisely because it rules out the possibility of considering the social character of the relationships under scrutiny and the social positions of the actors involved. In this context, the exercise of 'mirroring' back can be not only mechanical, but can also be a way of appearing to understand the Other while in fact re-inscribing (her) Otherness. All of this is demonstrated forcibly in Oprah and Harville's final summary of the lessons of the programme:

Harville That's why marriages don't work. There's no commitment to mutual healing and mutual helping.

Oprah 'Cause that's what marriage is? A commitment to . . .

Harville That's what marriage is. Marriage – marriage is a structure for healing. And if you do meet each other's childhood needs, you'll have the marriage of your dreams. And if you don't, you'll have the marriage of your nightmares. And you can predict that. (p. 38)

To posit marriage as 'a structure for healing' seems, at best, wishful thinking and, at worst, actively deceitful. Surely it contradicts the evidence amply provided in this and many other programmes from the *Oprah Winfrey Show* that, far from being a structure for healing, marriage can be seen as a structure for 'wounding' and for the disempowerment of women and children. Harville himself, makes this point in his theory of the childhood 'wound' and cycles of abuse, albeit not with the intention of critiquing the institution or framework of marriage in itself.[33] Not only does this facile exchange contradict the predominant experience of marriage,[34] but it also contradicts the historical meaning of the legal/economic/social contract of marriage which has served as a structure for ensuring patrilinial inheritance and for the inscription of women (and their children) as property.[35]

Epilogue

As our analysis shows, the twin frameworks of therapy and presumed heterosexuality have all but ruled out the possibility for questions to be raised about power relationships and patterns of social inequality. It seems to us that it inevitably becomes a contradiction in terms to seek to challenge common sense and common forms of oppression through frameworks which mitigate against such questions. We would suggest that a very different picture of Dale, Cari, Jay and Madelene's situations would have emerged, given a framework which questions the social character of individual patterns in relationships, which interrogates gendered and other forms of inequality and which challenges expertise and dominant social institutions.

The close reading which we have given to this one programme reveals a significant disjuncture between Oprah's explicit goals for her show and the contradictory effects of its framework. Indeed, what we have seen is that the framework and format of the show can easily subvert the challenging educational objectives of the kind of socially responsible television Oprah is aiming to produce[36] and can disempower precisely those people whom she is aiming, through the show, to empower.

Notes

We would like to thank members of the Politics of Sexuality Group for their critical support and the many people who have encouraged us to continue with this work. We would also like to thank staff at the British distributors of the *Oprah Winfrey Show*, Midlantic Films and Vicky Spiratos at Burrelle's Transcription Services for their patient assistance in finding programme titles, first transmission dates and transcripts.

1. The criteria for 'adultness' are completely unclear. For example, a programme on women and men who had been fired from their jobs because they were lesbian or gay was broadcast as 'Adult Oprah', while a programme entitled 'Lesbian and Gay Baby Boom' was broadcast in the afternoon. Similarly programmes on child sexual abuse have been broadcast at both times.

2. Mellencamp (1992) and Squire (1994), for example, have commented on Oprah's women-centredness in both topic choice and personal manner; and Squire particularly locates Oprah within the general sphere of Black feminism.

3. Paolo Freire has developed the concept of 'conscientization' in, for example, *Pedagogy of the Oppressed* (1972). Freire argues for a pedagogy which focus on the conditions of oppression and empowering people to understand their oppression through both education and other forms of struggle. We feel that Oprah's role as an educator through television, particularly one with a commitment to social issues, makes it important to make use of the term 'conscientization' to identify the radical potential of such programming.

4. Between March and September 1993, we videotaped every *Oprah Winfrey Show* broadcast. This paper is based on extensive viewing of these programmes (both as they went out and during a concentrated period when we watched 30 hours of programming in one week) and, in some cases, of the transcripts provided by Harpo Productions. We have also watched a number of programmes on several occasions. Our analysis should be understood as being generated from viewing within the British context, where it can be said that television has a rather different cultural meaning than it does in the United States. For example, the tradition of pubic service and socially responsible

television broadcasting is one which has a certain hegemony in the UK (although this is currently under threat) compared with the American tradition of broadcasting for the 'lowest common denominator' and where television itself is generally seen as the 'idiot box'.

5. See also Squire's (1994) identification of a number of narratives which constitute the *Oprah Winfrey Show*.

6. We use the term 'kinship' in this chapter to describe both relationships between people in general and relatedness (or what is seen to count as being related to another person in familial terms).

7. It is beyond the scope of this chapter to consider this issue in depth. However, it is important to at least note that the presentation of therapeutic interactions as entertainment in itself constitutes a breach of the confidentiality which is usually considered to be axiomatic in therapy or counselling.

8. We recognise that making violence and abuse speakable cannot, by itself, solve the problems. Neither is the speakability of abuse unchallenged as we can see from the recent publicity given to 'false memory syndrome' (a notion which has infiltrated more than one of Oprah's programmes).

9. Note, however, Kelly , Regan and Burton's (1994) argument that neither 'victim' nor 'survivor' are appropriate descriptors for people who have experienced sexual abuse.

10. Another reason may be the ways in which therapy has become a key part of American popular culture and indeed has provided a kind of lingua franca for discussing personal and emotional difficulties. It is interesting to consider how this particular dimension of the language of the *Oprah Winfrey Show* translates in a British context where therapy has not become embedded in poular common

sense (or experience) to anything like the same extent.

11. It is significant, for example, that the Moynihan Report (1965) applied the term 'dysfunction' to African Americans.

12. It should be noted that the tradition of therapy, while claiming universality, is itself derived from European bourgeois culture.

13. This might appear very different if Oprah had a large number of people of colour appearing on the show as experts or guests. It is a question why she does not.

14. The phrase 'heterosexual matrix' is used by Judith Butler (1990).

15. Duncker uses this phrase to describe a central theme she sees in Margaret Atwood's fiction.

16. The *Oprah Winfrey Show* does also occasionally feature issues about women's abusive behaviour towards male partners or children. It is beyond the scope of this paper to examine these programmes and the ways in which they challenge or reinforce feminist critiques of patriarchal power. In any case, they do not represent either the vast majority of programmes or the more general picture of the ways abuse is gendered.

17. Unless otherwise indicated, all quotations have been drawn from the programme transcript produced by Burrelle's Information Services. However, where there were obvious mistakes in the transcript, we have made the appropriate corrections.

18. This is, of course, a liberal humanist argument in its assumption of a universal subject and in its presumption of human equality abstracted from the material inequalities which actually pertain in any given situation or between any given subjects. Indeed, the *Oprah Winfrey Show* is characterized more generally by liberal politics.

19. We use the term 'liberal equivalence' to describe the tendency to equate situations which involve unequal power relations as if they were equal. We see this as characteristic of liberal politics more generally and of the *Oprah Winfrey Show* specifically (see also note 21).

20. For example, Cari was wearing an obviously expensive (possibly designer) suede outfit and Dale, a suede jacket. All of the guests looked as if they were very well-heeled indeed. This was reinforced in more subtle ways by their manner of self-presentation, the language they used to describe themselves and the activities they referred to doing in their day-to-day lives.

21. See also Kelly 1986 and Kelly, Regan & Burton 1990 for further discussion of this point.

22. This formulation is, we presume, not intended as a critical commentary on the sexual politics of marriage where, indeed, two have been considered one and that *one* is the man. Indeed, as we have saggested above, where 'blame' is to be apportioned, that *one* is much more likely to be the woman. And in any case, within this logic, even if the 'wounding' parent had been the father, it would have been seen as the child's fault if not the mother's for marrying an abusive partner.

23. Although we would disagree with individualized cycle of abuse approaches and with Harville's particular version of it, it is nevertheless clear that many children, if not most are indeed damaged by 'family life'.

24. Twelve-step programmes such as Alcoholics Anonymous have provided the main paradigm for popular self-help books and organizations in relation to a wide variety of problems.

25. This includes Harville and Helen's 'ideal relationship'. For example, in a subsequent extract from their video it emerges that they have been conflicted about Helen's habitual lateness, but while Helen has had to learn to accept Harville's impatience with this, he has apparently not had to learn anything:

Helen I mean, you know, he can pick up a paper. He's always complaining that he doesn't have time to read. And he could just flow with it. And I had to learn to first acknowledge that you were never going to flow with my being late.

Harville Yeah.

Helen Then second, really respect and honour it. And then — and now, I think it's rather charming that you — and dear.

Harville That I won't flow with your being late (p. 27).

26. We were initially perplexed about the shift of attention from Dale to Cari as object of the 'you'. What was immediately visible was that, following Oprah's question, Dale looked towards Cari to answer. What we were not clear about at first was whether he had instigated the shift or Oprah had. It was only when we watched the video in slow motion we were able to detect that Oprah had turned her gaze on Cari as she asked the question. We wondered why Oprah shifted the focus in this way. It seemed to us there were two possible reasons: firstly, the common sense of the programme as we discussed above and specifically Harville's framework seemed to assume that relationship problems stem from *women's* negative pattern. Secondly, it may be that Oprah was simply more drawn to and interested in Cari (perhaps because presented herself assertively and immediately tapped into the ethos of the programme).

27. Interestingly, Harville's view that one

needs to resolve problems in one relationship before moving on to another one through a 'goodbye process' excludes the very relationship, i.e. with the parents, which he identifies as the origin of all 'problem patterns'.

28. For example:

Dale I want to say good-bye to feeling third and fourth choice ...

Harville And tell *her.*

Dale ... where our son came first, which was understandable. But her parents came second; her friends came third.

Harville And say *your* friends. *Your* friends.

Dale Your friends.

Harville Your parents.

Dale Your parents came third, and then me in every consideration and every way she . . .

Harville You. You.

Dale ... handled all of our ...

Harville Say *you.*

Dale You – in every way that you handled all of our – our friendships. It was always your friends . . .

Cari If I got it, you are saying good-bye to being third, fourth and fifth. My putting our son, which was understandable, but my family and friends ahead of you . . . And basically to sum it up, that I never, ever made you number one. (pp 24–5).

29. See, for example, Spender 1980; Cameron 1985; Swann and Graddol 1988. These authors, among others, have pointed out that men/boys tend to talk more than women/girls, that they tend to interrupt women/girls more than the reverse, and that the kind of contributions that girls/women make in conversation tend to be geared towards bringing the other out while men/boy's conversation tends to be more self-referential.

30. More specifically, Dale criticises Cari for having friendships which, in his view, she prioritises over him. Indeed, he points out that even their son Drake claims more of Cari's attention than he does (though he acknowledges that this is understandable).

31. This is not to suggest that lesbian and gay relationships are not characterized by problems relating to a range of inequalities, or that sexist inequality is the only form of inequality inscribing compulsory heterosexuality. We are also well aware that heterosexual couples (and all couples) can actively struggle against sexist and other forms of inequality within their relationships. By 'struggle' here, we are not arguing that individuals can simply choose for their relationships to be exempt from being shaped by social inequalities. What we are suggesting is that the personal is political and that relationships are therefore a site of personal/political struggle.

32. It is interesting to note that this positioning of women as both problem and problem solver is a leitmotif within popular women's magazines (see Winship 1987). Clearly the intertextuality between the *Oprah Winfrey Show* and women's magazines in this and other respects is important both for the ways in which viewers might read the show and how the show can be understood as being addressed primarily to women.

33. Indeed, to draw on Sandra Harding's (1992) taxonomy with respect to critical approaches to the analysis of science, Harville takes what may be described as an *empiricist* critique of marriage, i.e. he critiques 'bad marriages' but not 'marriage-as-usual'. Many feminists, by contrast, have critiqued both the institution and the fundamental social character

of marriage in itself.
34. See Shere Hite (1991, 1994), among many others, whose work demonstrates this point.
35. Marriage has also served as a structure for the eugenic reproduction of particular social and cultural formations (i.e. 'desirable' populations). This is reflected in rules or social conventions about who is allowed, disallowed or forced to marry whom.

36. This is not to suggest that Oprah is not interested in producing entertainment and in gaining mass audiences. As Oprah might well ask, how useful is socially educative television which no one watches? The question remains whether there is any popular appeal discourse which would not throw up similar contradictions to those which we have discussed in relation to therapy.

References

Anthias, F. and Yuval-Davis, N. (1992) *Racialised Boundaries: Race, Nation, Gender, Colouring Class and the Anti-Racist Struggle*. London: Routledge.

Barrett, M. and MacIntosh, M. (1982) *The Anti-Social Family*. London: Verso.

Butler, J. (1990) *Gender Trouble: Feminism and the Subversion of Identity*. London: Routledge.

Cameron, D. (1985) *Feminism and Linguistic Theory*. London: Macmillan.

Chodorow, N. (1978) *The Reproduction of Mothering*. Berkeley: University of California Press.

Chodorow, N. (1989) *Feminism and Psychoanalytic Theory*. New Haven: Yale University Press.

Collins, P. H. (1990) *Black Feminist Thought: Knowledge, Consciousness and the Politics of Empowerment*. London: Unwin Hyman.

Delphy, C. and Leonard, D. M. (1993) *Familiar Exploitation: A New Analysis of Marriage in Contemporary Western Societies*. Cambridge: Polity.

Duncker, E. (1993) Heterosexuality: fictional agendas, in Wilkinson, S. and Kitzinger, C. (eds) *Heterosexuality: A Feminism and Psychology Reader*. London: Sage.

Epstein, D. and Steinberg, D. L. (1995a) 12 steps to heterosexuality: common-sensibilities on the *Oprah Winfrey Show, Feminism and Psychology*, 5, (2) pp. 275–80.

Epstein, D. and Steinberg, D. L. (1995b) Heterosensibilities on the *Oprah Winfrey Show*, in Purvis, J. and Maynard, M. (eds) *(Hetero)Sexual Politics*. London: Taylor & Francis.

Freire, P. (1972) *Pedagogy of the Oppressed*. Harmondsworth: Penguin.

Hite, S. (1991) *The Hite Report on Love, Power and Emotional Violence*. London: MacDonald Optima.

Hite, S. (1994) *The Hite Report on the Family: Growing Up Under Patriarchy*. London: Bloomsbury.

hooks, b. (1982) *Ain't I a Woman*. London: Pluto.

Kelly, L. (1986) *Surviving Sexual Abuse*. London: Polity.

Kelly, L., Regan, S. and Burton, L. (1991). Short summary of findings from an exploratory study of the prevalence of sexual abuse in a sample of 16–18 year olds. Mimeograph. Polytechnic (now University) of North London.

Kelly, L., Regan, S. and Burton, L.

(1994). The victim/survivor dichotomy: beyond an identity defined by violation. Paper given at the British Sociological Association Conference, University of Central Lancashire.

Mellencamp, P. (1992) *High Anxiety: Catastrophe, Scandal, Age and Comedy*. Indianapolis: Indiana University Press.

Rubin, G. (1975) The traffic in women, in Reiter, R. (ed.) *Toward an Anthropology of Women*. New York: Monthly Review Press.

Spender, D. (1980) *Man Made Language*. London: Routledge.

Squire, C. (1994) Empowering women? the *Oprah Winfrey Show, Feminism and Psychology: Shifting Identities: Shifting Racisms (Special Issue)*, 4, (1) 63–79.

Swann, J. and Graddol, D. (1988) Gender inequalities in classroom talk, *English in Education*, 22, (1) 48–65.

Winship, J. (1987) *Inside Women's Magazines*. London: Pandora.

3

Technologies of Heterosexuality: Eugenic Reproductions Under Glass

Deborah Lynn Steinberg

Straight selections: eugenics and (hetero)sexuality

The common sense and traditional meaning of 'eugenics' as both a philosophy and a historical set of practices have been embedded in the rationality of twentieth-century science and medicine. Eugenic science has simultaneously emerged as a project of social engineering based on medical scientific theories of heredity, of natural inheritance, and a more general logic of selection and impetus to control the reproduction of desired and stigmatized social categories and characteristics. Eugenic discourses have linked notions of natural (i.e. genetic) 'fitness' and judgements of social acceptability in a project of social engineering. In Foucauldian terms, the eugenic gaze is at once a praxis of hierarchical observation and normalizing judgement, a scientific and socializing disciplinary regime of reproduction.

Conventionally, eugenics is primarily understood as a (discredited) genetically based science of racial and racist selection, though one whose tentacles of reproductive control have also incorporated class and ableist elements (Mort, 1987, Morris, 1991; Proctor, 1988). Less commonly is eugenics directly associated with or seen as expressive of a dominant discourse of family, that discourse of 'legitimate' kinship in which class, gendered and racialized inequalities are normalized and in which heterosexuality is assumed and (re)inscribed. In other words, in its widest sense, the project of eugenics is the project for the reproduction of 'legitimate' family and the social relations of inequality which underpin it. Here, scientific notions of heredity and modes of medical control over reproduction can be understood as components of a much more complex logic of controlled reproduction which is, itself, embedded within what Adrienne Rich (1978) has termed 'compulsory' and Judith Butler (1990) has termed the 'matrix of heterosexuality'. Eugenic ideas and practices, then, are about not only racialized and classed but also gendered and heterosexist notions of nature, and the heritability of normality and abnormality. If the policing (coerced or voluntary[1]) of the putative boundaries of race and class is a defining feature of eugenic theory and practice, it is underpinned by and mediated through the presumption and policing of heterosexuality.

I am not the first to suggest that new reproductive technologies, including *in vitro* fertilization (IVF)[2] bespeak or are at least linked with a logic of social engineering.[3] However, it is significantly the case that most debates around IVF and related practices have not been concerned with the ways in which these practices may reflect, reproduce and, perhaps most importantly, (re)normalize eugenic sensibilities. Nor have critical studies either of the history of eugenics or of reproductive technologies considered the reproduction of heterosexuality as a specifically eugenic project in the terms I discuss above. I would suggest, however, that whether or not heterosexuality has been theorized specifically as hereditary, it is not only assumed to be so in and of itself, but is intrinsically bound up with those characteristics (desired or derided) which have been understood more conventionally as appropriate (or inappropriate) objects of eugenic practices.

This paper argues that IVF and related practices are underpinned by a eugenic logic and sensibility in which the reproduction of heterosexuality is both an end in itself and an organizing logic. Drawing on examples from a survey I undertook of criteria for patient screening in British IVF clinics, this paper will show that IVF practice is permeated with notions of reproductive 'fitness' which are elaborated within and through the boundaries of conventional heterosexuality. Specifically, I shall argue that while the survey reveals a continuum of overt to covert forms of patient screening, there are significant contradictions regarding what practitioners regard as discriminatory or legitimate screening; and that these contradictions reflect a commitment to the principle of screening within which it is possible to be engaged in the very forms of selection to which practitioners may state opposition. In this context I shall consider the implications of selection policies in relation to the social profiles of IVF patients; and, perhaps most importantly, the ways in which IVF selection practices can be seen to relate in direct and indirect ways to the reproduction of ableist, class oppressive, (hetero)sexist and racist social divisions.

Professional cultures and sexual boundaries: IVF and feminist critique

Since 1978, with the birth of Louise Brown, the first 'test-tube baby', the advent and growth of IVF and related practices has generated, particularly during the 1980s, a significant body of critical feminist activism and literature. This literature reflects the perspectives both of feminists who have been interested in exploring potential benefits for women (see, for example: Stanworth, 1987; Birke *et al.*, 1990) and feminists who consider that these technological innovations are fundamentally oppressive in gendered and other respects (e.g. Corea, 1985; Spallone and Steinberg, 1987; Klein, 1989). Much of this literature has focused on several interrelated questions: the impact of IVF related treatments on women in various respects (e.g. health, social status) ; the attitudes of women towards IVF; and motives women have for undergoing treatment. In this context, questions of women's reproductive rights and the scope afforded in the context of IVF treatment for women's reproductive choice have been central. A somewhat less developed, though no less significant, aspect of feminist critical studies of IVF has focused on the professional cultures of IVF treatment, that is, on questions around the motivations, rights and choices of practitioners in the field and on the ways in which they do or do not understand their practices in gendered, racialized, classed and other ways (see, for example, Spallone, 1989 and McNeil *et al.*, 1990). This paper contributes directly to the latter project, that is, to debates around practitioner values and cultures in relation to women's fertility (specifically IVF). However, I would suggest that it is crucial to consider and understand access policies of clinics. It is important to note that patients can only choose from the choices offered by medical professionals.

A second underdeveloped area of debate, of particular importance for this study, concerns questions of the regulation and recuperation of conventional (heterosexual) definitions of family through reproductive technologies (see, for example, Stanworth, 1987; Klein, 1989; Spallone, 1989; Haines, 1990). However, the predominant focus in this literature is on the ways in which family ideology relates to the reproductive choices of infertile women (who are largely white, middle class and heterosexual). As I have argued elsewhere (Steinberg, 1994) the concentration on this particular group of 'consumers' has, at times and in significant ways, obscured both the questions of *professional* agency and, specifically, the ways in which the regulation of heterosexuality is central to a broader selection-orientated professional ethos. It is therefore my intention in this paper to bring critical questions about the reproduction of heterosexuality through reproductive technologies to the centre – to examine reproductive technologies as technologies of heterosexuality.[4]

Regulating sexualities: reproductive medicine and social control

Any evaluation of contemporary practices in reproductive medicine needs to be considered in the context of the historical relationship between medicine, women's reproductive autonomy and health; the role of medicine as an institution of social control and in the formation of dominant discourses of family and breeding. Feminist and other commentators have, for example, given complex accounts of the heritage of compromised autonomy, bodily alienation and professional disenfranchisement for women, both as practitioners and patients through the medicalization and masculinization of health care, and particularly of sexuality and reproduction (see, for example, Oakley, 1976; Witz, 1992; Donnison, 1993). In this context, the significant role of professional medicine in the (re)production of class, gendered, racialized and sexualized social divisions[5] in the formation and policing of dominant discourses of family and (hetero)sexuality are widely documented (Butler, 1990; Fried, 1990; Mort, 1987; Oakley, 1976). Barker, (1981) has argued in the context of the contemporary character of racism in Britain, that class and racialized divisions have specifically been mediated through (medical and) scientific discourses of breeding and nation.[6] Mort (1987) and, more recently Anthias and Yuval Davis (1993) have explored the ways in which discourses of breeding and nation interface with and intensify gender divisions more widely. Mort's work, moreover, identifies classed and gendered discourses of breeding as sexualized, specifically as discourses of sexual purity and pollution. The history of reproductive medicine, in other words, has been deeply invested in and formative of eugenic ideologies of kinship, family and reproductive heritage and these, in turn, have mediated and been mediated by cultural sensibilities around 'dangerous' and 'acceptable' sexualities. Medicine as a profession and reproductive medicine in particular, have played central roles in the mediation, (re)production and regulation of sexuality and particular definitions of 'legitimate' family. These, in turn have had serious implications for the shaping of a range of social inequalities and specifically for the importance of medicine in that process.

This history raises important questions for an evaluation of contemporary innovations in reproductive medicine. As I noted above, criteria by which IVF and related practices are given to or withheld from women patients are established centrally by medical professionals (though other institutions, including the law (Human Fertilization and Embryology Act 1990), are implicated). In this context, it is important to evaluate the social relations of diagnostic and treatment decisions made by practitioners, i.e. the criteria by which practitioners select or de-select potential patients, specifically with reference to questions about the regulation of family and sexuality.

This study

Between January and April 1990, I conducted a postal questionnaire-survey, with open-ended questions, of all registered clinics offering *in vitro* fertilisation (IVF) and gamete intra-fallopian transfer (GIFT)[7] in Britain.[8] The survey had several aims: firstly, to gain some insight into the attitudes of IVF/GIFT professionals[9] regarding their practices; secondly, to gain information beyond that provided in the Voluntary Licensing Authority (VLA)[10] Reports about the practices at the clinics; thirdly, specifically to investigate screening policies, that is, criteria and rationales for accepting or rejecting potential patients and embryos. With respect to patient screening, questions were asked about physiological and non-physiological criteria (e.g. age, marital status, socio-economic status, race, etc.) for providing IVF/GIFT. Questions were also asked about policies around genetic screening criteria for both patients and embryos. A total of 75 questionnaires were sent out, out of which 35 (47 per cent) were returned and 24 (32 per cent) were completed.[11]

The survey took place during the period leading up to the passage of the Human Fertilisation and Embryology Act (HFE) Act 1990. Thus, responses were at a particularly sensitive and key historical moment of negotiation of 'legitimate' IVF and related practices. Although not raised as a major issue during the dominant debates over statutory regulation of IVF, responses to this survey suggest that the issue and practices of selection, both of patients and of embryos, have been central to the practice, ethos and future direction of IVF and GIFT. As we shall see, while there appear to be a number of differences amongst clinic screening policies, there are a wide range of similarities in practitioner responses, suggesting a shared professional 'common sense' about 'appropriate' reproduction (i.e. who should and should not be parents) and about the 'appropriate' role of practitioners in managing it. While the responses represent a small number in 'real' terms, nevertheless they suggest fairly widespread assumptions by practitioners that IVF professionals are entitled (perhaps even obliged) to have and exercise power, through the medium of IVF/GIFT practices, over the reproductive decision-making of others. This paper will concentrate on responses of practitioners around non-physiological criteria for screening patients and their evaluations of the importance of genetic screening of patients and embryos.

Finally, it must be noted that preceding studies (e.g. Arditti *et al.*, 1984; Corea, 1985)[12] of IVF patients have indicated the predominance of white, middle-class, able-bodied women living in heterosexual couples amongst those undergoing treatment. A similar social profile of IVF patients emerges from the media coverage of this field of medicine. For example, pictorial representations of parties assembling large groups of IVF children (which also feature white, male IVF doctors) or announcements of the births of various IVF children, as well as descriptions in nearly all IVF literature of IVF 'couples' (see Steinberg, 1993) suggest this profile. It is in this context that I am interested to consider ways what responses to this survey suggest about the relationship between patient-screening practices and the dominant profile of IVF patients.

Reproducing heterosexuality: reproducing heterosexism

The regulation of heterosexuality in patient profiles is both direct and explicit.[13] With one exception, all clinics (23 out of 24) refused to treat women who were not either married or in long-term (marriage-like) heterosexual partnerships. It is interesting that the one respondent who indicated that his/her clinic would treat all categories of women listed in the questionnaire (married, single, divorced and widowed women as well as single lesbians and lesbian couples) was from a private clinic. It is, of course, possible that this apparently liberal access policy may have been motivated by financial factors. Indeed, this same respondent, unlike all the others, also indicated that all listed physiological conditions were used as indicators for IVF treatment. In other words, this respondent seemed willing to treat any woman without restriction.

There were two related arguments used to justify the restriction of treatment to married women or women in long-term heterosexual relationships. The first expressed an unwillingness in principle to assist any but heterosexual married (or akin to married) women to reproduce. The second, more subtle version of this position put forward what I would term the 'scarcity' argument about IVF/GIFT provision.

'Ethically dubious' women

Many clinicians took the position expressed in the Warnock Report (1984), and eventually in the Human Fertilization and Embryology (HFE) Act 1990,[14] that children should be raised by heterosexual couples and that women living in anything other than this kind of arrangement should not be assisted to reproduce:

> I would personally have reservations about doing for [lesbians] – I feel a child should much preferably have a father as well as a mother in their formative years. [divorced women], same effectively as [lesbians]. (C17)[15]

> We do not consider categories [single, divorced, widowed, lesbian women] as ideally suited to managing GIFT treatment and having a child. (C22)

> Like to think child born to stable relationship with a mother and father. (B9)

> Ethical considerations. (B28)

Respondents indicate two possible sources for such a policy. One, as suggested by C17 comes as a result of clinicians' personal views about appropriate parenting, or as another respondent put it 'personal choice' (C18). Only one practitioner (see (B14) below) indicates any reservations about imposing personal views about who should be appropriate parents or potential patients. These responses are significant not only for the ways in which they seem to reproduce dominant common-sense definitions of 'legitimate' family, but also for what they suggest about the discretionary character of professional power and accountability *vis-à-vis* patients. Clearly these respondents implicitly define the value judgements on their patients' social profiles as a legitimate component of their medical responsibilities. In this respect the reproduction of 'acceptable' heterosexualities is contiguous with the reproduction of professional power and domain.

Other respondents attribute the source of heterosexist selection policies to ethical committees:

> At present we are planning for group a, b [married, married-like] to avoid confrontation with ethical committee and other [indecipherable]. (C23)

> Ethical committee advice. (B3)

One response suggested that selection of heterosexual patients reflected NHS policy:

> Policy aimed at meeting NHS commitment of service primarily. (C35)

Others referred to fears of adverse media attention:

> You must be joking. I have conscientious objections to treating women in these ethically dubious groups. I certainly do not wish to end up in the national press! (CAA)

> Exclusion predominantly because of fear of public reaction and reservations from some team members. Acknowledge little evidence suggesting excluded groups could not make satisfactory parents/family units. (B14)

The last comment suggests that even where a practitioner does seem to have reservations about exclusionary policies, the ideology of the traditional nuclear family and heterosexist pressures seem too great to allow for resistance.

A second type of justification for heterosexist selection policies were arguments about the 'scarcity' of provision:

> More than enough work for 'straight couples'. No sperm freezing facilities easily available. (C16)

> Lack of time and facilities. At present we are limited to the above [married, cohabiting (heterosexual) couple]. (C10)

> Pressure of numbers in totally NHS clinic. (C19)

> Service developing and enough work by providing a and b. (C29)

> Totally NHS funded clinic with a long waiting list of heterosexual couples, therefore some criteria for inclusion had to be applied and the decisions were taken after discussion with colleagues. (B24)

The 'scarcity' argument, however, only explains the perceived need to restrict services. It does not explain the categorical exclusion of all women not living in heterosexual couples. Indeed, the policy could just as easily have been run on a first come, first served basis, or, indeed, based on physiological health considerations.[16]

A final reason suggested for heterosexist exclusions implied self-selection:

> We have no requests from the groups bracketed above. (B19)

In the context of a complex system of professional referral, it is important to ask what 'no requests from the groups' means. There are several possible interpretations. It is possible that GPs make no requests for IVF or GIFT on behalf of patients who are not heterosexual (as this is the regular avenue for specialist consultation). If this is the case, this would indicate that a heterosexist selection ethos (and practices) not only operate at specialized gynaecological and obstetric levels, but at all relevant levels of the medical hierarchy.

However, this practitioner might also be suggesting that only heterosexuals are presenting themselves to GPs (with infertility problems and/or requesting IVF or similar treatment). If this is the case, this raises questions about a possible pattern of self-selection. Indeed, self-selection on this basis would be in keeping with a range of pointedly heterosexist elements of contemporary British society. These include financial constraints on many single and lesbian mothers, for example, who tend to experience greater poverty than white, middle-class, heterosexual, partnered women; legal constraints, such as the instability of custody for lesbians (Rights of Women 1986); and the broader social disapprobation of lesbian parenting and lesbian life. More subtly, it may well be that the heterosexist representations and marketing, which reproduce the language and narrative of 'couples' (Franklin, 1990) of IVF and GIFT services is likely to reinforce the perception that the obstetric community would be unlikely to be sympathetic to lesbians' and single women's desires for children, or to their experiences of 'infertility' (a perception that would be born out by some of the disapproving comments of this sample of practitioners).[17]

Picking 'proper' parents

Patient screening is not, of course, limited to the overtly heterosexist practices of exclusion outlined above. Indeed, my study suggests that patient screening revolves around more subtle indices of not only conventionally heterosexual conceptualizations of 'proper families', but indeed of distinctively romantic notions of marriage (coupledom), home and hearth.[18]

Screening for 'Stability'

Nearly all respondents (22 of 24) claimed that the mental and psychiatric state of patients and their partners was used as a criterion for IVF and GIFT treatment. Half also indicated that this was a 'very important' consideration. There were two reasons given for this selection criterion: ability to cope with the strain of treatment and, significantly, ability to care for children:

Depends on ability to cope with stress of treatment and failure and ability to cope with baby/babies. (C16)

Ability to bring up child. (C19)

Only relevant where this would affect ability to deal emotionally with treatment/failure/pregnancy or with ability to care for child. (C22)

Pressure to avoid at all costs adverse parenting situations. (B14)

If psychiatric opinion indicates that pregnancy would be detrimental or that there would be disadvantage to the child. (B19)

Wish to bring children up in stable [healthy?] family. (B3)

These practitioners clearly saw themselves as responsible for the creation of families and both obligated and entitled to judge parenting abilities to this end. The reference to 'pressure to avoid. . . adverse parenting situations' distinctly suggests a worry about being held accountable for and implicated in 'bad parenting' practices. However, what, in Britain today, constitutes 'bad parenting' is constituted not only within medical but also through legal and popular discourses. In addition to a long history of medical opinion on and regulation of familial relations (from psychiatry to paediatrics to obstetrics and gynaecology) has been a similar range of governmental policies around child protection and definitions of a proper family. Recent legislative policies such as the Children Act 1989, for example, effectively define proper families as heterosexual nuclear units (see Langan, 1992, p. 78). Section 28 of the Local Government Act 1988 defines lesbian and gay households as 'pretended family relationships' (see Stacey, 1992) and lesbians, as I note above, are particularly vulnerable to losing custody of their children and being defined as unfit mothers. As I also point out above, the Warnock Report 1984 and eventually the HFE Act 1990 define the 'best interests of the children' in heterosexist terms. Furthermore, in practice, many commentators have noted that the authority of social workers to intervene in and regulate 'adverse parenting situations' is directed primarily to poor and black families, particularly those headed by single women (see Bryan *et al.*, 1985, pp. 112–20; Mama, 1992; Dominelli, 1992) It is notable in this context that two additional respondents indicated that the advice of social workers (as well as GPs and psychiatrists) regarding the suitability of prospective patients to parent were sought (A10; B16A).

Thus, concerns about the mental and psychiatric state of prospective patients and partners, and screening on this basis can be seen to reflect and (re)produce two related dominant common senses: a long standing regulatory discourse of parental 'fitness' and specifically a professional discourse which constructs medical professionals as primary arbiters of 'good' and 'bad' parenting and, in turn, constructs judgements about parenting as medical matters. In this context, the dominant white, middle-class, heterosexual profile of IVF/GIFT patients 'fits' the dominant discourse of 'parental fitness' and is clearly consistent with judgements about 'ethically dubious women' discussed above.

It must be said that not all practitioners indicated that IVF and GIFT treatment would be ruled out entirely for those judged to be mentally and psychiatrically 'unstable'. One respondent commented that 'if at that time, [the prospective patient/partner were] psychiatrically unstable, I would delay until improved as it is a stressful procedure' (C29). Another stated that patients (and partners) 'must be normal to "endure" IVF cycle. Would treat mental state prior to IVF' (B9). The juxtaposition of 'normal', in this last response, with ability to cope with IVF is interesting. Indeed, all of the responses discussed so far suggest that notions of personal and parental 'normality' are framed within an understanding of IVF/GIFT treatment as a project for the reproduction of 'traditional' family units. In so doing, IVF and GIFT practitioners join the ranks of other professionals (e.g. psychiatrists and social workers) whose job descriptions more obviously revolve around defining and regulating what is and is not considered 'normal' with respect to parenthood. Here this agenda is extended to the literal, hands-on, process of (re)generating familial relationships.

Regulating relationships: evaluations of emotional dynamics

Most respondents (17 of 24) indicated that the 'emotional dynamics of the family/couple', that is, evaluation of the quality of marital (or marriage-like) relationships, were a criterion for treatment:

Stable union required. (C16)

Vital that they should co-operate and work together to give support. (C23)

Would *obviously* depend upon stability of relationship. (A10) [my emphasis]

Would like to think they were stable. (B9)

Both must be wholeheartedly in favour of using this procedure. (B14)

Couple needs to be well motivated and in unison with the desire
for a family and the desire for such treatment. (B24)

Clearly, single women are excluded in this ethos of teamwork – a
concept, like 'stability,' discursively tied to (heterosexual) couples. Here
the emerging definition of an appropriate relationship is one in which
two 'think and feel as one' and in which there is an unequivocal desire
for children. This notion epitomizes the conventional, romantic
definition of marital union. Indeed, there is no consideration within
these criteria of the possibility that few relationships lack ambivalence
or are entirely stable and synchronous. Implicitly, these comments seem
to indicate that prospective patients must at least act the stereotyped
ideal of marital accord in order to be considered for treatment.[19] It is
interesting that respondent A10 seemed to feel he/she was stating the
'obvious' in considering marriage assessment as part of IVF and GIFT
protocols. This is a testament both to the ubiquity and power of
conventional family discourse (despite the fact that most families do not
conform to the ideal) and to practitioners' apparent sense of entitlement, if not obligation, to make such assessments as part of their
medical responsibilities.

Class and the reproduction of sexual divisions[20]

The reproduction of class divisions as sexual divisions has been
explored by Mort (1987), among others. The ways in which professional practices in the sphere of reproductive technologies are mediated
by and mediate class relations is clearly significant to an understanding
of their sexual politics. Of all the possible screening considerations
addressed in my study, the question of class-based selection practices
emerged as, perhaps, the most subtle, least 'intended' of those I queried.
Yet, while practitioner responses did not indicate wilful exclusions of
working-class/poorer-potential patients, class emerged as an effective
and significant dimension not only of exclusionary access policies, but
also as an intrinsic (if not explicit) part of the discourse of 'proper'
families which emerged more pointedly around questions of patients'
sexual/social status.

Two sections of the survey addressed the question of selection of
patients on the basis of class/economic factors: respondents were asked

about the cost of treatment by NHS or private provision of services; and whether financial status, ability to pay for treatment, educational qualifications, occupation and standard of accommodation were used as criteria for selecting or refusing prospective patients. Here respondents were asked if they selected on these bases and how important they considered these criteria.[21] The answers were somewhat contradictory. One would, perhaps, expect that those respondents who identified their clinics as private (20 of 24 total responses) would have regarded the ability to pay as important and therefore as a criterion for selection. However, ten respondents (six more than the number of NHS clinics in the sample) said ability to pay was not important and two more than that (twelve) indicated that this was not a criterion for selection. This discrepancy is significant because it suggests a breach between processes (e.g. costs) which may pre-emptively exclude poorer candidates from treatment and perceptions of those who implement or are responsible for those processes. Similar discrepancies were revealed by responses to all of my suggested categories.[22]

Nevertheless, whether or not respondents saw (or see) themselves/ their clinics as operating a direct selection policy on the basis of these considerations, clearly the single greatest factor which accounts for the dominance of (white) middle-class and heterosexual patients in the IVF context is the direct cost of treatment cycles, together with the hidden costs of treatment.[23] Costs of treatment in 1990 ranged, in private clinics (over 50 per cent of my sample) at between £250–£1750 per cycle, with the price of drug treatments extra. It is important to note, in this context, that most patients will undergo several cycles in order to have at least a 10 per cent chance of having a live birth. At most NHS clinics from my response pool, costs of drugs are extra and borne by patients. This has obvious implications for those groups, including black people, single women and lesbians,[24] most likely to be found in the poorer sectors of the population.

High-technology treatments like IVF and GIFT, moreover, require high levels of financial investment within the research and clinical context. Such investments, in an ever shrinking NHS budget, can only divert attention and resources away from primary medical care, specifically in this context from primary infertility prevention (such as mass screening for sexually transmitted diseases). It can be argued that the hegemonic association of progressive medicine with developments of increasingly sophisticated technological processes and expertise marginalize alternative, less glamorous, and indeed, less medicalized approaches to health care. Indeed, characteristic of a medical model is a definition of ill-health in terms of individual pathology (Illich, 1976), a definition which sidesteps the complex social conditions/relations of adversity and class inequality (e.g. poor housing, poverty, environmental pollution and oppression) which are associated with ill-health. Locker (1991) argues that 'numerous studies have shown that social class measured by occupation, education, income or area of residence, is closely related to health. . . . As a consequence, social and political change may be necessary to modify the health experience of these groups' (pp. 20–21). Certainly treatments like IVF and GIFT do not represent strategies aimed at social and political change in the class conditions which might foster impaired fertility.

Thirdly, as a middle-class constituency, the medical profession has traditionally acted as an agency of social control that has been particularly directed toward controlling working-class people and aimed at reinforcing middle-class morality. As Frank Mort argues, the profession has laid 'claim to a middle-class monopoly over the issues of health and hygiene' (Mort, 1987, p. 42). This general observation can be related directly to women's bodies, sexuality and reproduction. Anne Witz (1992) has noted that the politics of expertise and professionalization are class relations – relations which, I would suggest, are inevitably (re)produced in high-technology infertility treatments such as IVF and GIFT.

It can be argued that the policies delimiting access to IVF and GIFT on the bases discussed so far in this paper reflect and reinforce what Mort terms 'medico–moral regulation' (1987), that is the growing hegemony of medicine as an apparatus of social control over sexuality and reproduction. Historically constituted, in class- and race-specific ways, ideas about who can legitimately reproduce and parent (and who should be medically assisted to or prevented from doing so) (see, for example, Davis, 1990; Fried, 1990; White, 1990) have been the context in which IVF has been developed as a 'regulatory' approach (that is a mode of managing women's reproductive processes), as well as elaborated in the subsequent policies of access revealed in this survey.

In this respect, like much traditional medicine, neither IVF nor GIFT can be said to address inequalities experienced by poor and working-class people (inequalities which foster ill health, including infertility). They are firmly entrenched in (and elaborate) the dominant paradigm of professional medicine as well as the notion of scientific 'progress' which is, itself, embedded in the promotion and production of 'high' technology. This is a matter not just of access but of form, resources and priorities. Indeed, for this reason, it could be argued that a democratization of access to IVF and GIFT, even if it were possible or likely with increasingly privatized medical care does not, in itself, alter the fundamental classist character of the high-technology approach to health care that they embody. Nor does it address the integrally heterosexist character of class relations both within and outside the sphere of professional medicine. Moreover, while it has been argued that medicine has been about class regulation and control, there have also been studies which have shown the class-specific appeal of medical models (see Reissman, 1992 and Martin, 1987). Reissman has noted, for example, that middle-class (white and heterosexual) women have historically had a disproportionate investment in the medicalization of pregnancy and birthing. In this context, the disproportionate profile of middle-class IVF and GIFT patients may also reflect (intentionally and/or effectively selective) class/heterosexist relations which have characterized the process and reception of medical professionalization more generally.

Sexual regulation and racialized reproductions

Of all the questions asked in the survey, those regarding selection on religious or racial bases seemed to touch the nerve of an important tension that characterized all responses. All respondents either indicated 'no' (that race and religion were not criteria for treatment and that they were 'unimportant' considerations), or they declined to respond to the question at all. Significantly, while most respondents seemed pointedly untroubled at the idea of selecting patients on heterosexist criteria or on genetic bases (see below), the notion of selecting on racial or religious grounds was greeted as offensive by many.

Within a general expression of objection to the question, comments varied in significant ways. There were terse assertions that race and religion were 'not relevant' (C22) as selection criteria as well as the apparently liberal, democratically minded statements: 'Service for all' (C35), and 'if treatment is needed it should be given' (C10). These statements seem implicitly to claim both an anti-discriminatory and, in the latter case in particular, a narrowly physiological orientation in both the clinic policy and the medical context more generally.

While the tone remained consistent, it appeared that the prospect of selection on racial grounds provoked more pointed objections than did the prospect of doing so on religious grounds. One respondent, for example, on the question of racial selection expressed what seemed a more pointed criticism of the question, asking 'why should we?' S/he then provided a more ambivalent response to the question of religious exclusion:

> We don't not wish to play god. Customer (*sic*) is usually right. We worry about group whose religion nominally precludes assisted conception because it divorces them from moral support if family remain unsympathetic. (B14)

Another respondent with similar concerns wrote: '[religion] irrelevant if couples decide to continue after counselling'. I would suggest that, at least in part, the concerns expressed around religious beliefs in the context of IVF and GIFT reflect both the view of IVF/GIFT patients as 'couples' and 'family' members and the high visibility of objections to these treatments by right-wing Christian groups such as the Society for the Protection of Unborn Children (SPUC). It would be difficult to imagine reservations about giving medical treatment to a patient whose family or religious community were unsupportive in any other context. For example, would doctors feel reluctance or sensitivity of this kind in the case of a Jehovah's Witness who, in their view, needed and, importantly, presented themselves for treatment which violated the religious beliefs of their families or community? Moreover, the question of embryo 'personhood', raised by powerful religious lobby groups, was, at the time of this survey, reflected in legislative debates about the possible banning of IVF-based (embryo) research. In this climate, I would suggest that religious sensitivities on the part of practitioners are likely to have been high.

The quotation above also raises the question of the perception by practitioners of their own role and position in the context of their patient's reproductive decision-making. Statements such as: 'we do not wish to play god' and 'customer (sic) is usually right' deny that practitioners do make reproductive decisions for others. Another respondent, in a similar vein, commented: 'multi-racial and multi-religion country, therefore [screening on these bases] not appropriate' (B24). Yet, this is also a country where people have different sexualities and familial lifestyles. Nevertheless, all of these clinics discriminate on the grounds of sexuality and domestic arrangements, and as I discuss below, increasingly select patients and embryos on genetic grounds. Clearly there are circumstances in which discriminating or 'playing god' is considered more acceptable. Racial exclusion is seen here as discriminatory and illegitimate and an inappropriate exercise of practitioner power while heterosexist exclusion, however, apparently is not.[25]

Why would practitioners feel concern about 'playing god' in the racial and religious context, but not in the context of sexuality (or genetic 'health')? I would suggest that the notion of racial exclusion raises the spectre of selection practices under National Socialism and of, what I would term, the 'unacceptable face' of eugenics. As I discuss in more detail elsewhere (Steinberg, 1993), one of the characteristic arguments put forward by IVF practitioners in their books and articles is the rejection of any relationship between 'Nazi eugenics' and IVF practices. To this end, concerns with reproducing heterosexual family units and genetically 'healthy' offspring (see below) do not seem to raise criticisms in the way that a notion of racial selection does. In this context, sexual and genetic selection seem to be constructed as non-discriminatory and entirely legitimate precisely because they do not seem obviously to participate in the notorious discourse of racial hygiene. It would seem then, from the perspectives of my respondents, that heterosexist and genetic screening are understood as conceptually (and materially) separate from racism, indeed as having entirely different logics and ethos.

My respondents overwhelming claimed, then, that they and their clinics would find overt selection of patients on racial/religious grounds unacceptable (indeed, for many, repugnant). Taking it for granted that these responses are offered in good faith, nevertheless the overt and conscious rejection of racist selection criteria does not necessarily indicate the absence of racism in the overall selection process. Certainly the categories of selection respondents find acceptable are implicitly and historically racialized. The dominant discourse of family underpinning heterosexist selection policies is a case in point; dominant notions of 'legitimate family' are not only about heterosexuality and child-rearing, but are also racialized (white) and classed (middle class) (see, for example Carby, 1981; Collins, 1990; Anthias and Yuval-Davies, 1993). Secondly, the effective selection by economic status (discussed above) would disproportionately affect women of colour.[26] Thus, mechanisms for effective selection based on class/economic factors might serve simultaneously to exclude or marginalize in racialized ways. Thirdly, these issues must, of course, be seen in the context of the history of professional medicine which, as discussed above, has been widely critiqued not only as an agency of social control but also for its institutional racism both generally and with particular reference to obstetric and gynaecological specializations. Finally, as I noted earlier, media portrayals of IVF 'birthday parties' in Britain since the birth of Louise Brown have shown a striking predominance of white patients, children and practitioners. This stands as a notable contrast to the disproprotionate representation of black women patients with respect to procedures such as sterilization (Davis, 1990; Fried, 1990; White, 1990). This both suggests at least some kind of selection process and reinforces a common sense of IVF as designated white as well as heterosexual.

Genetic screening: selective rationalities normalized

Responses to my questions about genetic screening and counselling[27] reveal some variation of opinion about their perceived importance and role in IVF/GIFT practice. However, they also provide a keen illustration of the shared commitment to the *principle* of screening not-withstanding contestations about its appropriate form, context and targets:

Question: How important is genetic screening/counselling in IVF/GIFT treatment?

Not very important except where age or family history of [?] indicate it. (C19)

Only important where there is a high risk or suspected risk of genetic abnormality (e.g. recurrent miscarriage). (C22)

Very important. (C35)

For average couple it is irrelevant. (B16A)

Many of those over 35 years as would be the case for non-IVF pregnant women. 43 per cent of our IVF cycles are to women 35 years and older. (B16A)

If genetic problem offered, otherwise I don't see the relevance. Not appropriate in terms of IVF, only in usual cases for anyone wanting a pregnancy spontaneously. (B9)

Not important unless history of problems. (B3)

Should be available if requested or patients in high risk group. (B14)

With the exception of C35, these comments explicitly reveal that perceptions of legitimacy in relation to screening on genetic bases are negotiated through two key discourses: one of 'risk' and the other of voluntarism.

Languages of 'risk'

The designation of genetic screening for those who fall into the category of 'high risk' is an interesting construction of such screening as of limited importance. On the one hand, it appears that an 'average' couple is perceived of as having no genetic impairment. Genetic risk, therefore, seems to be perceived as a special case, rather than as a factor which would be routinely expected, at least as a potential problem, in the IVF/GIFT context. In this context, screening would, similarly, seem to be perceived as important only in exceptional cases. However, in order to designate prospective patients and/or their partners as 'high risk' in the first place, it would be necessary to undertake some form of genetic (family history) inquiry. Thus, this discourse of 'risk' depends on the widespread practice of precisely what it is perceived to limit.

Voluntary screening

That genetic counselling and screening should be voluntary rather than routinely imposed was explicitly indicated by most respondents:

If couple accepted the risks I would proceed. (C29)

It is indicated in some but patients need to decide and choose. (C23)

Helpful in relation to couple's being more able to make an informed decision with respect to less 'crippling' anomalies and enables difficult decisions to be undertaken jointly and other more serious situations. (B24)

One recurrent argument was that genetic counselling and screening are not routine for pregnant women (and their partners) outside the IVF/GIFT context so routine screening witthin IVF/GIFT treatment would not be justified:

We don't routine (*sic*) screen the normal fertile population. It is discriminatory to screen the infertile. (B14)

No evidence that there is increased risk of genetic disorder after GIFT treatment compared with spontaneous conception therefore why do counselling/screening? (C16)

One respondent suggested that routine counselling and screening might undermine the morale of patients:

Offered routinely it *may* upset some of the patients who are trying not to build up to (*sic*) much hope. (C29)

It would, of course, make sense that in a context where patients are intensely invested in having children, the possibility of being screened before or after conception for genetic 'abnormalities' might well be extremely distressing, particularly in the latter situation where they might be advised or feel compelled to terminate a 'high-risk' pregnancy.

Indeed, the language of 'risk' is a loaded one. As a diagnostic discourse, it resolutely individualizes the character of disability and thus sidesteps an interrogation of the social attitudes, conditions and inequalities which shape the experiences of disabled people. It is both imbedded in and reinscribes a pervasive common sense that disability is a natural and inevitable disaster. The call for voluntary screening places putative emphasis on patient's choice and on the perception that genetic counselling and screening enable patients to make difficult decisions. Yet, it is questionable what 'choice' might mean in the context of the language of 'risk'. In this context, a practitioner's willingness to proceed 'if couples accepted the risks', underestimates the power of negative medical discourses of disability, and medical judgements of expressed in the ableist language of 'risk'.[28] Considering the ableism endemic in our social institutions and dominant social (including medical) attitudes, how many patients would be willing to proceed with a pregnancy if advised that there was 'risk' of producing disabled offspring?[29]

It is my feeling that most practitioners' support genetic screening as a way to spare patients/offspring not only the perceived negative character of disability, but the negative social attitudes and conditions surrounding the lives of people with disabilities (and their primarily female carers). However, if the language of 'risk' assumes the natural negativity of disability, it also assumes the importance, even necessity, of preventing or terminating a pregnancy which 'risks' the reproduction of disability. The primary focus of concern in the context of genetic 'risk' assessment, whether performed on prospective parents or on embryos is the genetic profile of offspring. At the heart of these practices is a concern to prevent the birth of disabled children. Ironically, this inescapably eugenic sensibility naturalizes the very conditions and attitudes that practitioners may, through the practice of genetic screening, wish to spare prospective patients and their children. While practitioners may support genetic counselling/screening practices specifically out of a recognition of the harshly punitive realities of living as or caring for a person with disabilities in an ableist society, the underpinning ethos of genetic screening can also be seen to contribute to those very realities. If the emphasis on voluntary screening bespeaks a personal opposition to ableist discrimination, my respondents nevertheless clearly inhabit a discourse which normalizes it.

Significantly, no respondents indicated that they thought these questions 'provocative' (including the respondent who made this comment about the section of the questionnaire addressing other possible screening criteria, including race). While there were differences in the relative importance given to the role of genetic screening and counselling in the IVF and GIFT context, none stated that they had reservations about the use of such screening *per se*. While most respondents explicitly rejected the notion of routine screening, genetic considerations were clearly perceived as an important and consistent component of IVF and GIFT treatment by all of them. It is important to point out here, moreover, that concerns about the genetic profile of offspring are consistent with the other patterns of practice emerging from my survey. Indeed, the concern with medicalized quality control of offspring, in this respect, fits with more emphatically supported concerns to diagnose the quality of marriages and the fitness of prospective patients (and partners) to parent.

Finally, it is interesting and disturbing to note that cultural/medical languages of 'risk' have both sexualized and gendered as well as ableist resonances. Even before the era of HIV/AIDS, 'dangerous' sexualities – homo and hetero – have constituted 'medico–moral' discourses of class, race, family and breeding (see, for example, Walkowitz, 1980; Mort, 1987; Russett, 1989; Jackson, 1994). Female bodies (see, for example, Nead, 1988; Oakley, 1976; 1984; Moscucci, 1990; Donnison, 1993), disabled bodies (see, for example, Proctor, 1988; Morris, 1991) and homosexual bodies (see, for example, Weeks, 1991; Watney, 1989; Patton, 1985) have been constituted historically as sites of physical and social risk, as transmission vectors of physical and social disease, as signifiers of individual and social disorder and dysfunction. The advent of genetic diagnostic medicine within obstetrics and gynaecology is underpinned by and reproduces a complex discourse which links notions of risk, parental and professional responsibility (or even blame) and breeding – notions which, themselves, reflect and reproduce classed, racialized and sexualized social divisions. It is beyond the scope of this paper to explore this issue properly with respect to current professional practices within reproductive technological medicine. Nor does the empirical evidence of this study lend itself, alone, to an examination of the ways in which these questions constitute (or are challenged within) practitioner sensibilities and the professional culture of IVF. What clearly does emerge, however, is that genetic indices constitute a distinct dimension of a broader professional ethos selection orientated around explicit policing of heterosexuality and more subtle forms of racialized and classed regulations of reproductive sexuality. It is in this context that it is possible to suggest that if genetics is an 'acceptable face' of selection (along with heterosexuality), it, like heterosexist selections, may serve to mediate, rationalize and obscure other, less socially palatable forms of screening.

Technologies of heterosexuality

Responses to my survey suggest, therefore, that IVF and GIFT projects are not simply about enabling the infertile to biologically reproduce, but comprise an extensive social reproduction package. I have argued from my survey findings that heterosexist norms have been central to IVF and GIFT practice in Britain. I have also indicated that racism, class and ableist inequalities form part of the matrix of this field. This survey provides direct evidence of selection overtly on heterosexist grounds and effectively on financial grounds. While it does not provide direct evidence of racialized selection, it does suggest that racialized selection may be more subtly mediated through ideas about what constitutes 'fit' parenting and through class relations at several levels. Similarly, I have argued that genetic selections (on a voluntary basis) like heterosexuality, are perceived as more or less acceptable indices of screening and, like more overt forms of heterosexist selections, may serve to mediate, rationalize and obscure other, less overt forms of selection. I have also argued that while respondents may differ on the importance they place on forms of screening, they nevertheless see screening in principle as an intrinsic (indeed necessary) dynamic and logic of their practices. What is clear is that practitioners in this field are positioning themselves, their patients and IVF/GIFT treatment within conventional, white, middle class and heterosexist kinship discourses (which have, themselves been historically constituted by medical and scientific professions). In these ways, practitioners, even when opposed to particular forms of discrimination or eugenic practices, are nevertheless involved in the (re)production of key social divisions through the administration of IVF and GIFT and are positioned within a discourse in which eugenic sensibilities inhere.

The question of 'choice'

It would seem imperative, in the light of the arguments made in this paper, to return to the issue of choice which I raised at the start of this paper, and to consider two related questions: whether a democratization of access to IVF related treatments is possible and whether this would more fundamentally subvert the selective/eugenic rationality IVF related practices.

For example, it is certainly possible to imagine regulations against direct screening on some of the grounds discussed above (e.g. banning the selection of patients on heterosexist grounds and providing IVF/GIFT services on the NHS). Clearly such a move would seem to subvert important barriers against access to treatment for groups which are clearly marginalized by current screening priorities and the high costs of treatment. There are, however, a number of problems with such an argument. Firstly, as I argue throughout this paper, the mechanisms of screening in this context are not always overt or direct. How would it be possible, in this context, to develop effective anti-discriminatory regulations against the considerable discretionary power of medical professionals in defining and applying any criteria for treatment? Moreover, unless one assumes that public medicine has or will have unlimited resources, the idea that unlimited access to high-investment, high-technology treatments like IVF is, at best, utopian.[30] The limitations on the possibility of democratization, in other words, are extensive and complex. Moreover, the questions of feasibility and the political economy of public-health provision cannot be divorced from other considerations – the historical power of reproductive medicine, its centrality in the formation of dominant discourses of family (which are reflected in the overt heterosexist screening practices revealed by my respondents but which are also inform other areas of medicine and other powerful social institutions). Democratizing access to IVF/GIFT treatment would not seem to substantially subvert these relations. Nor would it address the social relations, causes and context of infertility, or the social relations, formal properties and risks of treatment itself.

To ask whether it is possible to democratize access to IVF-related treatments is, in essence, to entertain the possibility of divorcing this sphere of reproductive medicine from conventional discourses of family and from the historical role of medicine as an agency of sexual and reproductive regulation and control. To argue for democratization would seem to accept that such a divorce is possible. I would suggest that a widening access to IVF/GIFT treatments is not only not enough, but indeed, as a proposition, sidesteps the more fundamental questions about the power of medical discourse and professionals, the character and political economy of medicine generally and reproductive medicine specifically, and the wider social climate around notions of 'fit' parenting (in which the former have been centrally implicated).

To define reproductive choice/rights in terms of democratization of access to treatment would seem to assume that women's reproductive agency is both without and transcendent of context. It would, furthermore, separate the policing of heterosexuality through access policies in this specific context from the wider institutionalized reproduction of heterosexuality/heterosexism which is further shaped by the advent and management of reproductive technologies. The results of this survey confirm and illustrate that the professional praxis of IVF is infused with a eugenic sensibility in which conventional constructions of heterosexuality are central. It would seem unlikely that granting 'equal' access (were this possible) to lesbians, single women, and those who are marginalized on racial, classed and other bases would fundamentally shift the heterosexist selective rationality conceptually underpinning this and other reproductive technologies.

Notes

1. Eugenics is predominantly associated with coercive state/medical control over the reproduction of particular populations. It is interesting to consider whether it is the issue of coercion or the logic of selective breeding which causes most disquiet. One of the ways in which practitioners have rationalized contemporary selection within IVF (such as genetic screening of embryos) is by disassociating their practices from the *involuntary* character prominent in the history of eugenics (see Steinberg, 1993). The consequent construction of 'bad' eugenics as coercive and 'good' eugenics as voluntary would seem not only to impute a *prima facie* benignity to the logic of selection but also to ignore the ways in which voluntary eugenics on a wide scale might reflect a significant shift in the common sense of reproduction. Coercion becomes unnecessary where there is a general acceptance and belief that eugenic screening is necessary for 'responsible' and 'healthy' reproduction.

2. *In vitro* fertilization consists of a series of procedures including: the administration of hormone drugs to induce ovulation of more than one egg; the surgical removal of eggs; the fertilization of removed eggs in a culture medium and re-insertion of fertilized egg(s) into the woman. These procedures have an extremely low success rate and are generally performed several times (Morgan and Lee, 1991)

3. See, for example, Arditti *et al.* 1984; Spallone and Steinberg (eds), 1987; Spallone, 1989. Erica Haimes (1990) has also discussed the impetus, from many quarters, to harness the disruptive potential of such practices for the reproduction of conventional forms of family.

4. I use the concept 'technologies of heterosexuality' in the Foucauldian sense of 'technologies of the self' (see, for example, Rabinow, 1984, pp. 331–80).

5. Consider, for example, the complex power relations of expertise (McNeil, 1987) underpinning the professionalization of medicine; medical-scientific theories of class, race, gender and other categories of 'difference', particularly in the context of the history of racial hygiene and eugenics movements (Mort, 1987; Proctor, 1988).

6. While not specifically focusing on science or medicine, Cohen (1989) has extensively discussed the ways in which notions of breeding related to class became interpellated within the imperial context to notions of race.

7. Gamete intra-fallopian transfer (GIFT) is similar to *in vitro*

fertilization. Women undergo a regimen of superovulation treatment and surgical contraction of their ova. However, whereas IVF involves fertilization of ova by sperm in a Petri-dish culture medium before the fertilized ova are vaginally transferred, with GIFT ova and sperm are injected directly into the fallopian tubes (Morgan and Lee, 1991, p. 127).

8. All the clinics surveyed were registered and licensed by the Voluntary [Interim] Licensing Authority [VLA/ILA] and listed in the *Fourth Report of the Voluntary Licensing Authority for Human In Vitro Fertilisation and Embryology (1989)*.

9. Clinics were registered under the name of one clinician (usually the head of the team), thus responses were based on the perspective of an individual on the upper end of team hierarchies. This must be considered to be a significant limitation in the research. However, team leaders may be most likely to reproduce dominant professional common senses and to disproportionately shape local and general professional cultures.

10. The Voluntary Licensing Authority was formed by IVF, other medical scientific practitioners and some lay-members in 1985, in anticipation of the imposition of statutory regulation of IVF and related practices. It provided a model of professional self-regulation, including licensing of clinics and publication of annual reports, which also included a code of IVF practice.

11. This is an average response rate to a postal questionnaire (Moser, 1958; Moyser and Wagstaffe, 1987). However, since the questionnaire was sent to *all* registered clinics, the percentage return rate is also a percentage of *all* clinics (rather than a

sample) offering these services in Britian at the time. In the light of this, I would argue that it is possible, while taking into consideration the important limitations of postal surveys, to draw conclusions about IVF practice in the UK from the returns which I have received. The remaining 11 returned questionnaires were accompanied with letters or comments declining to participate in the survey for reasons ranging from lack of time to length of questionnaire to lack of established service provision. Elsewhere (Steinberg, 1993) I have discussed in detail the structure and format of the survey as well as a number of feminist methodological issues relating to researching professional groups and important advantages and limitations in undertaking a questionnaire survey approach.

12. An earlier study which I conducted suggested similar patterns with respect to patient profiles and access policies around donor insemination. (See Steinberg, 1986, 1987).

13. An important question in the survey concerned categories of women accepted for or rejected from treatment. The question read as follows:
Does your clinic offer IVF/GIFT treatment to: (a) married women; (b) unmarried but living with male partner; (c) single women; (d) divorced women (with donor sperm); (e) divorced women (with ex-husband's sperm); (g) widowed women (with donor sperm); (h) widowed women (with husband's sperm); (i) lesbian couple; (j) lesbian (single). Please specify any reasons for including or excluding any of the above for/from treatment.

14. The HFE Act 1990 stipulates that in making treatment decisions practitioners must take into

consideration 'the child's need for a father'. For extended discussion of the heterosexual politics of the HFE Act, see Steinberg, 1993.

15. To protect confidentiality all responses were coded. Those quoted in this paper do not represent a sample. Rather, I have reproduced *all* responses provided to the questions analysed here.

16. This is not to suggest, however, that physiological criteria are unproblematic. The persuasiveness and ubiquity of the 'scarcity' argument was also indicated in Christine Crowe's study of IVF patients in Australia (Crowe, 1987, p. 87).

17. A telling and related example of media hostility to the desire of women who are not married to have children was the 1991 'Virgin Birth' controversy. Here single women's access to donor insemination was brought under attack in tabloid and 'quality' press as well as television coverage of the allegedly selfish and deviant desires of some women to conceive without sexual intercourse and to mother without male partners. This controversy was significant in the parliamentary decision to add a clause to the Human Fertilisation and Embryology Bill pressuring practitioners to treat only married women (or women with male partners) with IVF, DI and related procedures.

18. This is reflected, in part, in responses to my questions about whether or not practitioners gave consideration to patients' (and partners') mental and psychiatric state and the emotional dynamics (of the couple's relationship) in making treatment decisions. A related criterion, intelligence, was also indicated by most respondents.

19. Christine Crowe's early study of women undergoing IVF treatment in Australia suggested that outward appearances of conformity to such idealised definitions of coupledom and desire for children constituted a significant expectation and dynamic of the treatment experience (Crowe, 1987).

20. I am not, in this context, using the word 'class' in a strict Marxist sense, i.e. to denote a relationship to the means of production. I am using it, rather, to indicate relative income and social status.

21. Here they were given a choice of 'very', 'somewhat' and 'not' important.

22. One respondent wrote 'as long as patient and husband can get to the clinic, it doesn't matter about occupation. [Twenty?] patients have taken two or three weeks holiday for the treatment' (C10). This suggests a breach between practitioner's stated intent to be non-discriminatory and the ways in which they may be implicated in discrimination. Clearly, it is only patients/partners in particular occupations who can afford and arrange to have '2 or 3 weeks holiday for the treatment' (and to do so repeatedly to accommodate the likelihood of repeated cycles of treatment).

23. Aside from the stated costs of treatment and even for patients undertaking treatment on the NHS, there are a range of 'hidden' costs which may include: travel to the clinic and accomodation (if the clinic is not local); the costs of additional procedures (as I note, drugs costs are ususally extra); the possible loss of the (woman) patient's income as it may be difficult to continue treatment cycles while in paid employment; and child-care costs if there are other children.

24. Lesbians, like single heterosexual women, are disproportionately to be

found among poverty statistics. It is worth noting in this context that the emerging 'pink pound' is *not* lavender.

25. One notable response raised questions about whether clinics do directly exclude potential patients on racial or religious grounds. In the margin of the questionnaire, next to the questions referring to screening patients on racial and religious grounds, this respondent wrote: 'Provocative questions. If I answered these questions I would be breaking the law' (CAA). This response hinted that selection practices on racial grounds might indeed be carried out at this and perhaps at other clinics and that admitting to this would create legal trouble for the clinic. Certainly in a pre-legislative context, where clinics would be pressured to present the most benign face of IVF and GIFT practice, if such selection practices were being carried out it might seem politic to deny them, or to refuse to answer the question. This respondent was the only one to object to all of my questions on selection policies, except those on genetic bases, as 'provocative' and who refused to answer any of them. However, as with all the other respondents, the questions on racial and religious selection clearly provoked the most objection.

26. Government statistics and a wide range of commentators and monitoring groups have identified the disproportionate representation of black people, in particular women and their children, in poverty statistics.

27. Genetic counselling is an advice service offered by medical scientists (usually trained genetic counselling specialists) in which a medical history is taken of a woman and man who wish to reproduce together. The process is used to determine an 'inheritance pattern' of traits which are socially and/or medically defined as undesirable. Based on this pedigree, counsellors assess the statistical probability of producing 'genetically damaged' offspring; hence the terminology of 'risk' and 'risk groups'. Genetic screening involves the use of a variety of diagnostic tests to acquire genetic information about an individual. In the reproductive context it is used to identify carriers of heritable genetic conditions which may be transmitted to offspring.

28. In other words, the notion of 'risk' in itself constructs the condition in question as inherently and inevitably negative. I would argue that such constructions contribute to a social climate which is deeply intolerant of disability and which discriminates profoundly against people living with disabilities (see also Morris, 1990).

29. It must be noted that while a hegemony of voluntarism seemed to emerge in the survey, some respondents indicated that genetic counselling and screening results *were* used directly as criteria for treatment, and some stated that IVF or GIFT were used specifically for genetic reasons.

30. While I was completing this paper, I was told anecdotally by a GP friend, that in one region, a decision has been made by the health authority that instead of limiting services (a necessity in economic terms) by screening patients on the grounds discussed in this paper, one cycle of IVF/GIFT treatment would be available to any patient for whom it would be deemed physiologically appropriate. While this move obviates overt practices of selection, to offer one cycle is almost no better than offering none – as the likelihood of live birth from one cycle of treatment is virtually nil.

References

Anthias, F. and Yuval-Davis, N. (1993) *Racialized Boundaries: Race, Nation, Gender, Colour and Class and the Anti-Racist Struggle*. London: Routledge.

Arditti, R., Klein, R. D. and Minden, S. (1984) *Test-Tube Women: What Future for Motherhood?* London: Pandora

Barker, M. (1981) *The New Racism: Conservatives and the Ideology of the Tribe*. London: Junction Books.

Birke, L., S. Himmelweit and G. Vines. (1990) *Tomorrows Child: Reproductive Technologies in the 1990s*. London: Virago

Bryan, B., Dadzie, S. and Scafe, S. (1985) *Heart of the Race: Black Women's Lives in Britain*. London: Virago.

Butler, J. (1990) *Gender Trouble: Feminism and the Subversion of Identity*. London: Routledge.

Carby, H. (1981) White women listen: black feminism and the boundaries of sisterhood, in CCCS.*The Empire Strikes Back: Race and Racism in 70s Britain*. London: Hutchinson, pp. 212–35.

Cohen, P. (1988) The perversions of inheritance: studies in the making of multi-racist Britain, in Cohen, P. and Bains, H. S. *Multi-Racist Britain*. London: Macmillan.

Collins, P.H. (1990) *Black Feminist Thought: Knowledge, Consciousness and the Politics of Empowerment*. London: HarperCollins.

Corea, G. (1985) *The Mother Machine: Reproductive Technologies from Artificial Insemination to Artificial Wombs*. New York: Harper & Row.

Crowe, C. (1987) 'Women want it': in vitro fertilization and women's motivations for participation, in Spallone, P. and Steinberg, D. L. (eds). *Made to Order: The Myth of Reproductive and Genetic Progress*.

Oxford: Pergamon, pp. 84–93.

Davis, A. (1990) Racism, birth control and reproductive rights, in Fried, M. G. (ed.). *From Abortion to Reproductive Freedom: Transforming a Movement*. Boston: South End Press, pp. 15–26.

Dominelli, L. (1992) An uncaring profession? an examination of racism and social work, in Braham, P., Rattansi, A. and Skellington, R. (eds) *Racism and Anti-Racism: Inequalities, Opportunities and Policies*. London: Sage.

Donnison, J. (1993) *Midwives and Medical Men: A History of the Struggle for the Control of Childbirth*. New Barnet, Herts: Historical Publications.

Franklin, S. (1990) Deconstructing 'desperateness': the social construction of infertility in popular representions of new reproductive technologies, in McNeil, M., Varcoe, I. and Yearley, S. (eds). *The New Reproductive Technologies*. London: Macmillan, pp. 200–29.

Fried, M. G. (ed.) (1990) *From Abortion to Reproductive Freedom: Transforming a Movement*. Boston: South End Press.

Haimes, E. (1990) Recreating the family? policy considerations relating to the 'new' reproductive technologies, in McNeil, M., Varcoe, I. and Yearley, S. (eds.). *The New Reproductive Technologies*. London: Macmillan, pp. 154–72.

Illich, I. (1976) *Limits to Medicine: Medical Nemesis: The Expropriation of Health*. Harmondsworth: Penguin.

Jackson, M. (1994) *The Real Facts of Life: Feminism and the Politics of Sexuality c.1850–1940*. London: Taylor & Francis. (especially chapter 3)

Klein, R. D. (ed.) (1989) *Infertility: Women Speak Out about Their*

Experiences of Reproductive Medicine. London: Pandora.

Langan, M. (1992) Who cares? women in the mixed economy of care, in Langan, M. and Day, L. (eds) *Women, Oppression and Social Work: Issues in Anti-Discriminatory Practice.* London: Routledge.

Locker, D. (1991) Social causes of disease, in Scambler, G. (ed.). *Sociology as Applied to Medicine.* London: Baillière Tindall, pp. 18–32.

Mama, A. (1992) Black women in the British state: race, class and gender analysis for the 1990s, in Braham, P., Rattansi, A. and Skellington, R. (eds.) *Racism and Anti-Racism: Inequalities, Opportunities and Policies.* London: Sage.

Martin, E. (1987) *The Woman in the Body: A Cultural Analysis of Reproduction.* Boston: Beacon Press.

McNeil, M., Varcoe, I. and Yearley, S. (eds.) (1990) *The New Reproductive Technologies.* London: Macmillan.

Morgan, D. and Lee, R. G. (1991) *Blackstone's Guide to the Human Fertilization and Embryology Act 1990: Abortion and Embryo Research, the New Law.* London: Blackstone Press.

Morris, J. (1991) *Pride Against Prejudice: Transforming Attitudes to Disability.* London: Women's Press.

Mort, F. (1987) *Dangerous Sexualities: Medico–Moral Politics in England since 1830.* London: Routledge & Kegan Paul.

Moscucci, O. (1990) *The Science of Woman: Gynaecology and Gender in England 1800–1929.* Cambridge: Cambridge University Press.

Moser, C.A. (1958) *Survey and Social Investigation.* London: Heinemann.

Moyser, G. and Wagstaffe, M. (eds) (1987) *Research Methods for Elite Studies.* London: Unwin Hyman.

Nead, L. (1988) *Myths of Sexuality.* Oxford: Blackwell.

Oakley, A. (1976) Wisewoman and medicine man: changes in the management of childbirth, in Oakley, A. and Mitchell, J. (eds) *The Rights and Wrongs of Women,* Harmondsworth: Penguin, pp. 17–45.

Oakley, A. (1984) *The Captured Womb: A History of the Medical Care of Pregnant Women.* London: Blackwell. (section 1)

Patton, C. (1985) *Sex and Germs: the Politics of AIDS.* Boston: South End Press.

Proctor, R. N. (1988) *Racial Hygiene: Medicine Under the Nazis.* Cambridge: Harvard University Press.

Rabinow, P. (ed.) (1984) *The Foucault Reader: An Introduction to Foucault's Thought.* Harmondsworth: Penguin.

Reissman, C. K. (1992) Women and medicalization: a new perspective, in Kirkup, G. and Keller, L. S. (eds). *Inventing Women: Science, Technology and Gender.* Cambridge: Polity, pp. 123–44.

Rich, A. (1978) Compulsory heterosexuality and lesbian existence. *Signs* 5 (4): 631–60

Russett, C. E. (1989) *Sexual Science: The Victorian Construction of Womanhood.* Cambridge, MA: Harvard University Press.

Scambler, G. (ed.) (1991). *Sociology as Applied to Medicine.* London: Baillière Tindall.

Spallone, P. and Steinberg, D. L. (eds) (1987) *Made to Order: The Myth of Reproductive and Genetic Progress.* Oxford: Pergamon.

Spallone, P. (1987). Reproductive technology and the state: The Warnock Report and its clones, in Spallone, P. and Steinberg, D. L. (eds) *Made to Order: The Myth of Reproductive and Genetic Progress.* Oxford: Pergamon, pp. 166–183.

Spallone, P. (1989) *Beyond Conception: The New Politics of Reproduction*. London: Macmillan.

Stacey, J. (1991) Promoting normality: Section 28 and the regulation of sexuality, in Franklin, S. *et al.* (eds) *Off-Centre: Feminism and Cultural Studies*. London: HarperCollins, pp. 284–304.

Stanworth, M. (ed.) (1987) *Reproductive Technologies: Gender, Motherhood and Medicine*. Cambridge: Polity.

Steinberg, D. L. (1986) Report in progress: policies of access to AID as a medical treatment in the UK. *Women's Studies International Forum.* 9 (5/6): 551–5.

Steinberg, D. L. (1987) Selective breeding and social engineering: discriminatory policies of access to artificial insemination by donor in Great Britain, in Spallone, P. and Steinberg, D. L. (eds) *Made to order: The Myth of Reproductive and Genetic Progress*. Oxford: Pergamon, pp. 184–89.

Steinberg, D. L. (1993) 'Pure culture': a feminist analysis of IVF Ethos and Innovation. PhD thesis, Department of Cultural Studies, University of Birmingham.

Steinberg, D. L. (1994) Power, positionality and epistemology: towards an anti-oppressive feminist standpoint approach to science, medicine and technology. *Women: A Cultural Review.* December.

Walkowitz, J. (1980) *Prostitution and Victorian Society: Women, Class and the State*. Cambridge: Cambridge University Press.

Watney, S. (1989) AIDS, 'Moral panic' theory and homophobia, in Aggleton, P. and Homans, H. (eds) *Social aspects of AIDS*. Philadelphia: Falmer.

Weeks, J. (1991) *Against Nature: Essays on History, Sexuality and Identity*. London: Rivers Oram

White, E. C. (ed.) (1990) *The Black Women's Health Book: Speaking for Ourselves*. Washington: Seal Press.

Witz, A. (1992) *Professions and Patriarchy*. London: Routledge.

4

Invasion of the Monstrous Others: Heterosexual Masculinities, the 'AIDS Carrier' and the Horror Genre*

Peter Redman

'At first glance, everything looked the same. It wasn't. Something had taken over the town.' Thus begins Don Siegel's classic 1956 science fiction film, *Invasion of the Body Snatchers*, a story in which aliens take over human bodies and rapidly threaten to engulf the whole of America and all that is decent, loyal and true. Looking back at the responses to AIDS and HIV in mid- to late-1980s Britain, it is difficult not to draw parallels between popular representations of the epidemic and films like *Body Snatchers*. The tabloids were full of hysterical headlines warning of the dangers of predatory and sexually violent 'AIDS carriers': '18 vice boys in AIDS revenge' (*Sun*, 24 November 1986), 'AIDS: the mass killer stalking a city's women' (*Daily Mail*, 6 February 1988), 'AIDS Victim Raped Teenage Boy' (*Daily Mail*, 6 February 1988), and on and on. If these headlines were to be believed, civilized society and family life were under serious threat from without. Dangerous and shadowy figures threatened to undermine both the moral and physical health of the nation. Nor were more 'serious' commentators immune. A stock-in-trade of popular commentary during the 1980s was the notion that the epidemic would 'leak' from 'high risk groups' into the 'mainstream population'. For instance, an editorial in the *Independent* (30 January 1988) informed us

*An earlier version of this chapter appeared in *Cultural studies from Birmingham*, 1, 1991, 8–28 under the title 'Invasion of the monstrous others: identity, genre and HIV'.

The West faces the prospect of a steady 'leakage' into mainstream society which could prove difficult to contain. . . . The victims who could reasonably be deemed guilty are those – homosexual, heterosexual or drug-abusing – who have refused to adjust their behaviour. . . . They are endangering their own lives and those with whom they come into contact.

Even the prominent American gay rights activist, Randy Shilts, could not resist the temptation to identify a so-called 'patient-zero', an airline steward who supposedly 'introduced' the virus into the US (Shilts, 1987). All of these commentaries had one thing in common: the 'AIDS carrier', a predatory and frequently violent figure who threatens to 'spread' HIV from 'deviant' subpopulations to the morally healthy 'mainstream'.

While some of the early anxiety about HIV may, with hindsight, seem overblown (at least in the case of the UK), it is not my intention to belittle the seriousness of the epidemic nor the gravity of the losses that it has caused. Instead, this chapter is an exploration of the figure of the 'AIDS carrier' and its role in the popular struggles over sexuality and 'the family' that punctuated the 1980s. The chapter is primarily concerned with the question of why the 'AIDS carrier' became so central to popular representations of the HIV epidemic. After all, the meanings of HIV were being fought out between a variety of competing voices that ranged from virology and epidemiology to the self-definitions of AIDS activists and community groups. How was it then that the 'AIDS carrier' came to dominate public perceptions to the extent that it did? Why was it that people most vulnerable to the epidemic were (and according to the *Sunday Times*, are) so insistently constructed as part of 'deviant subpopulations' whose 'moral depravity' seemingly posed such a threat to the whole fabric of society? Why didn't these other, more inclusive voices dominate popular perceptions?

This chapter locates its answers to these questions in a complex interaction between venereology, the politics of the New Right, and the popular purchase of the horror genre. As such it argues that the figure of the 'AIDS carrier' is complexly overdetermined, and that its ubiquity cannot be reduced to any one cause. However, this chapter also argues that the figure of the 'AIDS carrier' is inextricably bound up with the fears, anxieties and secret desires of hegemonic forms of heterosexual masculinity, articulated through the figure of the 'AIDS carrier' as monster. As such, this chapter argues that the popular fascination with and stigmatization of this figure needs to be understood as an attempt to shore up the boundaries of hegemonic heterosexual masculinity in the face of its own internal contradictions. From this vantage point, this chapter argues that popular responses to HIV in the 1980s can be understood as a key cultural site in which the meanings of heterosexual masculinity (and, with them, heterosexual male identities) were produced, reproduced, defended and, perhaps, challenged.

The venerealization of HIV

As is now fairly well documented, the construction of HIV-infection and AIDS as conditions of abnormality has its roots in the first medical attempts to model the then unknown disease syndrome. Between 1979 and 1981 the US disease surveillance organization, the Centers for Disease Control (CDC), started receiving reports of unusual outbreaks of two conditions, Kaposi Sarcoma (KS) and *Pneumocystis carinii* pneumonia (PCP), previously fairly rare illnesses. One of the most significant of these reports was published in the CDC's journal the *Morbidity and Mortality Weekly Report* (MMWR) in May 1981. The report detailed the appearance of PCP (a pneumonia associated with suppressed immune-systems) in five gay men. The report's significance lay in an accompanying editorial note. This claimed that 'the fact that these patients were all homosexuals suggests an association between some aspect of a homosexual lifestyle or disease acquired through sexual contact. . .' (quoted in, Oppenheimer, 1988, pp. 270–71). As Gerald Oppenheimer has argued, this extrapolation, based as it was on only five cases, was extremely pre-emptory. Why was it made?

In an analysis of early epidemiological research on AIDS, Oppen-heimer argues that this elision between AIDS and gay men's sexuality took place against a background of increased medical interest in gay men and sexually transmitted diseases (STDs). He writes:

> Analysts linked (an) epidemic of STDs among gay men to gay liberation and the attendant life-style of bars, discos and bathhouses and of anonymous sexual partners. These charges reinforced a set of assumptions, often expressed in medical texts

. . . by venereologists, that gay men, because of their 'pathetic promiscuity' and supposed hedonism, are more vulnerable to sexually related diseases than *are heterosexual men and women* (Oppenheimer, 1988: 271).

In effect, these early cases of PCP were made sense of through a set of *venereological* categories, categories that from the outset constructed HIV-infection and AIDS as peculiar to gay men, as sexual in origin, and as related to a 'deviant' and 'exotic' lifestyle.

As I will argue in the next section, venereological discourse has a long history of constructing people with sexually transmitted diseases as 'the cause of' or a 'source' of disease. Such assumptions were replayed in the early epidemiological research on the mystery epidemic. For instance, a CDC report from 1982 identified large numbers of sexual partners and drug-use as significant variables among men presenting with opportunistic infections associated with immune dysfunction. Another CDC survey of gay men, published in 1983, identified multiple sexual partners, regular use of bathhouses, drug-use and exposure to faeces during sex as key variables (see Oppenheimer, 1988, p. 273 and p. 277; Whippen, 1987). Such findings fed into a 'lifestyle' explanation of immune breakdown. Analysts hypothesized that it was a 'fast-lane' gay male lifestyle composed of sex and drugs, possibly in association with infection by a viral agent, that was suppressing gay men's immune systems and leaving them vulnerable to opportunistic infections like PCP and KS (see Oppenheimer, 1988).

What was surprising about all this was that heterosexual cases of the unknown syndrome were reported as early as August 1981. By June 1982, 22 per cent of CDC reported cases were heterosexual men and women. Early models of the disease syndrome simply failed to take these cases into account. If they had done, it is possible that AIDS and gay sexuality would never have been so thoroughly conflated. As Meurig Horton and Peter Aggleton have argued (1989), in such circumstances, AIDS might well have been constructed in the same terms as Hepatitis-B infection. Hepatitis B is transmitted in a similar manner to HIV but has never been thoroughly elided with gay sexuality. Instead, it is seen as a viral agent capable of sexual transmission. As it was, even after a viral agent (HIV) was identified as the cause of AIDS, HIV infection continued to be constructed in venereological terms. Venereological discourse constructs a model of disease transmission in which infection is seen to pass from 'abnormal' and 'diseased' subpopulations to the 'general public'. With the identification of HIV, this venereological model ensured that gay men were constructed as the 'source' of the virus, and a 'threat' to 'mainstream society'. Subsequent medical research on HIV in Africa constructed the continent in much the same way. In 1985, for example, an article in *Science* put forward the hypothesis that HIV might have mutated from a supposedly similar virus found in African green monkeys, giving rise to a slew of scientific and popular represenations that conflated African cultures with disease, an excessive or deviant sexuality, and a supposed 'primitivism'. As Chirimuuta and Chirimuuta have argued, '[The green monkey hypothesis] cohabit[s] easily with racist notions that Africans are evolutionary closer to subhuman primates, or with images gleaned from Tarzan movies of Africans living in trees' (Chirimuuta and Chirimuuta, 1989, p. 71).

However, the fact that the 'abnormality' version of HIV derives from venereology does not in itself explain why this particular medical model had such a purchase on the popular imagination. In fact, HIV has been and is made sense of through the languages and practices of several medical disciplines (principally, virology and immunology), yet it was a venerealized account that popular representations of HIV drew on the most. The question remains then as to why it was the venereological model and not virology or immunology that exerted such a grip on the popular imagination.

'Threat', 'promiscuity' and 'reservoirs of disease': the venereological model and social anxiety

I would argue that an important part of venereology's popular purchase lies in the fact that, since the Victorian period at least, sexually transmitted diseases have been constructed as an index of wider social and moral health. For venereologists as much as public moralists, sexually transmitted diseases have been a site of social anxiety. Venereological research from the Victorian period to the present has been shot through with fears about social breakdown and moral decline. In effect, sexually transmitted disease appears to be a potent metaphor for fantasies about a social fabric that is being remorselessly undermined.

Lucy Bland and Frank Mort (1984) have traced such venereological anxieties in their modern form to an increasing preoccupation in the nineteenth century with 'national health'. One of the major themes of this preoccupation was the isolation of sexually 'deviant' populations from the 'healthy' majority. Victorian fears centred on the 'threat' posed by prostitution. Prostitutes were seen as potential 'conduits of infection', a channel of moral and physical contagion connecting the 'residuum' (the urban poor) to the middle classes (see Bland and Mort, 1984, pp. 133–5). Bland and Mort argue that fears of the residuum had, by the inter-war period, been translated into fears of 'social problem groups', with the 'amateur-prostitute' or 'good-time girl' replacing the professional prostitute as the central object of medical and social concern. In the inter-war period fears about young single women were duplicated in growing fears about young people, black immigrants and, from the 1970s, gay men. (For an overview of these post-war developments see Chief Medical Officer for England and Wales, MOH, *Annual Report*, 1964; 1969; 1971; 1980).

These fears indicate that, at least from the Victorian period onwards, venereology has been obsessed with a 'threat' to moral and physical health posed by 'deviant' or 'abnormal' subpopulations. This agenda has been very different to that of other medical disciplines. Virology and immunology, for example, focus almost exclusively on the operations of disease at the level of the cell, and have little interest in the social dimensions of health. Venereology, on the other hand, has historically identified sexually transmitted disease as an index of social life, and it has sought to find the causes of sexually transmitted disease in social and moral issues. In the post-war years, venereologists have identified a cluster of social and moral factors that supposedly underlie rising STD rates. Foremost among these are social change, increasing social movement and, most important of all, 'promiscuity'.

In post-war venereological literature notions of social change and an increasingly mobile population translate most often into notions of 'family breakdown', 'teenage rebellion' and black immigration. A research paper from 1965, for instance, points to the following as factors behind STDs in young people: 'Teenagers must adjust themselves to a greater independence to a weakening and breakdown of family bonds, to the disappearance of religious influences, to commercial pressures from exploitation of the growing teenage market'

(Catterall, 1965, p. 626). In a popular book on venereal diseases published in 1967, the same author blamed the 'so-called teenage revolt' for STDs among young women. In a remarkable passage, he even suggests that young women caught STDs as a result of drifting to London, where 'the majority tend to associate with itinerant men and with foreigners and coloured immigrants, who appear to add glamour to their aimless lives' (Catterall, 1967, p. 103).

Writing as he was in the 1960s, Catterall felt that, 'the most important group in the spread of venereal diseases is without doubt the unmarried, promiscuous, immigrant men' (Catterall, 1967, p. 111). Venereologists had two explanations for this. On the one hand, black (particularly African–Caribbean) immigration was seen as resulting in the introduction of more 'primitive' and 'uninhibited' sexual customs into Britain. On the other hand, migration – like young women's move to the city – was believed to have a disinhibiting effect. Both viewpoints were articulated in the following, clearly racist, research paper published in the *Practitioner* in 1965.

> The reasons for high venereal disease rates amongst immigrants are not far to seek. Some, by no means all, come from lands where promiscuous behaviour is common and venereal disease rates are also high and these persons tend to continue such behaviour after arrival. Immigrants as a whole are mostly males who have left their home lands in search of work. They are thus removed from parental, marital, tribal, religious and other influences which are inhibitory to promiscuity. (Wilcox, 1965, p. 636)

However, even more than social change and mobility, it is promiscuity that has been central to post-war venereological anxieties. For example, in his standard introductory text, *Sexually Transmitted Diseases,* C.B.S. Schofield argued that 'Many of the facets of current societies predispose towards an increase in promiscuity. The increase in the incidence of sexually transmitted diseases is a result of the increase in indiscriminate promiscuity which is the basic problem, the acquisition of disease being merely fortuitous' (Schofield, 1979, p. 33).

The Annual Report of the Chief Medical Officer for 1970 was similarly assertive on this question, warning its readers that 'If we lived in a monogamous and sexually continent society these diseases would not spread' (MOH 1970, p. 66).

The importance of promiscuity within venereological discourse lies in the central role played by the figure of the promiscuous person. The 'carrier' provides a key link in venereology's model of disease transmission in which STDs spread from 'deviant' subpopulations to the 'mainstream'. For example, the Annual Report of the Chief Medical Officer for 1974 warns that 'there is some evidence that this increase (in syphilis) is beginning to spill over into the female population, presumably due to spread via bisexual males' (MOH 1974, p. 77). In this instance the 'promiscuous' bisexual occupies much the same position as the prostitute in the Victorian period, the 'good-time girl' in inter-war venereology and the 'AIDS carrier' of the 1980s.

The 'promiscuous person' appears in venereological discourse as a lone figure spreading disease to an unwary public. For example, in an analysis of epidemiological surveys of STDs among gay men, Tony Coxon quotes the following extract: 'The AP ('active') homosexuals are many times . . . as promiscuous as the AR ('passive') homosexuals, and therefore much less frequent in this subpopulation.' (Coxon, 1988, p. 134).

In effect, this suggests that there are less gay men who like to fuck than there are gay men who liked to be fucked, and the picture it conjures up is thus one of a few highly promiscuous gay men infecting a much larger population with sexually transmitted diseases. As Coxon points out, there is no real evidence that supports this division of gay men into 'active' and 'passive' partners. The research simply replays the notion of a passive wider community under threat from a diseased minority. It is, then, in the figure of the lone promiscuous person that venereology finds its perfect illustration of threat and invasion.

The promiscuous person, the diseased subpopulation, and the breakdown of moral and social ties, have all provided a vocabulary through which venereology has carried on an extended social commentary over the last forty years. At the heart of this social commentary, the threat of sexually transmitted disease has acted as a metaphor for the erosion of social and moral boundaries. Venereology's anxiety about social and moral issues has thus provided an area of common ground between the discipline and other key political and social groups, most recently the tabloid press, and the moral Right and its popular constituencies. In articulating fears about the 'break-up' of the family, or the 'threat' of black immigration, gay liberation or 'permissiveness', venereology has shared a common vocabulary with the moral Right. In the process, sexually transmitted diseases have become a way of speaking about a wide range of contentious social issues, a fact that has been particularly apparent in relation to HIV.

The construction of HIV infection as a condition that comes from dangerous subpopulations and threatens 'normal' society, allowed HIV to be appropriated by a highly conservative moral agenda. During the 1980s the social agenda of the moral Right was dominated by issues that centred on 'the family' and sexuality. The decade was punctuated by a series of struggles (over HIV, teaching about homosexuality in schools, child sexual abuse, sex education, abortion and infertility treatment) that sought to reassert traditionalist familial ideology in the face of perceived threats from feminism, gay activism and the liberal professions. (For a discussion of the moral Right's mobilization round these issues, see Altman, 1986; Campbell, 1988; Durham, 1991; Watney, 1989.) The construction of HIV as a disease of 'abnormality' fitted effectively into this pre-existing agenda. The representation of gay men and black people as diseased subpopulations whose excesses threatened 'normal' heterosexuals and 'normal' families echoed the moral Right's own fears about the erosion of 'family values' and a traditional 'British way of life' by dangerous outsiders. For the Right generally, and the tabloid press in particular, the HIV epidemic became a way of speaking about these issues in a way that was legitimized by medical authority.

In this light, it is possible to interpret the prevalence of a venerealized version of HIV as a consequence of the fact that HIV became rapidly swept up into the wider ideological struggles of the 1980s. The ability of venerealized accounts of HIV to be appropriated into other settings simply meant that a venereological model of the epidemic had wider access to public 'air-time' than virology- or immunology-based models whose scope tended to be more restricted to medical issues. However, the fact that a 'medico–moral alliance' (to borrow Frank Mort's phrase) managed to set the moral agenda round HIV in the 1980s, does not in itself explain why this moral agenda had such a purchase on the public imagination. As I will go on to argue, venerealized accounts of HIV seemed to arouse the most intense of feelings, evoking a mixture of disgust and wide-eyed fascination. To understand this we need to turn to an analysis of the unconscious fears and desires played out in genre representations.

HIV, heterosexual masculinities and the horror genre

In March 1988 the *Sun* newspaper carried a story on the alleged homosexual rape of a stagehand at the Theatre Royal, Norwich. The story had all the ingredients of a solid tabloid melodrama. The rape victim had apparently committed suicide because 'he thought he might be turning homosexual', or because 'he was scared he had caught AIDS'. His alleged attacker was a 'gay pal' of 'star', Wayne Sleep, 'who once danced on stage with Princess Di' (*Sun*, 4 March 1988). The story was clearly a heady concoction of royalty, violence, 'deviant' sexuality and AIDS, a concoction that managed to transform a personal tragedy into public entertainment. The strong undercurrent of voyeuristic fascination that characterizes this story leaves it particularly open to critical analysis. The focus of the piece is not on the suicide but the alleged rape, a focus that reveals a simultaneous sense of loathing, and a fascination with the details of the incident. For instance, we are told how the victim was tricked into staying the night in a hotel room and how the alleged attacker 'aroused Robinson, smeared him with vaseline and satisfied himself with anal sex'. The pseudo-clinical tone of this sentence carries a sense of distaste; its detail, however, reveals a wide-eyed fascination.

The interplay of loathing and desire revealed in this story has been central to dominant, venerealized accounts of HIV. The alleged attacker is identified as a person who may have the virus, one of the 'AIDS carriers' of popular mythology who spreads disease into the 'heterosexual population'. Yet despite the fear and loathing that are implied, his actions are constructed as covertly titillating. What is it that is going on in such representations of gay sexuality and HIV? Judith Williamson (1989) has argued that the themes of the venerealized account of HIV (its emphasis on invasion, boundary loss and threat from dangerous outsiders) point to the fact that it has been constructed through the conventions of the horror genre. She argues that the venereological model of transmission which sees disease spreading via carriers from subpopulations to a healthy mainstream explicitly replays one of the major storylines of this genre. For example, Rosemary Jackson identifies two key versions of the horror story. The first, as in the Frankenstein or Jekyll and Hyde stories, deals with threat from within the self, 'through excessive knowledge or rationality, or the misapplication of the human will' (Jackson, 1981, p. 58). The second version deals with threat from outside the self, the 'not-I'. As in the Dracula story, 'the self suffers an attack of some sort which makes it part of the other' (Jackson, 1981, p. 58). The venereological model of transmission clearly draws on the second of these versions. In HIV commentary, Africa, 'high-risk groups' and the 'gay community' all connote 'alien territories', the diseased world of the monstrous, while the figure of the 'AIDS carrier' stands for the monster itself.

Recognizing that venerealized accounts of HIV are located firmly within the conventions of the horror genre is crucial to an explanation of the popular purchase of these venerealized accounts. Critical commentary on the genre tends to stress that the horror story is fundamentally concerned with the instability of identity, the threat of boundary invasion and boundary dissolution. For example, Rosemary Jackson argues that the central preoccupation of the genre is the 'problematic relation of the self to other, the "I" and the "not-I", the "I" and the "you"' (Jackson, 1981, p. 72). I would argue that the fascination that venerealized accounts of HIV engender is based in precisely this preoccupation with identity instability and boundary invasion.

Rosemary Jackson's assertion that identity is fundamentally unstable draws heavily on a psychoanalytical model, one that argues that a conscious sense of a unitary identity is constructed and preserved through the exclusion or repression of particular, disruptive or threatening desires. Such desires do not go away but constantly return to threaten the equilibrium of conscious identity. It is for this reason that Jacqueline Rose has argued that the unconscious constantly 'reveals the "failure" of identity' (Rose, 1983, p. 9). The endless return of repressed or excluded desires means that the boundaries of conscious identity have to be endlessly policed, held down and re-secured. Identity itself is never simply achieved or finished. Thus Rose writes:

> 'Failure' is not a moment to be regretted in a process of adaptation, or development into normality. . . . Instead 'failure' is something endlessly repeated and relived moment by moment

throughout our individual histories. It appears not only in the symptoms, but also in dreams, in slips of the tongue and in forms of sexual pleasure which are pushed to the sidelines of the norm. (Rose, 1983, p. 9)

From this perspective the horror story can be read as replaying this constant failure of conscious identities. The loss or breakdown of boundaries which is central to the genre, parallels the endless disruption of identity by the unconscious.

In *The Politics and Poetics of Transgression*, Stallybrass and White argue that this constant failure or slippage of identity is what underlies relations of fear and desire for the Other. One of the key ways in which the conscious self is policed is by 'splitting-off' and 'projecting' on to others desires that are threatening to the self. However, as Stallybrass and White argue, 'a fundamental rule seems to be that what is excluded at the level of identity-formation is productive of new objects of desire' (Stallybrass and White, 1986, p. 251). Since the repressed or excluded elements come from within the self they can never be wholly repudiated or left behind. In fact, Stallybrass and White argue that the very act of repudiation acts as a form of ownership. They write, 'These low domains, apparently expelled as "Other" return as the object of nostalgia, longing and fascination' (Stallybrass and White, 1986, p. 191).

The result of this is that the Others excluded as most threatening become simultaneously desirable. Far from being watertight and secure, the boundary between self and Other becomes a 'hybrid zone', 'inclusive, heterogeneous (and) dangerously unstable' (Stallybrass and White, 1986). From this perspective it would appear that venerealized representations of HIV play on a fundamentally unstable relationship between self and Other, a simultaneous fear of and desire for the 'Others' of venereological discourse: in particular, gay men, black people and young single women.

The question that emerges from this is one that asks precisely which desires are being excluded and projected on to the 'Others' of venerealized accounts of HIV. One of the most obvious explanations is that venerealized accounts of HIV police heterosexual male identities against the threat of repressed or split-off homoerotic desires. In *An Introduction to the American Horror Film* Robin Wood identifies sexuality or 'sexual energy' as one of the crucial factors that is heavily policed in contemporary culture and which returns to consciousness in the horror genre (Wood, 1985, p. 198). Wood argues that homophobia (like that visible in popular representations of HIV), 'is only explicable as the outcome of the unsuccessful repression of bisexual tendencies: what is hated in others is what is rejected (but none the less continues to exist) within the self' (Wood, 1985, p. 200). Similarly, Eve Kosofsky Sedgwick's work on the late-19th and early-20th century cultural construction of Anglo-American forms of heterosexual and homosexual masculinity, has underlined the ways in which hegemonic forms of heterosexual masculinity are centrally defined through an opposition to male–male erotic and emotional contact (Sedgwick, 1985; 1991). Sedgwick argues that such forms of heterosexual masculinity are characterized by homophobic panic, a panic caused by a 'strangling double bind' at the heart of masculinity: namely a simultaneous desire for and fear of erotic attachment to other men (see Sedgwick, 1991, pp. 186, 187). Sedgwick explains this with reference to Freudian psychoanalytic theory, arguing that boys' identification with the phallus (the desire to be the fantasized, all-powerful Father) is always in dangerous proximity to the desire *for* the phallus (desire for the Father) and risks constant collapse into the latter. As she writes, 'there is no secure boundary between wanting what somebody else (i.e. Daddy) has and wanting Daddy' (Sedgwick, 1985, pp. 105, 106). Thus in a culture where male–male sexual contact is deeply stigmatized, it is inevitable that the insecure boundary between identification with and desire for the phallus becomes a site of anxiety, fear and denial: in short a site of homophobic panic.

Homophobic panic is clearly central to the popular responses to HIV that characterized the 1980s and underlines the ways in which HIV can be understood as a cultural site in which the boundaries of heterosexual masculinity were produced, reproduced, defended and undermined. However, sensitivity to the content of venerealized accounts of HIV should make us wary of an explanation that begins and ends with homophobia. While not as centrally, black people and young single women (a figure that merges with the prostitute), as well as gay men, have been constructed as 'Other' within popular representations of the epidemic. What is common to these three groups is the representation of their sexualities as active, excessive, promiscuous and dangerous. From this perspective, what is being 'excluded' or 'split-off' in venerealized accounts appears to be the threat of that which is powerful and boundaryless.

Rosemary Jackson has argued that the threat of boundarylessness is one that is central to the horror genre's preoccupation with identity loss. She writes: 'Fantasy (i.e. the horror genre), with its tendency to dissolve structures, moves towards an ideal of undifferentiation, and this is one of its defining characteristics. It refuses difference distinction, homogeneity, reduction, discrete forms' (Jackson, 1981, p. 72).

Barbara Creed has linked this 'ideal of undifferentiation' to Kristeva's notion of 'abjection': that is, 'that which does not "respect borders, positions, rules". . . that which "disturbs identity, system, order"' (Creed, 1986, p. 45). Creed argues that the abject is, ' "the place where meaning collapses", the place where "I" am not' (Creed, 1986, p. 461). As such, it stands in opposition to a stable coherent sense of identity and continuously threatens it. The function of the horror story, she argues, is to bring about an encounter between the abject and the conscious self (Creed, 1986, p. 49). In other words, the horror story plays with the threat of boundary or identity collapse.

Such fears of boundary-loss can be quite clearly identified in venereological literature. Venereology's preoccupation with themes of social change, mobile populations and promiscuity, all reveal a fear of constraints or boundaries breaking down. The category of social change, for instance, suggests anxieties that focus on the undermining of traditions, conventional forms of authority and social restraint. Anxieties centring on mobile populations suggest fears of miscegenation, the blurring of cultural identities and fixed categories moving out of their allotted spaces. However, fears of boundary loss become most explicit in relation to promiscuity. The 'promiscuous' person suggests a figure who refuses to respect boundaries, by insisting on uncontrollable and uncontained sexual contact. These three factors which underlie venereology's explanation of rising rates of sexually transmitted disease, can thus be understood as having a latent content that reveals a preoccupation with boundarylessness, undifferentiation and merging of identities.

This state of boundarylessness has clear echoes of the first stages of human existence, in which the infant has no sense of itself as separate from its primary carer (in our culture a position usually occupied by the mother). Following Kristeva, Creed links a fear of this state with the child's attempts to break away or separate from the mother. Creed argues that in the process of this attempt to separate, the mother becomes associated with the 'abject', and the 'abject' comes to signify 'the subject's fear of his (sic) very own identity sinking irretrievably into the mother' (Creed, 1986, p. 50). The horror genre's emphasis on boundary loss replays precisely this set of fears, a reworking that becomes clearest in acts of 'possession' where the monster takes over or incorporates the subject into the world of the Other. As Rosemary Jackson has written, 'What is represented in the vampiric myth in *Dracula* is a symbolic reversal of the Oedipal stage and of the subject's cultural formation in that stage' (Jackson, 1981, p. 120): in other words, a reversal of the process by which the infant gains subjectivity or a sense of differentiation from 'the Mother'.

The importance of this analysis lies in the fact that it provides an explanation for the fear of the Other as powerful which continually resurfaces in venereological literature and in venerealized accounts of HIV. In the vampire-myth version of the horror story and in films like *Invasion of the Body Snatchers*, identities are not only broken down (through dismemberment or death) they are actively taken over by an Other more powerful than the self. In venerealized representations of HIV the figure of the vampire or the alien is paralleled by the figure of the promiscuous person or the 'AIDS carrier': the hyper-penetrative gay man, the insatiable black man, the disease-ridden woman. More than any other group, however, this threat is epitomized by gay men. This fear reaches its peak in heterosexual men's fear of anal penetration. A whole range of commentators have been convinced that it is anal sex which 'causes' HIV. For example, George Gale, writing in his column in the *Daily Mail*, wrote: 'When asked, as a member of a symposium on AIDS, what message anti-AIDS advertising should put out, I caused great offence, not only among homosexuals, by saying: "Sodomy kills". [But] That is the truth' (*Daily Mail*, 11 March 1988). Sir Reginald Murley, again writing in the *Daily Mail*, parallels this, claiming: 'the clarion call for prevention in this country clearly needs to be directed against intravenous drug users and buggery' (*Daily Mail*, 7 November 1989). The fear and loathing expressed in these statements for what is a perfectly normal sexual activity for large parts of the population, speaks volumes about the extreme defensiveness that anal sex can provoke.

One of the key reasons that gay anal sex is so disturbing for heterosexual men is that it implies penetration by another. It suggests 'being taken', a symbolic and literal loss of boundaries to someone who is more powerful. Following Barbara Creed it is possible to suggest that this is not just a fear of gay men inspired by repressed or excluded homoerotic desires. Instead it can be understood as a psychic structure, a set of identity boundaries that relate to the child's attempts to separate from the mother who is experienced as engulfing and powerful. This psychic structure is, however, one that relates most specifically to heterosexual men. Writing in the tradition of feminist object relations theory (see, for example, Chodorow, 1978; Dinnerstein, 1978) Jessica Benjamin has argued that, in western cultures it is possible for boys to separate from their mothers by adopting fantasy position of power and control over them. As an escape from the threat of a separate and powerful mother, the boy is able (in effect) to reverse roles and imagine that the mother 'is not separate – she belongs to me. I control and possess her' (Benjamin, 1983, p. 294). Benjamin suggests that this 'is a way of repudiating dependency while attempting to avoid the consequent feeling of aloneness' (Benjamin, 1983, p. 296). From this perspective, hegemonic heterosexual masculinities are said to be organized round endless attempts to shore up a position that refuses to recognize dependency, and that attempts to preserve boundaries that are impenetrable, a position that is continually undermined by longing, fascination and nostalgia for dependency or a state of undifferentiation.

I would suggest that the venereological model, with its emphasis on a 'normal' society threatened by diseased subpopulations and dangerous foreigners, addresses precisely this psychic structure. If this is the case, it is possible to understand the popular purchase of venerealized accounts of HIV in terms of their access to these unconscious fears and desires, and it is this which gives HIV-related representations of gay men, black people and single women their particular fascination. What is perhaps most important about this is the recognition of the fact that heterosexual masculinities are actively (re)produced and resecured in and through such horror-based representations. These do not 'reflect' a struggle to police heterosexual boundaries that is going on elsewhere, they are themselves a site where such policing actively takes place. Thus this is a specific instance of what Valerie Walkerdine describes as the need to 'engage with the production of ourselves as subjects in and through our insertion into cultural practices' (Walkerdine, 1984, p. 165).

Conclusion

In this chapter I've attempted to illustrate the complex ways in which a venereological version of HIV (in particular the heavily fantasized figure of the 'AIDS carrier') has succeeded in dominating popular representations and understandings of the epidemic. In so doing it should be clear that the success of horror-based representations of HIV cannot be reduced to any one cause. For example, if AIDS cases had first been identified among heterosexual injecting drug-users, it is quite possible that HIV would not have been venerealized. 'Junkie pneumonia', for example, has never attracted the same interest as HIV. Similarly, if the epidemic had not occurred in the historical conjuncture of the New Right, it is possible that a venerealized account would never have been swept up into wider ideological struggles. For instance, the moral panic surrounding HIV in the 1980s was far more intense and socially-loaded than earlier post-war anxieties about sexually transmitted disease. Thus an analysis that reduced the role of medical, social and political factors in producing the meanings of HIV to the workings of unconscious processes would be worse than useless. However, it seems to me that the purchase of horror-based representations on the popular imagination and their power to fascinate, demands to be interpreted primarily in terms of psychic processes: the unconscious identifications, psychic conflicts and fantasy resolutions articulated by the horror genre.

Understanding responses to HIV in terms of the unconscious anxieties of hegemonic heterosexual masculinities is important precisely because it draws attention to the ways in which heterosexual (and by extension, homosexual) masculinities are actively produced and reproduced in and through popular narratives and wider cultural struggles. The fear and loathing directed at gay men in the context of HIV may not seem to hold out much promise for a world in which heterosexual masculinities are differently organized. However, the fact that hegemonic heterosexual masculinities are actively *produced* (and not immutably fixed) does point at least to the possibility of change. I am not suggesting that this is an easy nor an inevitable process, and, as a heterosexual man, I cannot pretend to know quite what such a reorganized form of subjectivity would look like or what it would feel like to live. Indeed, Kaja Silverman (1992) has warned against the belief that men's unconscious investments in contemporary hegemonic forms of heterosexual masculinity are easily shiftable, pointing out that 'the subject can continue to "recognize" itself and its desires within certain kinds of sounds, images, and narrative paradigms long after consciously repudiating them' (Silverman, 1992, p. 48). Nevertheless, as Silverman goes on to argue, it is surely not too utopian to acknowledge that a first step towards the reorganization of hegemonic heterosexual masculinities might lie in making visible the anxieties, projections and disavowals that are so obsessively occluded within popular representations like that of the 'AIDS carrier' as monster.

References

Altman, D. (1986) *AIDS and the New Puritanism*. London: Pluto Press.

Benjamin, J. (1983) Master and slave: the fantasy of erotic domination, in Snitow, A., Stanell, C. and Thompson, S. (eds), *Desire: The Politics of Sexuality*. London: Virago.

Bland, L. and Mort, F. (1984) Lookout for the goodtime girl: dangerous sexualities as a threat to national health, in *Formations of Nations and People*. London: R.K.P.

Campbell, B. (1988) *Unofficial Secrets, Child Sexual Abuse: The Cleveland Case*. London: Virago.

Catterall, R.D. (1965) Venereal diseases and teenagers, *Practitioner*, 195, November.

Catterall, R.D. (1967) *The Venereal Diseases*. London: Impact Books.

Chirimuuta, R. and Chirimuuta, R. (1989) *AIDS, Africa and Racism*. London: Free Association Books.

Chodorow, N. (1978) *The Reproduction of Mothering: Psychoanalysis and the Sociology of Gender*. London: University of California Press.

Coxon, T. (1988) The numbers game: gay lifestyles, epidemiology of AIDS and social science, in Aggleton, P. and Homans, H. (eds), *Social Aspects of AIDS*. Lewes: Falmer Press.

Creed, B. (1986) Horror and the monstrous feminine: an imaginary abjection, *Screen*, 27 (1).

Dinnerstein, D. (1978) *The Rocking of the Cradle*. London: Souvenir Press.

Durham, M. (1991) *Sex and Politics: The Family and Morality in the Thatcher Years*. Basingstoke: Macmillan.

HIV, AIDS and Sexual Health Programme, 'Briefing Pack', Health Education Authority, May 1990.

Horton, M. and Aggleton, P. (1989) Pervert, inverts and experts: the cultural production of an AIDS research paradigm, in Aggleton, P., Hart, G. and Davies, P. (eds), *AIDS: Social Representations and Social Practices*. Lewes: Falmer Press.

Jackson, R. (1981) *Fantasy: The Literature of Subversion*. London: Methuen.

Ministry of Health, *Annual Report*, (1964), (1969), (1970), (1971), (1980), 'On the state of the public health', being *The Annual Report of the Chief Medical Officer of the DHSS*. London: HMSO.

Oppenheimer, G.M., (1988) In the eye of the storm: the epidemiological construction of AIDS, in Fee, E. and Fox, D.M. (eds), *AIDS: The Burdens of History*. Berkeley: University of California Press.

Rose, J. (1983) Femininity and its discontents, *Feminist Review*, (14).

Schofield, C.B.S. (1979) *Sexually Transmitted Diseases*. London: Churchill Livingstone.

Sedgwick, E.K. (1985) *Between Men: English literature and Male Homosexual Desire*. New York: Columbia University Press.

Sedgwick, E.K. (1991) *Epistemology of the Closet*. Hemel Hempstead: Harvester Wheatsheaf.

Shilts, R. (1987) *And the Band Played On*. New York: Penguin.

Silverman, K. (1992) *Male Subjectivity at the Margins*. London: Routledge.

Stallybrass, P. and White, A. (1986) *The Politics and Poetics of Transgression*. London: Methuen.

Walkerdine, V. (1984) Some day my prince will come, in McRobbie, A. and Nava, M. (eds), *Gender and Generation*. Basingstoke: Macmillan.

Watney, S. (1989) Taking liberties: an introduction, in Carter, E. and Watney, S. (eds), *Taking Liberties: AIDS and Cultural Politics*. London: Serpent's Tail Press.

Whippen, D. (1987) Science fictions: the making of a medical model for AIDS, *Radical America*, 20 (6).

Wilcox, R.R. (1965) Venereal diseases and immigrants', *Practitioner* (195), November.

Williamson, J. (1989) Every virus tells a story: the meanings of HIV/AIDS, in Carter, E. and Watney, S. (eds), *Taking Liberties: AIDS and Cultural Politics*. London: Serpent's Tail Press.

Wood, R. (1985) An introduction to the American horror film, in Nichols, B. (ed.), *Movies and Methods*. Berkeley: University of California Press.

5

IMPEDIMENTA
Dramaturgy of the Divine Offspring

Deborah Lynn Steinberg

Umbilicus
(Creation Myth I)*

God Spoke

ate well
her bones dissolved
vestigial (so they said)
before his thewed magnificence
before his daughter
before her sword
was his intention

So gave his name
Stone
Mountain
watching stones erode

watching the mountain move
because the mountain moves

(but not)
(not this way)

not the way he planned

eroding
every day a little smaller
under his feet

One day

FLESH

the sex unused
but not vestigial
(like they said)

for the young
(eyes like his)
idea

that great fraud
that warrior
wild

(but not)
(not like they said)

not

HIS

not

SPRUNG

breast of his breast
(or) of his hand
(or) of his head

---

* Athene, goddess of warfare, was born, so it is said, full
grown from the head of her father Zeus, who had swallowed
her mother (Metis, first wife of Zeus) after learning she was
pregnant.

Father Lamentations I

Do not mis/take her

For someone you know
she is a raving in your life

Or claim her straying
bitter gall

for your own body
you say you had her there

Broken down as if she could not
bear it if you were to go
too far

Malice for love
when she lifts her head in pure horror

For the romantic you are
you think you would do anything

To have her back
as one more arm
of your arms

Cant for song
she has no range for singing

Head in the clouds
her mouth spills words siphoned

Refined, no more than a vessel
a vestal degraded
and you came too late

To save her
for yourself

Daphne
(The Metamorphosis)

I was running

a man
his oratory
his arrogance
inbred, a culture
rated him larger than I
arranged his sensibilities
his sense of entitlement

he
changed me
in the manner of things
in the way of such things
into a rooted thing
I continued running
but in the larger scheme
of things
in the wider matrix
of things
I was rooted
in a vision that
has little regard
for those kinds
of roots

my leaves
erected him
wept for him he said
fondly
crowns of valour
for his head
proud flesh

those grown
those shed
on my branches
there is no need to wait
so long

he said
she cannot speak
in the manner of such things
she cannot move
in the matrix of such things
rooted to the ground

and I, a sturdy one, can cut her
loose
to die, he said
to kindle my fire

Dreaming

If I came to you dreaming.
I am dreaming I am strong.
Dreaming strength.

Dreaming I am placed somewhere in time
this time I will live

I am lying in a maelstrom
sweeping what I breath as air
out of myself

reach my strangled grasp [gasp] into another one.

What would you say to me?
Would you know me?
Would you try to know what I know,
hold my visions close
as if dreams are premonitions, structured,
linear, linking one thing to another?

I am dreaming I am strong
Dreaming strength
I burn with passion
I don't need drugs to stay awake

I am lying in a nightmare
I lie, out of breath
lying in the embrace of someone who
burns with hatred for me

If I came to you dreaming and what would you say
    to me?
Would you know yourself despite the language
    barrier
would you hold out
structured, linear

one thing linking to another
a reduction to the lowest common denominator?

I never asked myself what freedom is
or why you wanted to stay with me
or how you could live with such contempt
as you had, for me,
touching you
an it
even while you slept

even while you slept

The worst memory is this
your dream
of me, you said to yourself
this
is mine now, I can have this now

But someone has spoken of unspeakable thoughts
and I will remember them

he said (II)

he said

I'm sure I touched the very bones of love

you are the very bones of love

you hold the bones

when my hands are full

of other things

Fear

A burned place grave with ash
finally found when I was dreaming
someone's quiet flash of inspiration
nothing there of mine no feeling

No time for thought a frantic clasp
in darkness numbness stealing in
while I am lying there I gasp in
horror fall to pieces feeling
nothing

Oh if I could be someone else
or somewhere else I would be
if I could believe that stealth
would give me breath I'd breathe

A crescent moon engraved with diamond
cuts my hand I hold it wheeling
back upon my back to cut me open
mouthed to scream but I am screaming

Theatrics and Melodrama: False Perceptions and Twisted Memories

I. Towards a Classification of Personality Disorder

The Personality Disorder is
a phenomenally disturbing one.
The language used to camouflage
one of utter contempt
Stand apart with your
hand on her head
Guidance is so
important at this time.

Swallow her whole do
not attempt to converse with
her confused
when she climbs on
your knee and
spits in your eye

Still Life

I am still,
even today,
creeping back into the past
looking for something
that remains
without an adequate explanation

It is a strange skin
marked
with a necrosis which
does not seem able to heal

It is an ugly and laughed at
dislocation

waiting in disquiet
four thousand miles
and almost seven years
away

I am thinking about you and how
your anger on those
last days
before I left, dismissed forever
followed me
to another continent

It is this which I remember
instead of
those times I thought that it would be
your apartment which would hold
some enduring meaning for me
saying, here, it happened here
and the landscape of each room
like it was only yesterday

I regretted never asking for a photograph
to aid my memory
of you
it stops me gazing
at the cold embodied tabula rasa
of doubt and constructing
an alternative exposure
of you

trapped
still life
a nostalgic parody
a visual aid to my account
and my unbeautiful witness

It was because I never asked you

>   reduced as my imagination was and continued to be
>   until that day you told me
>   that it was all academic now
>   wasn't it?

that what I hold of you now
is your epithetical contempt
and the butt ends
scathing
on the underside of your jokes
this image of you that
thrums with life
and hates me profoundly

My basest memory recalls your
fascination
with my self obsession
which I could transform into something I could sing
an art
suggesting something about me
that was deeply mysterious
that you couldn't get enough of

In fact it was me who was loved
as a still life
captured in a static representation
a successful
reconstruction of myself
apart from me
a thing
which could be read between the lines
a demanding versified structure
a complicated map
all roads lead to me

If you have anything of me
I imagine it is
this
thing of my self
that couldn't love you back
but called it love
this relentless hunger
which
you increasingly came to understand as greed
this existential desperation
that wasted your time
prolonged past its
sell-by date
smelling of corruption
metaphorphosing an agar on which could grow

only bacteria and worms
afterwards I would tell you
I couldn't keep down
anything
I consumed

How could you not
ask yourself
what that meant about you?

And I think of your cruelty
from my not wanting to know you
and you
no longer wanting to know me

Because I was
paralysed
with this inability to listen
and my teeth chattering
an anaphylaxis of shock
a lost breath of fear

And how were you supposed
to deal with that
crude
disfigured streak
in me
that found no joy in you
and no power in our power?

When I think of you and me
all I can remember
is one thing
or another

but what do I know of us

and the terrible picture we made
together?

Possession

This dream is not my own dream
a vision of her love and
her love
before the appalled loss of equilibrium
a graveyard she said

lifted to reveal a woman

alive, but only just

a prison I was
sleeping in the sun
above her

a thin earth
risen to let her go
I knew that she could leave I told her
so

but her face
in shreds
and the blood everywhere

echoed there
in her ragged voice
as she heard it

distance there as I saw it
as I wrote and wrote
of
freedom

Miriam's Letter

dear one
daughter

how I
told you

once of
love and you

remembered
that

for months

and sang to
sleep your

dread
and tremor

though I
could not

understand it
then

or now

a long time
ago

when I
birthed this fire

spinal numbed
waist down

could not feel
a thing

you fell
into your father's hands

never looking
back

and I

how could I

have known that there
would be

a second chance
to birth you

falling

this time
falling back into my

my

(but)
my

reluctant
awkward hands

fall back

fall back

continue to
forgive me

mother

Father Lamentations II

Do not mis/take her	for someone you know she is a raving in your life
Do not mis/take her	or claim her straying bitter gall
Do not mis/take her	for your own body you say you had her there
Do not mis/take her	broken down as if she could not bear it if you were to go too far
Do not mis/take her	malice for love when she lifts her head in pure horror
Do not mis/take her	for the romantic you are you think you would do anything
Do not mis/take her	to have her back as one more arm of your arms
Do not mis/take her	cant for song she has no range for singing
Do not mis/take her	head in the clouds her mouth spills words siphoned
Do not mis/take her	refined, no more than a vessel a vestal degraded and you came too late
Do not mis/take her	to save her for yourself

Work

Let me tell you my body is myself
drinking because the ovens make me sweat

Lifting the flesh to and fro that I
am cooking on this production line

I watch my arms grow massive with
strength and I can stay on my feet

all day working the dough and I
can walk two miles to my home and

I can feel myself grow hungry

I am not ill
my eyes do not become
dotted with black spots and blue haze
I do not see the fat man who is

a skeleton grow ghastly in my sleep

I do not deny myself all human
contact to deepen my capacity to feel

every meal is not my last meal
desperate with the anticipation of desertion

I do not want to suffocate or drown
to paralyse myself voiceless, lipless

without extremities to move me
I do not think deprivation is love

I do not live deserted, but in exile

I do not call my hatred freedom

Acknowledgements

The JUNE collective, of which I was a member, was formed in San Francisco in 1989 and ran for approximately five years. We produced a members-only monthly journal for work in progress, feedback and general discussion. Much of the work was performed in San Francisco. We also produced compilation issues of members' work. I owe the JUNE collective an indescribable debt not only for the collection in this book, but for providing an extraordinary creative space and a community of *dramatis personae* who were at once friends, cast members, pen pals, performers and dramaturgical authors of self, memoria and prophesy.

Thank you also to the Politics of Sexuality Group for logos and direction and purpose.

Notes

The poems in this collection have been revised but were first written or appeared as follows: 'Umbilicus (Creation Myth I)' as 'God Spoke' in 1990, a version appeared in *JUNE: a cavalcade of monthly drama*; Father Lamentations I and II as 'Father Variations I and II' in 1991, a version appeared in *JUNE: a cavalcade of monthly drama*; 'Daphne (The Metamorphosis)' as 'Daphne' in 1985, a version appeared in *JUNE: a cavalcade of monthly drama*; 'Dreaming' in 1991; 'he said (II) in 1985; 'Fear' in 1991; 'Theatrics and Melodrama: false perceptions and twisted memories/page 1' in 1985; 'Still Life' in 1991, a version appeared in *JUNE: a cavalcade of monthly drama and compilation*; 'Possession' in 1991; 'Miriam's Letter' in 1991, a version appeared in *JUNE: a cavalcade of monthly drama*; 'Work' in 1991.

6

Masculinities and Schooling:
Why are Young Men so Homophobic?*

Anoop Nayak and Mary Jane Kehily

Introduction

Our starting point for this study is the question, why are young men in schools so homophobic? The paper grows out of school-based research which took place in two secondary schools in the West Midlands. We worked with 20 pupils; two Year 11 groups (age 15–16) and a group of sixth formers. We also interviewed teachers engaged in Personal and Social Education programmes. We used a range of qualitative approaches for data gathering including group discussion and semi-structured interviews with groups and individuals. A tape recorder was used for most sessions and combined with note taking during and after the research period. The methodological implications of researching sexuality in schools cannot be developed within the scope of this paper. However, we acknowledge the influence of feminist praxis in this field, particularly its emphasis on reflexivity, grounded theory and a recognition of the personal (Roberts and Bell, 1984; Harding, 1987; Hollway, 1989; Stanley and Wise, 1993).

Our work in schools suggests that sexuality is present in a variety of exchanges and encounters and performs a wide range of social functions. Although we are interested in pupil cultures more generally, here, we focus on the culture of masculinity and its significance for the

*An extended discussion of the themes of this chapter can be found in *Journal of Gender Studies*, 5(2), Playing it straight: masculinities, homophobias and schooling.

production of homophobias. Elsewhere it has been argued that pupil sexual cultures are active in shaping schooling relations (Epstein and Johnson, 1994; Mac an Ghaill, 1994; Redman, 1994; Kehily and Nayak, 1996). Our paper discusses the gendered dynamics of homophobia and the ensuing, and often dramatic, performances that take place. We attempt to trace the connections between homophobic thoughts, speech and actions. Our approach has been to work closely with the material generated and develop the themes signposted by our respondents. The paper looks at verbal and visual displays of heterosexism before moving on to consider the psychic investments in these processes. The variety of homophobic displays we encounter suggest young men have particular investments in these practices. We argue that these investments are played out internally and externally in an attempt to negotiate a coherent masculine identity.

Homophobic performances: some gendered dynamics

The ways in which attitudes towards homosexuality are expressed are neither monolithic or unambiguous. Even so, the pervasiveness of homophobic language and actions within schools cannot be underestimated. The variety of means through which these relations are articulated are noted by Epstein and Johnson:

> At its most general level, there is a presumption of hetero-sexuality that is encoded in language, in institutional practices and the encounters of everyday life . . . It is not necessary for homophobia to be expressed for heterosexism as a cultural structure to be active in a particular moment. It operates through silence and absences as well as through overt discrimination. (Epstein and Johnson, 1994, p. 198)

The distinction made by Epstein and Johnson between expressions of homophobia and daily cultural practices, which are themselves based around a norm of heterosexuality, is important. In our work with school pupils, though many subjects voiced derogatory comments about homosexuality, it seemed problematic to condemn these young people as outright homophobics. Our research suggests pupil cultures may employ sexual relations in both dominant and subversive ways (Kehily and Nayak, 1996). Here, sexuality is a resource that serves multiple purposes for pupils: for classroom humour, to disrupt sessions, to draw up boundaries against teachers and middle-class sensibilities, for the construction of masculinities and as a form of abuse towards other pupils or teachers.

In his study of the sex talk of young males, Julian Wood (1984) points to some of the alternative ways sexist language was employed, not only for misogynistic purposes, but to bolster masculine status and conceal vulnerabilities: 'We find that while the outward face of sexist talk is bravado, the inward face is another story. Furthermore, such talk and ideas weaken the ability to come to terms with the insecurities beneath them. The boast isolates the speaker from sympathy as well as from hurt.' (Wood, 1984, p. 79). From our research into the ways homosexuality is viewed in school this has real significance, where it is frequently young males that are most vociferous in their expression of homophobias. The question of gendered affiliations to homophobia was raised in our discussions with a group of fifteen-year-old girls.

The crucifix performance

In your class do you think that boys could be more homophobic or do you think that girls are?

Lucy   I think that boys are.

Susan   Yes, definitely.

Lucy   Because they go 'STAY AWAY' (*demonstrates crucifix sign with fingers*) or something like that.

ALL   Yes.

Susan   Like as if he's contagious.

Amy   If they're all sitting together like that (*ie. huddled up*), one of them will move away.

Seeing this expression of homophobia as a gendered performance (Butler, 1990), it is possible that, for the young men, the performativity is working at two levels; externally within the group and internally within the Self. Within the popular genre of horror, the crucifix as a religious symbol is used to ward off vampires, spirits and dark forces. The outward performance of making a crucifix sign resonates with psychoanalytical theories of sexuality concerned with creating an unambiguous sense of Self through displacing fears on to an imaginary Other. At an internal level this is intriguing, where within vampire mythology the ultimate fear is not death but that you will become a vampire. Here, the homosexual is fantasized as vampire, to be resisted and destroyed. This imaginary creation, through demonic signification, is an act Redman (Chapter 4) terms as the production of 'monstrous Others'. Using the crucifix as an imaginary form of defence positions homosexuality as threatening, evil and unnatural, while being able to visibly locate the desired heterosexual masculinity of young men. According to this group, girls had fewer reservations about sitting closely together and were less prone to the performative outbursts young males displayed against homosexuality. Indeed, homophobia seems to offer an opportunity for male exhibitionists to enforce heterosexual masculinities.

The connections between hegemonic masculinities and homophobia are all too clear when we consider that many of the characteristics ascribed to gay men are applied to women. We became aware of how homosexual labels could be attached to boys who conformed to authority or worked hard. The gendered dynamic of homosexual abuse was something a teacher, the PSE co-ordinator Miss Green, agreed with. We inquired: Gay seems to be used as a term of abuse within the school, a boy can be called gay if he gets on with his work and doesn't join in the fun with the rest of the lads.

Miss Green   That's right, I've heard it used that way or if they're just a very nice person, if they're gentle and not seen as macho.

There is, then, a contradiction between being 'nice' and conforming to dominant expectations of masculinity. The concept of being a 'gentleman' is regarded as a contradiction in terms. The relationship between sex talk and masculinity is referred to by Moore and Rosenthal: 'Boys who are not so strongly motivated towards sexual gratification or who do not talk – or brag – about their sexual experiences in this way risk derogatory labels that reflect unwelcome attributes such as unattractiveness ('nerd') or having homosexual leanings ('poofter')' (Moore and Rosenthal, 1993, p. 83). The problems that gay and many heterosexual young males have in negotiating this contradictory position suggests sexual conformity is a tightrope young males must carefully tread upon, as we shall see.

Miles talking

Miles   It's a sort of stigma, ain't it? A quiet person in a class
would be called 'gay' or summat. I was for a time 'cos I
was fairly quiet in the classroom and for a while everyone
was callin me a gay . . . To be honest it didn't really bother
me. I've never been bothered by insults or that, I just
thought they were stupid. I had my own group of friends
so it didn't really bother me; it wasn't my close friends who
were calling me gay. . . They [the name-callers] should be
allowed to leave and get a job, it would make life for
everyone else a lot easier. I think my grades have suffered
'cos of the disruptive members of the class. They're not
really interested in getting a qualification so it's, 'Well,
what can we do for a laugh today? Disrupt the history
lesson or something like that.' It just makes it impossible
for anyone who wants to get on with their work 'cos of the
things going on in the class, know what I mean?

When Miles talks about the ways in which 'gay' is used as a term of
abuse against him, the implications of this are fascinating. On the one
hand he claims it has little effect upon him (as a heterosexual male with
his own friendship group) when he states, 'To be honest it didn't really
bother me.' Later, however, he is aggrieved that sexual taunts have
disrupted his education and claims, 'I think my grades have suffered . . .
It just makes it impossible for anyone who wants to get on with their
work.' Establishing an identity as hard working may itself be a personal
strategy employed to avoid homophobic abuse by locating oneself
within a particular friendship group. It does seem that using sexuality to
abuse individuals is a serious issue for the victims of name-calling.
Clearly, resisting dominant codes of masculinity is a precarious business
within school where being labelled as 'gay' can have detrimental effects.
Once again, the connections between homophobias and masculinities
were recognized by young women.

Talking about Gavin

Libby   I'd hate to imagine, like, if one of the boys were gay in the
groups, the way the others would treat them.

Susan   I mean, they say Gavin's gay don't they?

All   Yes.

Susan   And he's not gay because I've known him since I was little because . . .

Libby   Yes, they don't even know him, but they say it anyway.

Susan   Like if a boy crosses his legs or makes a comment and everybody – like rumours just spread.

Why would it be certain people that would be called gay and not others, even if they don't know, like in the class?

Libby   I don't know, they've just got this picture of a gay person in their heads . . .

Susan   They pick on Gavin because he hasn't got a masculine voice and he doesn't – he's not very well built like everyone else in our year.

Amy   And if they walk funny, they're gay.

As the exchanges involving the case of Miles and Gavin demonstrate, actual sexual orientation is not the only factor that engenders name-calling. Other aspects of imagined gay behaviour are projected on to certain young men.[1] Young people are, then, encouraged to scrutinize their behaviour in order to survive the prospect of this type of peer labelling. The labelling itself is one premised on stereotypes, or, as Libby puts it, 'They've got this picture of a gay person in their heads.' This image operates as a blueprint for assumed gay behaviour. Young men who are considered gay are imagined to have high voices, camp walks, underdeveloped bodies, work hard and be relatively quiet in school. It seemed that these stereotypes of gay men had currency within schools and, if not necessarily believed, would rarely be challenged. The group of girls we worked with seemed more willing to deconstruct the stereotypical homosexual image. Here, the girls are speaking about male homophobia.

Shouting it out

Amy   They think that they can point out like gay people just by the way they walk or the way they act.

Susan	It's really pathetic!
Lucy	Like if he's got a squeaky voice, 'Oh he's gay!'
Sally	Just, like a, like a normal man . . . he could be walking down the street and you could think, 'Oh, I bet he's got a really nice girlfriend', but for all you know, he could be gay or he could be homosexual.
Susan	People still think they can tell.
Libby	People do shout it out and start calling them gay. Well, the boys do.

Once again, it seems that masculinity has particular investments in homophobia. When Susan and Libby are talking about identifying or shouting at gays we see how by 'people' they come to mean 'boys'. However, beyond the simple expressions of homophobia may lie other reasons for such name-calling. Attempts to conceal the anxieties Wood (1984) spoke of, an envy of other males who are doing well at school and a desire to create disruption or gain laughs are all part of these complex interactions. In the crucifix example, the performative level of homophobia was central. Here, shouting out that someone is gay is itself a reiteration of one's own heterosexuality, recognized through male bravado and display. For Andrew Jones (1993), physical demonstrations such as shouting are part of the wider social repertoire of bodily male practices. Haywood (1996) similarly claims that whenever a male was in a particular group talking about sex, he was always loud. It was significant that only groups of males who cultivated a masculinity where sexual proficiency and prowess was important, talked loud. Such practices are also a means of avoiding the threat of becoming a victim of this type of verbal abuse. Homophobic performances are, then, closely interconnected with the struggle for masculinities. Here, male sex talk is about as much about self as audience.

Looking big

Miles	Girls are called 'slag', it's just something to pass the time, they think, 'Oh look at him, he's quiet, not like everyone else and you get a laugh if you call him gay.'

Melissa   It's for attention I suppose.

Miles   And it makes them look big.

And what do you have to do to be popular?

Miles   Well, you got to be disrupting lessons, be cheeky to teachers, otherwise you're looked on as a wimp or something.

Melissa   'Cos I worked hard people called me a snob, 'cos I got good grades but I didn't want to work on a checkout for the rest of my life.

Our research seems to suggest that differing rules exist for young men and women when it comes to name-calling (Lees, 1986; 1993). It seemed there were also different social codes that valued male resistance in the classroom. Unsurprisingly, gender dynamics intervene where Miles is seen as 'gay', but Melissa is seen as a 'snob' for working hard. In Paul Willis' (1977) study of male working-class pupils, such school relations were integral to preparing 'lads' for the culture of the shop floor. For Willis, conventional masculinity is tied to notions of class, where 'manual labour is associated with the social superiority of masculinity and mental labour with the social inferiority of femininity' (1977, p. 148). Melissa suggests young men engage in various forms of verbal abuse 'for attention', which may explain the 'loudness' of much sex talk. The young women claim males call each other 'gay' as it can make 'them look big' (i.e. like men). The concept of 'looking big' has a physical quality to it and can be seen as a symbolic form of body-building for male reputations.[2] Here, masculinity must be worked at, yet is continually displayed as natural (Dyer, 1983). Masculinity is competitive and is used to make young men 'look big' often at the expense of others.

Although sex talk and particularly homophobic abuse were common amongst males it would be wrong to assume all young men had access to these speech forms within peer settings. It may be the case that only certain males may get away with using sex talk to enhance their reputations. Talking about sexuality as a means of confirming masculine power could backfire on some whose reputations were less macho. The different boundaries that exist when it comes to sex talk between male groups is hinted at by a seventeen year old in Willmott's study talking about masturbation:

> I suppose all boys do it. I know all my mates do. We talk about it sometimes, have a joke about it. I think you do get some boys who think, 'I'm not going to tell anyone in case they think I'm dirty, wanking myself off.' But me and my mates, *we tell everybody* [our emphasis] we wank off. (Quoted in Willmott, 1971, p. 54)

It then seems that sex talk can enhance the status of some young men but not others. Similarly, Wood (1984) found that certain males had more access to sexual demonstration than others, who had to wait outside the room while 'bundles' with girls were in progress (1984, p. 70). Of course this raises questions about the space young women have to negotiate these relations, but differences between male sexual power and its various articulations are focused on here.[3]

The performative aspects of homophobic male expression as learned in school may be carried out into other spheres of life. The following conversation about work spaces is worth citing as the interactions witnessed seem very similar to the types of sexual relations we found in schools. They also tell us more about the way many men may react to homosexuality generally.

Hotel homophobia

Susan   My mum runs a hotel and she had two [gay men] stopping in the hotel and they were sharing like a double room together and then the waiters in the hotel wouldn't serve them because they were going, 'I'm not bending down, or he might try and pinch my arse' or whatever. (*Laughs*)
And they make real jokes out of it and they really avoid them and they go in the girls' toilet, because they go, 'I'm not going near him!' And like, when he's up at the bar or whatever, they like ignored him. Like he was a social outcast.

In the extract the display of homophobia is central to establishing a heterosexual masculine identity. In actuality a highly contradictory form of masculinity is produced. Joking and anxieties operate simultaneously, while running into the 'girls' toilet' would hardly enhance masculine status in most contexts. In the same way that the crucifix narrative was able to show male fear yet remain in control, the hotel homophobia example does just this. There is a fear of becoming gay by entering the men's toilets or of catching homosexuality by coming into contact with the (presumed) gay men. The myth of homosexuality as a disease that can be passed on through any kind of physical contact is played out (see Goggin, 1993, p. 114). It is this mixture of fear, fascination, comedy and masculine display that we found to be regular features within classroom situations. That these reactions may continue into adulthood and other work forums is worrying.

Public masculinities, private insecurities

Amongst the homophobic language and actions that young men exhibited we found certain fixations. This included a desire to split off masculinity from any form of homoerotic attachment, a fascination with bodily practices and collective peer organization around and against homosexuality.

As we have already seen, male homophobic expression may be tightly bound up with attempts to increase status within the competitive pecking order of masculine groups Willis (1977) notes. The crudity of sexual labels may be used to construct hierarchical identities, defining the subjects abused and those doing the abusing. Within Chris Haywood's (1996) research humour was a means of othering, a form of display young men used to disassociate themselves from homoerotic attachments:[4]

Nik   What do you think of Adam Cobley?

Ross   He's a bum bandit.

Tibbs   He's a sphincter stretcher.

Stuart   Bent.

Why do you say that?

Ross   'Cos he's gay, he stretches sphincter.
         (Quoted in Haywood, 1996, pp. 237–8)

Similarly, the mention of one boy's name in our research was enough for others to define themselves against this individual and declare him a 'bum-chum'. It is interesting to consider why aspects of the body are frequently invoked in homophobia, sexism and racism. Perhaps these bodily references can be read psychoanalytically as a displacement of one's own bodily fears, desires and inadequacies. Within the school context we can see how 'weak' males are defined as 'gay' in order to consolidate the power and status of other males. The effect is to differentiate oneself by projecting vulnerabilities on to other young men. Although we recognize the significance of sex talk (Wood, 1984; Haywood, 1996) we have already seen the importance of performative homophobias and visual masculinities. Our work suggests sex talk is only one dimension through which young men construct and perform their masculinity. The role of bodily practices as a signifier of a person's sexuality is seen, where the way a male might walk, hold himself, sit, etc. provide for a visual grammar of understanding. Speaking about the outward encoding of masculinity beyond the level of conversation Askew and Ross (1988) found 'There was considerable non-verbal, aggressive or physical communication among boys. "Body language" such as stance, or tone of voice, played a large part in interaction' (p. 36).

The complex ways in which male peer groups collectively work with visual sign systems is interesting, where sitting close to another male can be viewed problematically. What is evident in our study is the active role pupils play in helping define the boundaries of sexual behaviour, what Redman describes as 'playground policing' (1994b, p. 147). For Skeggs (1991) young men's resistance often has negative implications for young women. The active cultures of pupils in producing sexual rules is also taken up by Epstein and Johnson (1994, p. 223) who note

> Stigmatization of gay and lesbian identities is a routine feature of student/pupil life . . . In this respect, as in others, the sexual cultu·e of school pupils, although always a resistance to schooling, is not necessarily transformative. It may, indeed, be very conservative, policing boundaries even more effectively than government decrees or school rules .

The complex negotiations that occur amongst pupils as to what is and what is not deemed acceptable are difficult to untangle. An example of male resistance to sexuality occurred when a teacher showed a video concerning HIV/AIDS during a PSE lesson. The teacher explained the film focused on two male characters, one gay and one heterosexual. The film worked with heterosexist reader assumptions that the gay man would be HIV positive. Instead, the narrative closure of the film saw the heterosexual man contracting the virus. The ways the film was interpreted by young males as being about homosexuality and subsequently dismissed, is telling of the self-policing processes pupils are engaged in. It is revealing to see the ways a predominantly male group negotiate to position themselves as masculine and heterosexual.

The HIV video

Jason   We had that film once.

Clive   Which one?

Savage   It was about homosexuals, weren't it?

Clive   That was in science.

Samantha   The only video we had in PSE was about crime and vandalism.

Jason   Was it in science? That one about, how do . . . I can't say it.

Clive   Homosexuality.

Jason   That's the one.

What was that then?

Shane   And you sat there and watched it?!!

Jason   We had to! We had to sit and watch it, we had no choice, we had to stay there and watch it.

What lesson was this?

Jason   Science, arh, we don't wanna know, we had to sit there and watch it.

Samantha   What was it about?

Jason   It was about these chaps, they told you they were gay.

Clive   Oh that. That was boring.

This extract raises a range of questions about male perceptions of homosexuality. What is it Jason cannot bring himself to say? Why does Shane challenge the others for watching the film? Why is Jason adamant to stress he was coerced into the viewing session? Why does Clive dismiss the video as boring? These questions can only be understood within the cultural matrix of masculinity, homophobia and schooling. Jason's heightened reaction to Shane's implicit charge that he secretly may have wanted to watch the film is illustrative of the competitive anxieties masculinities produce. The sequence is also indicative of the 'silences and absences' accompanying homophobias Epstein and Johnson (1994, p. 198) noted earlier. The ways pupil cultures may organize themselves collectively around issues such as homosexuality is intermeshed with gender dynamics. This is underlined in an exchange involving Melissa, Miles and Claire when we asked if homosexuality could be talked about.

Melissa   Yeah, we can talk about it with friends. You hear them say it's not right, but you can't say it's not right or it's right.

Miles   It's still a touchy subject. If you were like the person who started talking about it then they'd think, 'Oh he must be. He must be what he's talking about.'

Claire   But you can't say it's wrong. It's right for them and if it's right for them and they're happy, it's nothing to do with you or anyone else. It's what they want to do so who are you to say?

Melissa   In my year the boys tend to be more, 'Oh it's wrong, it's unnatural.'

It seemed that within female friendship groups homosexuality could be discussed in ways that young males were unable to amongst their respective peers. Miles admits that any reference to homosexuality could result in homophobic abuse with other males quick to assume that, 'He must be what he's talking about.' This tells us about the conversational boundaries that may exist within these social groups. Once more, it appears to be young men that are the most stringent guardians of heterosexuality and may perceive being gay as 'wrong' and 'unnatural' since it violates traditional masculinity. The reactions of

Miles would seem to suggest that talking about homosexuality within certain masculine peer groups in anything but an abusive or jocular way is virtually impossible. Talking about personal and emotional subjects can be problematic as it fractures the hard face of conventional masculinity. Wendy Hollway's (1989) study on heterosexual couples suggests men engage in emotional displacements. Carol Lee explains:

A friend once gave a description of the way men view emotions when he said: 'They're like accidents. They happen to other people. If you're lucky you never fall foul of them.' The more I thought about it the more apt his statement was in describing the attitudes of many of the boys I meet, who go to extraordinary lengths to avoid confronting their emotions. They build partitions of aggression or seeming indifference between themselves and the rest of the world so that no-one sees their vulnerabilities. These partitions are dangerous because they prevent both the world gaining a clear view of the person behind them and that person having a clear view of the world. (Lee, 1986, p. 34)

These 'partitions of aggression or seeming indifference' are lived out when young men speak about homosexuality. The film about HIV/AIDS showed some of these partitions being constructed by male pupils. Clive presents indifference, claiming he was bored, while Jason was aggressive, indignant that he was 'made' to watch the film. The showing of crucifixes to ward off homosexuality and the vocal attacks on anyone exhibiting potentially 'camp' behaviour demonstrates the psychic dramas played out by young men. The ways in which Miles is sensitive to homosexuality as a 'touchy subject' is also indicative of an awareness to these boundaries or partitions. Young men invest in masculinity in psychosexual ways where sexuality is itself a barometer for measuring male performance. Here, sexual reputation, wit, physical strength and swagger are vital ingredients.

The construction of homosexuality as biologically inherent was something that many young men invested in. This acted as a rationale for homophobic views and the demonstrative displays we have seen. That being gay was 'wrong' and 'unnatural' in the ways described was something that filtered into some teacher accounts too. The biological framework of sexuality was frequently worked and re-worked within school. Here, a teacher speaks about a gay pupil.

The case of Malcolm

Miss Green I remember one lad I taught, name was Malcolm.
Became a hairdresser. I always knew where I could find
Malcolm. He'd be smoking at the back of the school on
his own, but he was isolated. I knew why he was
isolated, the other kids had some gut feeling he was
different. I suspect Malcolm at the earlier age didn't
know why he was being isolated. Well, he wouldn't
know why he was different, but there must be kids here.

Malcolm is described to us as 'different', suggesting that homosexuality
is defined against a 'normative' version of heterosexuality. According to
the teacher Malcolm's sexuality could be spotted at some instinctive
level where 'other kids had some gut feeling'.[5] The isolation Malcolm
must have felt is akin to the 'burden of aloneness' which KOLA identify
as a feature of school existence for gay pupils (KOLA, 1994). There is
also a pathologizing of Malcolm as a victim of his genetic make-up, 'he
wouldn't know why he was different' yet the teacher knew and even
other pupils had some imagined sixth sense about it.

Heterosexuality then acts as the norm within schools and is the focal
point around which other sexual behaviours are located. The source of
its power is its taken-for-grantedness, the fact that it goes unexplained,
unchallenged and is assumed. This has the effect of seeing heterosexuality as natural, rather than socially constructed. Indeed, we have
already seen some of the social processes that are at play to produce
dominant masculinities and help enforce heterosexual behaviour within
schools. The ambivalence within young peoples sexualities was
something that Mac an Ghaill (1991, p. 297) found in his study on
young gay men as he explains:

> The students described the formation of their sexual identity as
> part of a wider process of adolescent development, with all its
> fluidity, experiments, displacements and confusions. For them
> sexuality could not be reduced to a conventional perception of a
> heterosexual–homosexual (straight–gay) continuum, on which
> each group's erotic and emotional attachments are demarcated
> clearly and unambiguously. They spoke of the contradictions . . .
> the complexity and the confusion of young males' sexual coming-
> of-age.

The ways in which heterosexuality is assumed, what Epstein and Johnson term the 'heterosexual presumption' (1994), has repercussions for the formation of gay and heterosexual identities.

Miles   In the first year if you got a girlfriend you're the laughing stock; now if you haven't got a girlfriend you're the laughing stock! (*All laugh*)

Heterosexual relations are then perceived as a natural culmination of growing up and becoming sexually aware. Within the culture of masculinity having a girlfriend is equated with being (hetero)sexual and so has status. Not having a girlfriend makes young men potential targets for homophobic abuse and unpopularity. For young males sex is reputation enhancing,[6] as long as it is strictly within the boundaries of heterosexuality. Sexuality may then be an uncertain realm where posturing displays, joke telling, abuse and intimate contact are under surveillance. The pressures to conform to masculine sexual expectations that young men place on themselves and one another results in inner tensions as we shall go on to explore.

Psychosexual dramas: why young men are homophobic

During the research it seemed as if young men were particularly uneasy around certain issues of sexuality, yet were frequently indulging in the types of spectacular and mundane displays we have identified. It seemed that if we could analyse some of the sources of these psychosexual anxieties we could go some way towards understanding the nature of male homophobic abuse. Where boundaries are drawn up and how they are maintained was of interest.

A safe distance

Claire   I got some gay friends and it didn't bother me, I got nothing against it anyway.

Miles   It would be different if it were your best friend who came and told you he was gay 'cos knowing people at a distance you tend to accept it. But if it was your best friend who told you it would immediately spring to your mind, 'Oh he wants to do it with me! (*All laugh*) I'm his best friend, why's he telling me this?'

We can see how the reaction of Miles suggests an internal anxiety towards being gay. At a general level this is not a problem 'with people at a distance'. However, masculinity is more troubled by the personal level. Having a close friend confide in his sexuality to you can create instability in conventional relationships. This may be why a best friend telling you he was gay would violate more codes than the fact of gayness itself. Miles outlines the basis of fear being that the friend would be making a provocative pass. Perhaps there is also the hidden fear that if a best friend confided in you about such an intimate sexual matter it would be very difficult to handle the emotional aspects of the discussion. Hidden self-anxieties surface when we follow the assumptions of these phobias through: your best friend is gay, and you like your best friend, could that mean you are gay? The closing comment by Miles also allows us an insight into the close but not so close friendships many males forge, 'I'm his best friend, why's he telling me this?' There is then an irony to the way masculine peer cultures may portray the best friend as trespassing conventional boundaries of intimacy by speaking emotionally.

The specific investments in certain homophobic rituals and displays is intriguing. The subjects of our research seemed to indicate that it was not homosexuality *per se* that many young males were against but its associations with femininity and self-identity. This would go some way to explaining the psychosexual struggles we have encountered and their ensuing ambivalences. It is at these internal levels that heterosexual masculinities are being worked through. Young women were frequently skilled in identifying these situational dilemmas and explaining these complex processes. Here, the young people are talking about why males indulge in homophobic abuse so vehemently.

Queers, peers and fears

Claire   It's more the boys. 'Cos you find the boys are more against gay yet they don't mind lesbians. They don't like gay people but they don't mind lesbians. It's because it doesn't affect them.

Melissa   It's a fear of what people think you are, I mean you might not be gay, but you would probably really worry about it.

Miles   But if you were gay, you've made your choice and you've made your choice not to listen to what other people think. If you weren't gay and everyone thought you were it would be unpleasant for you.

The comments made by Claire above, suggest the homophobias of young males is directional. In displaying their homophobia they are able to consolidate their masculine status at the expense of others. How else can we begin to understand the complexities of why it is that 'boys are more against gay yet they don't mind lesbians'. Undoubtedly this is a generalization (some males are lesbian haters and there is an invisibility of lesbianism in school) yet the threads of Claire's remarks are worth drawing out. She claims that young men are far less concerned about lesbians 'because it doesn't affect them'. This would indicate that a lot of male homophobia is concerned with constructing an imagined identity that is uncontradictory, unitary and essentially masculine. Homophobia, as a phobia, is then not simply about an abstract fear of gays generally (though this may be a feature) but is more specifically about internal fears of losing control and 'turning' gay. Homophobia is the process of expulsion or projection which transfers these inner anxieties on to Others. The ways in which Miles distinguishes between gayness generally and if a best friend was gay, and the differences between male attitudes to gays as opposed to lesbians bears testament to the psychic dynamics involved.

Melissa emphasizes the importance young men place on their masculine reputations when she notes that you might not be gay but 'it's a fear of what people think you are'. It is these psychic fears that are concealed behind many of the overt homophobic displays we have seen. This is not to explain away the implications of this as a form of abuse but to begin to open up a way of interpreting the seemingly irrational behaviour of young men. Melissa recognizes the ways masculinity feeds off and into homophobic anxieties when she claims whether you were gay or not 'you would probably really worry about it'. These fears are simultaneously produced and concealed by masculinity. Young men may worry about being gay and being called gay in part due to the intense hostility they express towards homosexuality and femininity.

The unconscious, yet highly stylized, positions of male homophobia may go some way to explaining male reactions (and resistance) to the film about HIV/AIDs. That the young men perceived the film to be about homosexuality demonstrates their hyper-sensitivity to this as a personal issue that affects their identities and reputations as gay or heterosexual. It also says something about the general invisibility of homosexuality within official school cultures that the video is perceived as a 'gay film'. The masculine need to challenge other males for watching the film locates Shane as unambiguously heterosexual and male. Finally, Jason's adamant claim that they had little choice in viewing the film and his intense emotional protests suggest his masculine identity was being appraised. If masculinity does not conform to the criteria of male peer groups, the consequences in terms of power, identity and status may be undermining.

Conclusion: splintered selves – handling the enemy within

> Within the dominant sense of masculine identity that rationalism has prepared, sexuality remains a troubling contradiction. It demands the very surrender and spontaneity which men have grown up to be suspicious of. It is only through turning sex into performance, and separating it from intimacy and personal contact, that they can still see it as an issue of control. (Seidler, 1987, pp. 96–7)

We began the paper with a potential paradox. That is, that homophobic abuse was rife within schools and particularly amongst certain male peer groups. However, we asserted it would be simplistic and condemnatory to see the pupils we interviewed as unequivocally homophobic. We have tried to indicate that beyond the outward expression of homophobia lie other sets of dynamics, masculinity being, perhaps, most central. The complex social make-up of masculinities sees many young men using homophobias to conceal uncertainties and attempt to assert a cohesive heterosexual identity. The competitive operations of masculinity illustrate that many young men are acutely aware of homophobic relations and adapt themselves to the conditions of their own making. Lynne Segal (1990) states that 'the more masculinity asserts itself, the more it calls itself into question' (Segal, 1990, p. 123). Beyond the dramatic displays of homophobia then, complex internal dynamics exist. The psychosexual struggles that young men are constantly engaged in within school suggest gender and sexual relations are filled with tension and anxiety. Young women, gays and individuals who are the victims of homophobic abuse, are the recipients of these violently expressed masculine fears.

Masculine displays of homophobia have consequences for pedagogic practice. These performances are as much about a construction of the Self, as they are about the construction of an Other. This has implications for curriculum change and the journey towards what Mac an Ghaill (1991) terms an 'emancipatory curriculum'. Our research suggests that the road to emancipation is strewn with various obstacles. One of our main concerns is the masculine investments in homophobias which could make many young men resistant to transformative sexual politics. This resistance stems from internal anxieties and inconsistencies around masculinity. The struggle to maintain and present a socially recognized masculine identity is voiced in the phobias and displays aimed at concealing the vulnerability of ambivalence. To establish a coherent masculinity these ambivalences must be contained in external social arenas as well at interior levels within the subject. In the constant struggle for a coherent masculine sense of self, subjects engage in various forms of splitting. Fears and anxieties are displaced on to Others as a way of protecting – and so denying – the fragility of Self. These processes of self-construction appear to go largely unacknowledged by the individuals concerned in the struggle to achieve the illusion of internal consistency. Homophobic performances are part of the self-convincing rituals of masculinity young men engage in. The continual rehearsal of these performances are indicative of the psychic rhythms of a dislocated masculinity. The repetition of homophobic sequences suggests the impossibility of achieving a unified self.

In her article 'Femininity as performance', Valerie Walkerdine considers why women and girls may psychically disassociate themselves from their academic achievements. According to Walkerdine this creates an 'unbearable contradiction' (1990, p. 144) where women may not recognize their academic selves, since the identity of 'femininity is equated with poor performance' (p. 134). This may result in complex processes of splitting and displacement:

> How is it that for many women, the powerful part of themselves has been so split off as to feel that it belongs to someone else?

Here is no simple passive wimp femininity but a power which is desired, striven after, yet almost too dangerous to be acknowledged as belonging to the woman herself. (Walkerdine, 1990, p.134)

It is worth thinking through Walkerdine's feminist–psychoanalytic theories alongside the homophobic performances of young men. If women are unable to locate a 'sense of self' within an academic identity, perhaps homophobic display is a way of acquiring a recognized masculine sense of self that is psychically compatible for young men. The psychic investments in positioning the identities of Self and Others leads Walkerdine to conclude that 'equal opportunities models based on choice simply cannot engage with the complexity of the issues' (1990, p. 145).

Although this may appear to lead us into a pedagogical cul-de-sac, this paper raises questions about the limitations of policy as an isolated mechanism of change. We argue that pedagogical practice must be contextual and sensitive to interactions pupil cultures are engaged in and the power relations working within groups and individual psyches. Our work recognizes the inconsistencies and anxieties produced through dominant constructions of masculinity. In Hollway's (1989) study of heterosexual power relations this itself is a starting point for political organization. Her concluding comments appear particularly apt for a consideration of masculinities and homophobic performances. 'The main point . . . is to show men's vulnerability . . . Making political this knowledge gives us a different view of men's displays of self sufficiency, their resistance, their distancing and rejections' (Hollway, 1989, p. 139). Hollway then goes on to explain that 'understanding is not synonymous with changing' emphasizing the importance of power as part of all social relations (p. 140). We regard male homophobic practices as offensive and damaging to self and others. The affects on gay students and those unsure of their sexual identities is particularly debilitating. However, to begin to recognize the identifications young men make in the dynamics of heterosexual masculinity, and the investments forged in homophobic display, may move us towards understanding the prevalence and persistence of these negative practices.

Notes

1. Within psychoanalysis this act of projection can be read as a way of expelling homoerotic desire and confirming a heterosexual, masculine sense of self.

2. Beynon and Atkinson (1983) have conducted ethnographic research on masculinity in school and stress the ways male reputations can be hardened through engaging with specific codes of violence. It would also appear that adherence to certain sexual codes is part of the symbolic 'body-building' process used to enhance masculinity.

3. For a more in-depth look at the ways young women are constructed through male sex talk see Lees (1986, 1993) and Wood (1984). Skeggs (1991) has demonstrated how young women negotiate sexism within educational arenas. Meanwhile Canaan (1986) has discussed how young women position themselves within heterosexual relations. She provides an analysis of the way sexual stories about 'the other kinda' girl (p. 203) can become significant markers for plotting the sexual practices of all young women.

4. Also see Easthope (1990) who discusses the peculiarities of male bonding in popular culture and the function of sexual jokes.

5. Witch-hunts of homosexuals have focused around assumptions of physical and/or biological difference. The need to emphasize gays as different in some way can be seen as a way of securing heterosexuality as 'safe' and free from such troubling ambiguities.

6. Although heterosexual activity is enhancing for young men, sex may be damaging to the reputations of young women. This itself goes some way to explaining the male sexual boast and the acute awarenes many young men had of being positioned as gay.

References

Askew, S. and Ross, C. (1988) *Boys Don't Cry: Boys and Sexism in Education*. Milton Keynes: Open University Press.

Beynon, J. and Atkinson, P. (1983) A school for men: an ethnographic case study of routine violence in schooling, in Walker, S. and Barton, L. (eds) *Gender, Class and Education*. Lewes: Falmer.

Brown, M. and France, P. (1985) Only cissies wear dresses: a look at sexist talk in the nursery, in Weiner, G. (ed.) *Just a Bunch of Girls*. Milton Keynes: Open University Press.

Butler, J. (1990) *Gender Trouble: Feminism and the Subversion of Identity*. London: Routledge.

Canaan, J. (1986) Why a 'slut' is a 'slut': cautionary tales of middle-class teenage girls' morality, in Varenne, H. (ed.) *Symbolizing America*. Lincoln: University of Nabraska Press.

Dyer, R. (1983) Don't look now, *Screen*. 23 (3/4).

Epstein, D. (ed.) (1994) *Challenging Lesbian and Gay Inequalities in Education*. Buckingham: Open University Press.

Epstein, D. and Johnson, R. (1994) On the straight and narrow: the heterosexual presumption, homophobias and schools, in Epstein, D. (ed.) *Challenging Lesbian and Gay Inequalities in Education*. Buckingham: Open University Press.

Easthope, A. (1990) *What a Man's Gotta Do: The Masculine Myth in Popular Culture*. Boston: Unwin Hyman.

Gill, I. (1989) Trying not just to survive: A lesbian teacher in a boys' school, in Holly, L. (ed.) *Girls and Sexuality: Teaching and Learning*. Milton Keynes: Open University Press.

Goggin, M. (1993) Gay and lesbian adolescence, in Moore, S. and Rosenthal, D. (eds) *Sexuality in Adolescence*. London: Routledge.

Griffin, C. (1985) *Typical Girls? Young Women from School to the Job Market*. London: Routledge & Kegan Paul.

Harding, S. (ed.) (1987) *Feminism and Methodology*. Bloomington: Indiana University Press.

Haywood, C. (1996) Out of the curriculum: sex talking, talking sex, *Curriculum Studies: Special Issue on Sexuality*. 4 (2): 229–49.

Holland, J., Ramazanoglu, C., Scott, S., Sharpe, S. and Thomson, R. (1991) *Pressure, Resistance, Empowerment: Young Women and the Negotiation of Safe Sex*. London: Tufnell Press.

Hollway, W. (1989) *Subjectivity and Method in Psychology*. London: Sage.

Holly, L. (ed.) (1989) *Girls and Sexuality: Teaching and Learning*. Milton Keynes: Open University Press.

Jones, A. (1993) Defending the border: men's bodies and vulnerability, *Cultural Studies from Birmingham* 2 77–123.

Jones, C. and Mahoney, P. (eds) (1989) *Learning Our Lines*. London: Women's Press.

Johnson, R. (forthcoming) Sexual dissonances: or the 'impossibility' of sexuality education, *Curriculum Studies: Special Issue on Sexuality*. 4 (2)

Kehily, M. and Nayak, A. (1996) 'The Christmans Kiss': sexuality, story-telling and schooling. *Curriculum Studies: Special Issue on Sexuality*. 4 (2): 211–27.

KOLA (1994) A burden of aloneness, in Epstein, D. (ed.) *Challenging Lesbian and Gay Inequalities in Education*. Buckingham: Open University Press.

Lee, C. (1986) *The Ostrich Position: Sex, Schooling, Mystification*. London: Unwin.

Lees, S. (1986) *Losing Out: Sexuality and Adolescent Girls*. London: Hutchinson.

Lees, S. (1993) *Sugar and Spice: Sexuality and Adolescent Girls*. London: Penguin.

Mac An Ghaill, M. (1991) Schooling, sexuality and male power: towards an emancipatory curriculum, *Gender and Education*. 3 (3).

Mac an Ghaill, M. (1994a) *The Making of Men: Masculinities, Sexualities and Schooling*. Buckingham: Open University Press.

Mac an Ghaill, M. (1994b) (In)visibility: sexuality, race and masculinity in the school context, in Epstein, D. (ed.) *Challenging Lesbian and Gay Inequalities in Education*. Buckingham: Open University Press.

Moore, S. and Rosenthal, D. (1993) *Sexuality in Adolescence*. London: Routledge.

Redman, P. (1994a) Curtis Loves Ranjit: coming to terms with pupils' sexual cultures. Paper prepared for BSA annual conference, Sexuality in Social Contexts, University of Central Lancashire, Preston, March.

Redman, P. (1994b) Shifting ground: rethinking sexuality education, in Epstein, D. (ed.) *Challenging Lesbian and Gay Inequalities in Education*. Buckingham: Open University Press.

Roberts, H. and Bell, C. (eds) (1984) *Social Researching; Politics, Problems, Practice*. London: Routledge & Kegan Paul.

Rogers, M. (1994) Growing up Lesbian: the role of the school, in Epstein, D. (ed.) *Challenging Lesbian and Gay Inequalities in Education.* Buckingham: Open University Press.

Sanders, S. and Burke, H. (1994) 'Are you a Lesbian, Miss?, in Epstein, D. (ed.) *Challenging Lesbian and Gay Inequalities in Education.* Buckingham: Open University Press.

Segal, L. (1990) *Slow Motion: Challenging Masculinities, Changing Men.* London: Routledge.

Seidler, V. (1987) Reason, desire and male sexuality, in Caplan, P. (ed.) *The Cultural Construction of Sexuality.* London: Routledge.

Skeggs, B. (1991) Challenging masculinity and using sexuality, *British Journal of Sociology of Education.* 11 (4) 127–40.

Stanley, L. and Wise, S. (1993) *Breaking Out Again.* London: Routledge.

Thomson, R. and Scott, S. (1991) *Learning about Sex: Young Women and the Social Construction of Sexual Identity.* London: Tufnell Press.

Walkerdine, V. (1990) Sex, power and pedagogy, in *School Girl Fictions.* London: Verso.

Walkerdine, V. (1990) Femininity as performance, in *School Girl Fictions.* London: Verso.

Weiner, G. (ed.) (1989) *Just a Bunch of Girls.* Milton Keynes: Open University Press.

Willis, P. (1977) *Learning to Labour: How Working-Class Kids Get Working-Class Jobs.* Farnborough: Saxon House.

Willmott, P. (1971) *Adolescent Boys of East London.* Harmondsworth: Penguin.

Wolpe, A. (1988) *Within School Walls: The Role of Discipline, Sexuality and the Curriculum.* London: Routledge.

Wood, J. (1984) Groping towards sexism: Boys' sex talk, in Mc.Robbie, A. and Nava, M. (eds) *Gender and Generation.* Basingstoke: Macmillan Education.

7

Educating Peter:
The Making of a History Man*

Peter Redman and Maírtín Mac an Ghaill

The History Man: Kent, 1980

It is morning, the double period before lunch time. We're sitting
in ragged rows in one of the old, nineteenth century classrooms
that forms part of the school house. I'm over to the side of the
room where I always sit, about halfway back, listening. The
teacher, John Lefevre, stands at the front of the class. It is history
A level, my subject, and he is debating with us. I don't remember
what about. Something has happened in the news and Mr
Lefevre, as usual, disagrees with the general opinion of the class.
Richard, one of the boys makes a point, and I wait to hear how
Mr Lefevre will respond. However, deciding to get back to his
teaching plan, Mr Lefevre terminates the argument.

'Believe me,' he says, 'If I wanted to, I could make a very
convincing case.'

'Go on then,' Richard says, and we laugh. Mr Lefevre holds his
ground.

'We don't have time, but believe me, I could make a very
convincing case.'

* Our thanks to the Politics of Sexuality Group for their comments on the first
draft. Particular thanks to Debbie Epstein, Deborah Steinberg and Lesley
Whitehouse for their comments on subsequent reworkings. An alternative version of
this chapter appears in *Discourse* 17 (2) 1996.

This phrase hits me between the eyes. It's not an evasion. In fact, it seems more compelling than a full reply would have been and I am both intrigued and excited by it. What would John Lefevre have said if he had the time? How could he claim so much authority for these ideas? Where did these ideas come from that gave him so much authority? The truth is that I was not used to hearing someone talking like this. People I knew did not assert their authority on the basis of ideas and I was fascinated by the sudden possibility of being able to put together an argument sophisticated enough to overshadow the common senses of my everyday life. 'Believe me, I could make a very convincing case' held out the promise of another world. I subsequently became similarly intrigued by a phrase in Malcolm Bradbury's *The History Man* which, of all things, we were reading for English A level and which, round the same time, was being serialized on television. The phrase ran something like, 'About this time, Howard started pushing people around intellectually at parties.' You could push people around intellectually? I hadn't realized.

This phrase of Mr Lefevre's was one of several throwaway remarks that I devoured and stored away. The strong impression they made on me were part of a wider interest that I had in him. For instance, I was fascinated by his physical appearance. He seemed to me very different from anyone else in the school. He was young, of average height, very thin, and had translucent, white skin. His hair was longer than most of the other members of staff and grew thickly, and he had a prolific beard. To my mind this gave him a somewhat romantic appearance, one confirmed by the large greatcoat he wore in winter, and by the pocket watch he used and the signet ring he wore. I decided that he modelled himself on the heroes of the nineteenth century Russian novels that he'd joked about reading too many of as an adolescent (how could you read too many Russian novels?). Equally I was intrigued by the way he occupied space as a teacher. My friends and I would make jokes about it. He had a habit of pointing at people doing something other than their work and saying, 'Put it away'. As he pointed the tip of his index finger would curl upwards, a gesture we would practise. Details like this and his slight frame gave him an air of vulnerability in the classroom, yet he also commanded a certain amount of respect, something which, for me at least, came from the fact that he could intellectually out-manoeuvre anyone in the room.

All of these things about him were glimpses of another world. He lent me occasional books, discussed what libraries I should join and generally took me seriously. Before I left school he told me that I was already working at degree level. It was one of the first unambiguous pieces of intellectual recognition I'd ever had. Equally, I remember him showing me some postcards of Samuel Palmer paintings. Of course, I'd never heard of Samuel Palmer but, more to the point, I'd also never met anyone interested in paintings. On another occasion, my friend Andrew heard him listening to BBC Radio 3 during the lunch hour one day. We were fascinated. I had never met an adult – other than the music teacher, who didn't count – who openly listened to a classical music station. There was something deeply transgressive about all of this, all the more so because he appeared wholly self-assured about who he was. It was, quite simply, another way of being.

This autobiographical fragment relates to Peter Redman's experience of a single-sex grammar school in the late 1970s and early 1980s. Our interest in the extract lies in what we would see as its potential to point to some of the complex routes through which boys become heterosexual, and the discontents that beset these heterosexual identities. This may seem like a surprising analysis. After all, the story is not about anything explicitly sexual. Why then do we feel that the story has anything to tell us about the social production of heterosexual masculinities? The answer to this question lies in the ways in which the story indexes a series of negotiations between the cultural, social and psychic realms, negotiations which 'speak' heterosexuality, although often in coded or indirect ways. It is these indirect, coded interactions that we aim to explore in this chapter, for we see heterosexual masculinities (including our own) not as pre-given biological entities or psychologically fixed character traits, but as, highly relational, embedded in the negotiations and contradictions of everyday life, spoken through culturally available forms, produced through and reproductive of wider social relations of power, and constantly worked at in cultural practices and the evasions, fantasies, anxieties and repetitions that characterize the endlessly unfinished business of the unconscious.

The rest of this chapter explores these themes in more detail. Its core argument is that, to understand how sexualities are lived and experienced, we need to grasp them as they emerge within specific cultural sites (in this case, schooling), and as they are produced in and through complex interactions: between the cultural meanings ascribed to sexuality and masculinity, between wider social relations and social processes, and between the unconscious's barrage of displacements, projections, repressions and splits. It seems to us vital that sexualities be understood in terms of these cultural, social and psychic dimensions, yet relatively few studies have attempted this task. There is a tendency for sociologically orientated work to focus on lived sexualities as the product of social structure, as 'learnt' from representations, or as negotiated within subcultural practices (see for example Connell, 1995; Mac an Ghaill, 1994; Tolson, 1977; Willis, 1977). In contrast, psychoanalytically inflected work has tended to focus on the unconscious leaving relatively unspecified the ways in which sexualities are concretely lived in and through social relations of power, available representations, and collective cultural practices (see, for example, Frosh, 1987; Sedgwick, 1985).

However, some studies have pointed the way towards a fuller theorization of the social, cultural and psychic dimensions of subjectivity (Dawson, 1994; Henriques *et al.*, 1984; Hollway, 1989; Silverman, 1992; Walkerdine, 1984). For example, Graham Dawson's work on masculinities and narratives of adventure argues that the forms through which masculinities are lived and felt must be understood as 'fully Janus-faced': that is, *simultaneously* cultural and psychic (Dawson, 1994, p. 48). Working within a culturalist rereading of Kleinian theory, Dawson argues that the culturally available 'discourses' of masculinity like that of the soldier hero (what he calls 'cultural imaginaries'), are invested with significance and 'rendered inhabitable' in part because they permit the organization of psychic defences. Yet, Dawson argues, at the same time, these cultural imaginaries have their own material histories, and the specific attributes they encode become 'attached to and absorbed into' the unconscious, thereby becoming part of the self (p. 47). Dawson writes

Whether in the reproduction of defensive formations, or in efforts towards new insight, reparation and integration, the emergence and life of . . . imaginary forms has both social and psychic determinations. If their moment of existence as imagos [i.e. unconscious representations] depends upon psychic configurations of anxiety and defence that construct the social identities of self and other, their moment of existence as cultural forms occurs under specific conditions of cultural production and consumption that are themselves shaped by configurations of economic, political and social circumstances. These material conditions govern not only the forms as such, but their availability and possible use by particular publics within existing patterns of social identity and recognition. It is only by supplying this full range of determining conditions that a fully historical account of the imagining of masculinities like the soldier hero becomes possible (pp. 51–2).

Following Dawson, this chapter attempts to chart some of the intersecting social, cultural and psychic processes through which heterosexual masculinities are produced.

As the 'John Lefevre' story indicates, our starting point is autobiography (or what we will go on to call 'auto/biography'). Autobiography is a beguiling research methodology. It seems to hold out the promise of self-discovery, of revealing the 'truth of one's being', a fact which no doubt also accounts for some of the pleasures of reading autobiographical and biographical texts. The danger for the researcher is that autobiographical writing veers into confessional self-indulgence. However, autobiography can and should have the more political and intellectually useful aim of locating subjectivity within history: that is, exploring the ways we both 'speak' and are 'spoken' by social structures, power relations, ideologies and discourses. As Graham Dawson argues, autobiography provides a particularly fertile methodology for exploring what it 'feels like' to inhabit socially available identities 'from the inside' (p. 233).

This is not to argue that autobiographical methodologies grant a privileged access to the 'real'. Despite the beguiling sense that reading autobiography puts us in touch with the 'authentic' inner voice of another individual, we need to be critically aware of the constructed nature of this voice. As Liz Stanley and David Morgan have emphasized, autobiographies are not 'immediately referential of lives' but are works of 'artifice and fabrication' which make use of 'genre conventions, temporal and other structuring (*sic*), rhetoric, and authorial "voice"', and which necessarily involve description, selection and interpretation (Morgan and Stanley, 1993, pp. 2–3). Liz Stanley draws attention to the ways in which autobiographical texts *construct* meanings by using the term 'auto/biography' (Stanley, 1993). However, in so doing, she does not suggest that auto/biography is 'too close to fiction' or 'too subjective' for proper academic enquiry. The claim to 'authenticity' in auto/biographical texts is no more disingenuous than that of other research methodologies (for example, participant observation or, for that matter, quantitative approaches like psychometrics), which in their conventional forms assert an ability to describe the world 'as it is'. The task, as Stanley sees it, is to use auto/biography critically by being reflexive about the textual production of meaning within autobiographical conventions.

What follows is then, a critical *reading* of the 'John Lefevre' story, that is an attempt to locate it within the wider social relations, cultural practices and unconscious dynamics of Peter Redman's school life. Both the original writing of the story (it was one of several we wrote in our attempts to explore our experiences of sexuality and schooling) and our final reading of it should thus be seen as simultaneously 'constructed' and 'objective'. We cannot avoid reconstructing or interpreting the past through the conventions and categories available to us, nor can we speak from anything other than a partial position. However, our practice can be reflexive (that is, aware of its own conditions of production) and our purpose critical (that is, orientated towards a better understanding of heterosexual masculinities, as a means through which to change them).

Becoming a history man: the intellectual as hero

Our reading of the John Lefevre story suggests that it is most obviously about 'proper' ways of being a man. It indicates the ways in which, although drawing on wider representations and the wider social relations of gender and sexuality, heterosexual masculinities are produced in close relation to schooling processes and within school and pupils' cultures. From this perspective, Peter's fascination with John Lefevre can be seen to stem from the fact that the teacher made available and validated a form of masculinity that was generally absent from the school, one that Peter could inhabit with a degree of comfort that he did not otherwise feel.

The forms of masculinity hegemonic in Peter's school were organized around several contradictory poles. At least in the first five years, the school's competitive academic culture tended to validate so called 'hard' subjects: maths, physics, chemistry. To be clever was to be good at these. Equally, the school's strong investment in the traditions of English public school life made a virtue of competitive sports – in particular rugby union and cricket – something that itself spoke very strongly of a white, English and middle-class masculine ideal. Thus, within the formal culture of the school, being a 'real boy' meant being either a scientist or an athlete.

In contrast to this, the predominantly white working-class/lower middle-class catchment area of the school meant that pupils' cultures tended to reproduce and validate masculinities that revolved round forms of white working-class male credibility: opposition to academic work and school authority, a taken-for-granted racism, football, 'the pub', girlfriends and, to a lesser extent (given the more academic orientation of a grammar school), fighting. These offered alternative or additional versions of masculinity to those preferred in 'official' school culture and promoted identities based on being 'hard' or, at least, 'one of the lads'. Combined with the forms of masculinity promoted by the school, they validated a somewhat contradictory and competing mixture of subject positions that, in different times and places throughout the school day, subordinated boys who weren't academically clever, who were interested in the arts and humanities, who weren't interested in sport, who weren't particularly 'laddish', who were overtly middle-class or overtly working-class, and who were either not English or not white.

In the context of these competing forms of masculinity, Peter found it relatively difficult to find a way of being a boy that he could occupy with ease. He was interested in the humanities, particularly history and English literature, was 'bad at games', and came from a religious and relatively middle class home background (his father was a Church of England priest) that carried strong popular connotations of effeminacy (the effeminate C of E priest is a standard comic character in British popular culture). All of these factors tended to place him in a subordinate position in relation to aspects of both informal pupils' cultures and the official culture of the school. In this environment, the 'muscular intellectualness' that Peter saw in Mr Lefevre was a way of asserting an alternative masculinity. Mr Lefevre took up space in the classroom not through his physical presence (in fact he was rather small and some of his mannerisms were thought to be funny), but through his ability to 'push people around intellectually'. His apparent self-confidence in what, to Peter, was an unknown world of political ideas, serious music, art history and Russian novels, gave him an aura of power. Mr Lefevre's presentation of self, or what Peter made of this, was thus a source of fascination precisely because it made available an alternative yet 'proper' form of masculinity that Peter found accessible and that was sustainable in the face of school and pupils' cultures: it added muscle to what was otherwise 'other'.

However, the accessibility of muscular intellectualness as an alternative form of masculinity was also dependent upon a sixth form reconfiguration of the masculinities validated in the pupils' cultures and the formal culture of the school. Peter had in fact been taught by Mr Lefevre for several years, but it was only in the school's sixth form that he began to identify or imagine him as a muscular intellectual. We would argue that this move from Year 11 to Year 12 (in effect, the move from compulsory state education to the labour market/further and higher education) marks a key cultural transition that involves young people in new social relations (in particular those of the labour market) and requires new forms of identity to handle them. Peter's entry into a grammar school sixth form marked a move into an environment in which academic success was newly validated as a route into a well-paid employment future. In such circumstances forms of masculinity orientated towards working-class 'lad' culture with its affirmation of manual labour skills (see Willis, 1977) lost currency, and more middle-class forms of masculinity organized round mental prowess gained ascendancy. Simultaneously, the fact that the sixth form was primarily a feeder institution for universities began to open up 'student' versions of masculinity which, although contradictory, allowed quite a lot of space for 'bohemian' identifications organized round politics, music, literature and art, forms that were self-consciously in opposition to science and commerce. Thus Peter's fascination with muscular intellectualness has to be seen against the background of the new forms of masculinity that became available in the school and pupils' cultures of the sixth form. Peter's reading of Mr Lefevre as a muscular intellectual was possible because these new forms of masculinity were beginning to be available to him. Muscular intellectualness was not a quality originating in Mr Lefevre but a discourse – a cultural code – that circulated in and through the meanings and practices of further/higher education, and the newly reconfigured pupils' cultures of Peter's sixth form. Peter's occupation of this newly available masculinity can thus be understood as a way of handling, or making imaginative sense of the cultural transition from compulsory to higher education, as well as an assertion of 'proper' maleness in the face of the masculinities validated within the school's and pupils' cultures.

While this analysis begins to clarify some of the connections between schooling and 'proper' gender designations, it does not immediately explain why these 'proper' forms of masculinity were heterosexual. What is it about occupying 'proper' forms of masculinity that almost inevitably implies a heterosexual identity? The answer to this seems to lie in the fact that, in mainstream contemporary Anglo–American cultures at least, heterosexuality and gender are profoundly imbricated. For example, Judith Butler argues that gender is routinely spoken through a 'heterosexual matrix' in which heterosexuality is presupposed in the expression of 'real' forms of masculinity or femininity. Thus Butler writes

> Although forms of sexuality do not unilaterally determine gender, a non-causal and non-reductive connection between sexuality and gender is nevertheless crucial to maintain. Precisely because homophobia often operates through the attribution of a damaged, failed, or otherwise abject gender to homosexuals, that is, calling gay men 'feminine' or calling lesbians 'masculine', and because the homophobic terror over performing homosexual acts, where it exists, is often also a terror over losing proper gender ('no longer being a real or proper man' or 'no longer being a real or proper woman'), it seems crucial to retain a theoretical apparatus that will account for how sexuality is regulated through the policing and the shaming of gender. (Butler, 1993, p. 238)

Eve Kosofsky Sedgwick's (1985; 1991) work on changes in Anglo–American male–male relations has begun to fill in some of the historical background to this imbrication of gender and sexuality. She argues that the current exclusion of male–male erotic contact from 'proper' forms of masculinity has its origins in an eighteenth-century shift from the religious to the secular discursive construction of sexuality, and that an important consequence of this 'endemic and ineradicable state of homosexual panic' has been the fact that homophobia is used to police the boundaries of acceptable heterosexual male behaviour and identity as well as more overtly (and often violently) being used to police homosexual behaviour and identity.

Thus, in structuring the attributes of 'real' boyness, the various forms of masculinity that were hegemonic in Peter's school can all be argued to have been crucially involved in policing the boundaries of hetero-sexuality as much as the boundaries of 'proper' masculinity. In particular, to be a 'real' boy at Peter's school was to be in opposition to the feminine and to 'feminized' versions of masculinity. For instance, the 'hard' scientific version of cleverness validated in the school existed in opposition to supposedly 'soft' subjects, like art, music and English literature. For the first five years in particular, the arts and humanities were seen as easy options, as essentially frivolous, or somehow lacking in due rigour and seriousness. They were, in effect, girlish subjects not fit for 'real' boys. Similarly, to be 'bad at games' implied a rather suspect lack of manly vigour and hinted at effeminacy, while to be uninterested in the core aspects of 'laddishness' (in particular school opposition, a certain level of working-class credibility, football and 'the pub'), was to be a ' bit of a poof'.

In this environment, Peter's fascination with the muscular intel-lectualness he identified in Mr Lefevre can be understood in terms of the access it promised to give him to the entitlements of conventional masculinity. The world of ideas and knowledge that Mr Lefevre seemed to inhabit no longer seemed effeminately middle class and thus the object of ridicule or embarrassment, but powerfully middle class, a source of personal strength and a means to exercise control over others. Thus, as a source of 'real' masculinity, muscular intellectualness 'defeminized' academic work in the humanities and refuted the label, 'a bit of a poof'. In claiming 'real' boy status, muscular intellectualness did not transform heterosexual masculinity's disavowal of the 'feminine' and the homosexual, it merely reproduced them in a new form.

In suggesting that masculinities are 'spoken through a heterosexual matrix' we do not wish to argue that laddishness, for example, is inevitably coded as heterosexual. Nor do we wish to suggest that everyone who inhabits hegemonic forms of masculinity experiences themselves as heterosexual and that everyone who inhabits subordinated forms of masculinity experiences themselves as homosexual. As the gay men's 'clone' style of the 1970s and 1980s demonstrated, highly physical and macho forms of masculinity can be successfully rearticulated so that they signify homosexuality. Equally, at Peter's school one group of friends organized themselves around a version of high camp that flaunted characteristics identified as quintessentially 'feminine' and 'poofy' by the forms of masculinity hegemonic in the school. Despite this, not all the group identified as gay either at the time or subsequently.

The existence of gay machismo and heterosexual camp should alert us to the fact that the subject positions made available by discourses of masculinity do not determine subjectivity. Within particular constraints, they can be read against the grain. In the examples given, both hegemonic and subordinate forms of masculinity are deployed as resources and their meanings are rearticulated: gay is macho; 'poofy' is superior, more refined. However, while the subject positions of hegemonic masculinities can be clearly subverted or lived in contra-dictory ways, they more commonly act as resources through which heterosexual subjectivities are produced, lived out and policed in local circumstances: they provide the social vocabulary through which heterosexual men are both 'spoken' and come to 'speak themselves' as heterosexual.

Being a history man and phallic anxieties

Peter's investments in muscular intellectualness can, then, be understood, in part, in social and cultural terms. As a 'local' version of heterosexual masculinity, muscular intellectualness provided Peter with an identity that bridged the transition from compulsory to higher education while also asserting a 'proper' heterosexual maleness in the face of the more mainstream masculinities validated in pupils' cultures and the formal culture of the school. However, while it is clearly crucial to grasp the ways in which heterosexual masculinities are produced in and through cultural forms and practices, we would argue that muscular intellectualness also articulated a battery of unconscious anxieties, fears and desires, and that Peter's investments in this version of masculinity lay, in part, in the ability of muscular intellectualness to organize an identity (however unstable) in the face of these unconscious contradictions. In particular, the active exclusion of 'the feminine' and the homosexual within the masculinities available in Peter's school (including muscular intellectualness) need to be understood in psychic as well as social terms. The unconscious dynamics underlying these masculinities were attested to by the violence with which they were defended. 'Proper' forms of masculinity were not simply asserted, they were policed. Deviations inspired fear and loathing, emotions that would sometimes spill over into violence. An out gay teacher at the school was the subject of routine persecution from boys, tacitly supported by some members of staff. Similarly, the members of a camp oppositional grouping were the subject of constant vilification. The extremity of these reactions was not necessarily uniform – for example, Peter had some partial alliances with the camp grouping – but feelings of fear and loathing were endemic and widespread. Strong feelings such as these speak of masculine identities beset by profound and irrational anxieties about the 'feminine' and the 'homosexual', and to grasp these we need psychoanalytic tools.

From a psychoanalytic perspective this policing of the 'feminine' and the homosexual can be seen to be articulating 'phallic' anxieties. The energetic exclusion of the 'feminine' and the homosexual from 'proper' forms of masculinity and the persecution of boys and male teachers who strayed outside their boundaries, strongly suggest attempts to secure ownership of male identities threatened constantly by collapse from within. The notion of the insecurity of heterosexual male identities is something of a truism in the recent 'men's studies' literature (see Davidson, 1990; Easthope, 1985; Pleck, 1981). However, it is Lacanian accounts that have produced what is arguably the most sophisticated and comprehensive theorization of the instability of gender and sexual identities. In Lacanian theory subjectivities are said to be produced in and through linguistic and cultural codes (what Lacan called the 'Symbolic order') rather than existing as pre-given, biological or psychological properties. Lacanians argue that gendered and 'sexualized' subjectivities are the product of the child's entry into the linguistic and cultural codes of society, codes which Lacanians argue are deeply inscribed within patriarchal power relations, which in turn become inscribed at the heart of gendered and 'sexualitized' identities.

The mode of this inscription is the 'phallus', a signifier said to be central to the whole field of representation, which connotes an ultimate patriarchal authority, power and control over meaning. Lacanians argue that, in entering the linguistic and cultural codes of society, the child must necessarily take up some kind of position in relation to the phallus. Indeed, they argue that the child can only speak itself as a subject through the terms made available by the phallic signifier: in other words the child can only speak itself through some relationship to patriarchy. Conventionally, the child is said to do this either by adopting the position of 'having the phallus' (that is, identifying itself as being the source of authority, meaning and power) or by adopting the position of 'lacking the phallus' (that is, identifying itself as being subject to patriarchal authority, meaning and power). Lacanians emphasize that the phallus is not an actual, material thing, but a signifier: something that exists only in the field of representation as a set of meanings. However, because the phallus is embedded in patriarchal relations, it is said to be obsessively confused with masculinity and the biological penis. The result of this is that biologically sexed men can more easily position themselves as 'having the phallus' than biologically sexed women (although, as we shall argue, this outcome is far from predetermined, inevitable, or secure).[1]

One of the more radical implications of Lacanian accounts is the fact that they see heterosexual men's relationship to the phallus – and thus the pivot around which their identities are said to be organized – as being profoundly unstable. Since the phallus is a signifier (a set of meanings built into language and culture) and not in actuality the male body, men's attempts to embody the phallus are inevitably doomed. In effect, men are faced with the endless task of living up to the phallus. They must endlessly and hyperbolically reassert their possession of the phallus in the face of the ever-present threat that their claim to ownership will be revealed as a sham (Frosh, 1994, pp. 77–80). From this perspective, heterosexual men's attempts to exclude the 'feminine' and the homosexual can be understood as attempts to disavow any connection with that which is culturally and historically constructed as lacking the phallus,[2] and which therefore threatens to undermine their claim to be the phallus's embodiment. Thus, from this Lacanian perspective, Peter's investments in muscular intellectualness – and, in fact, the range of competing masculinities validated in school and pupils' cultures – strongly suggest an attempt to secure ownership of the phallus and to 'suture' a male subjectivity to a stable position within available linguistic and cultural codes.

The production and reproduction of masculinities within the school can thus be said to be driven by unconscious processes – attempts to achieve stability in the face of the inherent instability of identity – as much or as well as by the collective negotiation of wider social relations at the local level of the school. This is not to say that the competing forms of masculinity available in the school are reducible to some point of origin in the unconscious. Clearly, the forms or 'discourses' taken by these masculine identities (muscular intellectual, sporting hero, 'lad', scientist) had their own material histories and were appropriated and reworked within the interactions and collective negotiations of school and pupils' cultures. However, boys' investments in these forms or discourses can be seen to articulate conflicts whose origins lie in the unconscious. These unconscious conflicts, in their turn, cannot be reduced to either an 'external' point of origin in the social world (the immediate social context of the school, or wider social relations) or to an 'internal' point of origin (the unconscious as the repository of instinctual or biological drives). Unconscious conflicts are articulated in and through the local forms of masculinity made available in the school (and elsewhere), and are the product of boys' and men's insertion into the patriarchal relations of the Symbolic order, but they are not the 'interior', subjective epiphenomena of 'exterior' social struggles. In Lacanian terms, the unconscious exists only in interaction with the social, and has no existence prior to or separate from it, but it is a distinct realm, subject to its own laws and with its own level of determination.

Desiring the history man: the 'irreducible ambiguity' of heterosexual masculinities

Our reading of Peter's story suggests, therefore, that it carries the traces of psychic, cultural and social determinants. It can be read as an attempt to 'own the phallus' through culturally available forms of heterosexual masculinity, while simultaneously revealing an attempt to negotiate the social structure: the transition from compulsory education. That these processes exist in a state of interaction is made obvious by the fact that Peter's new 'successful' attempt to own the phallus was made possible only through the forms of masculinity newly available in the cultural environment of a grammar-school sixth form which allowed different articulations of phallic authority from those available further down the school. However, we would argue that this analysis does not exhaust the content of Peter's story. In particular, we would suggest that the story points, if silently, to a desire *for* the phallus as well as to an identification with it, in the process foregrounding the psychic instabilities of heterosexual masculinities and, moreover, the provisional nature of all sexual identifications.

Following Freud, Kaja Silverman (1992) argues that, in negotiating its entry into the Symbolic order (in Freudian terms, the resolution of the Oedipal crisis), every subject takes up multiple and contradictory positions in relation to an Oedipal structure of identification and desire: both desiring the phallus/father and identifying with 'lack'/the mother, and identifying with the phallus/father and desiring 'lack'/the mother . It is for this reason that Freud made his famous statement that everyone has made a homosexual object-choice at the level of the unconscious. Entry into the Symbolic order implies some kind of resolution to these multiple identifications (and thus the adoption of some kind of orientation to having/lacking the phallus), but, according to Silverman, this does not imply that every biological male will identify with the phallus/father and desire 'lack'/the mother; nor does it imply that multiple identifications will be completely abandoned in favour of a single identification; nor does it imply a permanently fixed identification in relation to having/lacking the phallus. Thus, among an array of possible positions, some biological males will identify with the position of lacking the phallus despite their possession of a penis; some will identify with the position of having the phallus; some will move between the two or straddle both in contradictory ways; and some will shift identifications in a complex response to later experiences.

Perhaps the most radical implication of this argument is that it appears to be possible to inhabit positions wholly against the grain of the binary division, having/lacking the phallus. Not only can men invert this binary by identifying with the position of lacking the phallus (culturally coded as the 'feminine') while desiring that which has the phallus (culturally coded as the 'masculine'), they can also occupy contradictory or multiple positions in relation to it: identifying with the position of having the phallus (culturally coded as 'the masculine') while also desiring that which has the phallus (also the 'masculine'); or identifying with lacking the phallus (culturally coded as the 'feminine') while also desiring that which lacks the phallus (the 'feminine'). Indeed, Silverman goes on to argue that even apparently 'explicit' and 'stable' identifications (for example, the heterosexual man who identifies himself as wholly in possession of the phallus) contain a certain 'irreducible ambiguity'. For instance, identification with 'having the phallus' may also, simultaneously speak of or contain the traces of an earlier, pre-Symbolic desire for the phallus. It is as if occupying explicitly heterosexual forms of masculinity can 'look both ways': towards an overt identification with the phallus, and towards an unconscious desire for the phallus. Thus the boundary between 'identification with' and 'desire for' appears to be inherently unstable or, at the very least, to be disrupted by contradictory impulses, even if these are fragmentary or remnants from earlier psychic conflicts (see Silverman, 1992, p. 356).

Peter's story can be read as containing some of these elements. Most obviously, his fascination for Mr Lefevre can be said to have something of an 'irreducible ambiguity' about it, in which 'wanting to have what this man has' existed in close proximity to 'wanting to have this man'. As such, Peter's 'ownership' of the phallus through the position of muscular intellectual can be seen to be inevitably precarious. However, we feel that something more complex than this is also at work in the story. So far we have argued that this newly available, 'muscular intellectual' form of masculinity allowed Peter to own the phallus with an ease that had not been possible further down the school. That is to say, muscular intellectualness reconfigured phallic meanings in ways more accessible to Peter as a boy interested in the humanities, bad at games and from a relatively middle-class background. This suggests that, earlier in his school career, Peter attempted to occupy the position of the phallus but was fairly unsuccessful at this because the cultural forms available were not ones that he could inhabit with comfort.

We would not dispute this analysis, however our reading of the story suggests that there was also an element of *newness* in Peter's identification with the phallus. In suggesting this, what we wish to avoid is the implication that Peter's identification with the position of 'muscular intellectual' was simply the most recent in a line of phallic identifications stretching back into the 'Oedipal crisis'. It *is* possible to make such a reading of Peter's childhood, particularly his early investments in war stories and soldier heroes which, in their emphasis on an indestructible and all conquering power, clearly articulated phallic mastery. However, these identifications did not constitute a single, fixed route towards an inevitable adult heterosexuality. As a younger boy, Peter's fantasy identifications with the figure of the all-powerful soldier hero were shadowed by equally intense and pleasurable (if less socially sanctioned and therefore more secretive) fantasies about being beaten by powerful men, the quintessential position of 'being' the phallus – that is, proving the other's possession of the phallus by one's own subordination to it. Equally, in early adolescence Peter drew on public-school stories to organize homoerotic fantasies, fantasies that drew in part on the convention of the erotically desirable blond feminine youth, accessed via Thomas Hughes's *Tom Brown's School Days*.[3]

Such contradictory identifications point, in part, to Silverman's argument that the multiple identifications of the Oedipal scene are not abandoned in the 'resolution' of the Oedipal crisis, but persist in various repressed, projected or displaced forms. However, they also point to the possibility that the elements of the Oedipal scene can be reconfigured throughout life, thickening and cohering around particular (relatively) fixed identifications in key cultural transitions, and in response to changing material circumstances. From this point of view, Peter's identification with muscular intellectualness marked a moment of *concretization* but not an inevitable, preordained assumption of an adult heterosexual identity. This requires a radical reconceptualization of heterosexuality from that available in common sense where sexualities are presumed to be either biologically given or, in more psychologized versions, fixed in early infancy. We are not suggesting that sexual identities are in constant flux but we are suggesting that the popular notion that you can trace your sexuality along a fixed developmental path needs to be rethought. It may be necessary to begin to think about our sexualities as more contradictory than is currently allowed and to recognize the moments in which they achieve greater coherence or begin to come apart. We would argue that in understanding these moments of reconfiguration we need to grasp the complex interactions that exist between psychic and social processes, and to understand psychic identifications as both responses to the social world and the world of the unconscious.

Making a difference: understanding heterosexual masculinities

Our analysis of the John Lefevre story has sought to demonstrate that individual boys come to speak as their own particular positions within the available discourses of masculinity, because these (temporarily) resolve a complex interaction between the social environment, unconscious contradictions and aspects of individual biography . As such, we would suggest that heterosexual masculinities need to be rethought as profoundly contingent and local. They are produced in and through cultural forms and cultural processes, they are 'spoken' in multiple and often coded forms (for example, being a 'proper' boy; being an 'ordinary' Englishman) they are shot through with unconscious tensions and instabilities, and they exist only in relational form: that is, in interactions of opposition and similarity, resistance and control. This means that heterosexual masculinities are constantly worked at and worked over, never finally 'achieved'. They will display strong elements of continuity but, if we care to look, they will also reveal discontinuities, reconfigurations and contradictory desires. We would suggest that such a formulation goes some way towards grasping the real complexity of heterosexual masculinities as they are lived and experienced as concrete sexual 'identities', a complexity that is too easily denied in accounts that focus solely on social structure, cultural practice or the workings of the unconscious. As this argument demonstrates, it is not our intention to abandon the strengths of sociological and subcultural accounts in favour of a vulgar version of psychoanalysis which would see the subject positions of heterosexual masculinity as being fitted on to a subject already constituted as heterosexual in some formative moment in early childhood. From where we stand, the immediate theoretical and empirical task lies in beginning to specify the linkages and interactions between the unconscious, the cultural and the social as these are lived and felt by actual subjects in concrete social sites.

We do not claim to have done any more than scratch the surface of these issues. For example, a significant absence in the chapter is a full exploration of the ways in which heterosexual masculinities are produced in relation to girls and women. We may well want to consider the extent to which phallic identifications are motivated by a fear of 'maternal' power as argued within feminist object relations accounts (see, for example, Benjamin, 1990). Equally we need to theorize the cultural, social and psychic relations between the production of conventional forms of heterosexual masculinity and lesbianism, an issue almost totally absent from the existing literature. Most obviously, we also need to provide a full account of the consequences that heterosexual masculinities have for girls' and women's lives.

A similar set of questions can be raised in relation to class and ethnicity: in what ways does white middle-class Englishness 'speak' sexuality; in what ways are phallic anxieties and desires organized and 'spoken' through fantasies about classed and 'racialized' others; what are the consequences of these processes for Black and working-class lives? Similarly we need to be clear about the consequences that hegemonic heterosexual masculinities have for gay men and men who inhabit other subordinated forms of masculinity. These are all valid issues, not least because they question the relation of accounts such as ours to 'progressive' politics, in particular the diverse projects of the feminisms and the differing agendas of the various forms of lesbian and gay activism. There is an inherent ambivalence in heterosexual men writing even 'critically' about heterosexual masculinities. On the one hand, such writing may open up possibilities for change; on the other, it may also expose contradictions, vulnerabilities and previously 'naturalized' processes of subordination simply to recoup these for reconfigured but still hegemonic relations of gender and sexuality.[4] There is probably no way out of such double-binds, either at a personal or a public level. We believe that a better understanding of the interconnection between psychic, cultural and social dynamics is of crucial importance to sexual and gender politics and has the potential to make a real difference to schooling. We acknowledge the contradictions of holding such a position.

Notes

1. Because of limitations of space this is necessarily an abbreviated and oversimplified account of Lacanian arguments. For a fuller exposition and critique of Lacanian ideas see, Frosh, 1987, 1994; Gallop, 1982; Grosz, 1990; Mitchell and Rose, 1982, 1986; Silverman, 1992.

2. As Sedgwick points out, attention to other cultures and other historical periods shows that male-male erotic contact can be and is seen as a bulwark to rather than a diminishment of 'proper' masculinity (see, Sedgwick, 1991). Also, Herdt (1981) on male-male sexual contact among the New Guinean 'Sambia', and, Veyne (1985) on male sexual contact in classical Greece).

3. These erotic/masochistic fantasies were articulated through specific cultural forms. The fantasies of being beaten drew their vocabulary from obsessive rereadings of the Laura Ingalls Wilder children's books in which the threat of violent punishment is a regular theme. The erotically desireable blond youth is a common feature of nineteenth-century fiction and was a staple in 'Uranian' writing. Peter's schoolboy appropriation of it at the end of the twentieth century suggests that it is deeply sedimented in common sense. See Bristow (1991) for homoerotic undercurrents in public school stories and their conections to 'Uranian' fiction.

4. For a fuller analysis of these themes see Canaan and Griffin (1990)

References

Benjamin, J. (1990) *The Bonds of Love.* London: Virago.

Bristow, J. (1991) *Empire Boys: Adventures in a Man's World.* London: HarperCollins.

Butler, J. (1993) *Bodies That Matter.* London: Routledge.

Canaan, J. and Griffin, C. (1990) The new men's studies: part of the problem or part of the solution? in Hearn, J. and Morgan D. (eds) *Men Masculinities and Social Theory.* London: Unwin Hyman.

Davidson, N. (1990) *Boys Will Be . . .: Sex Education and Young Men.* London: Bedford Square Press.

Dawson, G. (1994) *Soldier Heroes: British Adventure, Empire and the Imagining of Masculinities.* London: Routledge.

Easthope, A. (1985) *What A Man's Gotta Do .* London: Paladin.

Frosh, S. (1987) *The Politics of Psychoanalysis: An Introduction to Freudian and Post-Freudian theory.* Basingstoke: Macmillan.

Frosh, S. (1994) *Sexual Difference: Masculinity and Psychoanalysis.* London: Routledge.

Gallop, J. (1982) *Feminism and Psychoanalysis.* London: Macmillan.

Grosz, E. (1990) *Jacques Lacan: A Feminist Introduction.* London: Routledge.

Henriques, J., Hollway, W., Urwin, C., Venn, C. and Walkerdine, V. (1984) *Changing the Subject: Psychology, Social Regulation and Subjectivity.* London: Methuen.

Herdt, G. (1981) *Guardians of the Flutes: Idioms of Masculinity.* London: McGraw-Hill.

Hollway, W. (1989) *Subjectivity and Method in Psychology: Gender, Meaning and Science.* London: Sage.

Mac an Ghaill, M. (1994) *The Making*

of Men: Maculinities, Sexualities and Schooling. Buckingham: Open University Press.

Mitchell, J. and Rose, J. (1982) Feminine Sexuality: Jacques Lacan and the Ecole Freudienne. London: Macmillan.

Morgan, D. and Stanley, L. (1993), Editorial introduction, Sociology 27 (1) 1–4.

Pleck, J. (1981) The Myth of Masculinity. Cambridge, Mass.: MIT Press.

Rose, J. (1986) Sexuality in the Field of Vision. London: Verso.

Sedgwick, E.K. (1985) Between Men: English Literature and Male Homosocial Desire. New York: Columbia University Press.

Sedgwick, E.K. (1991) Epistemology of the Closet. Hemel Hempstead:

Harvester Wheatsheaf.

Silverman, K. (1992) Male Subjectivity at the Margins. London: Routledge.

Stanley, L. (1993), On auto/biography in sociology, Sociology 27, (1) 41–52.

Tolson, A. (1977) The Limits of Masculinity. London: Tavistock.

Veyne, P. (1985) Homosexuality in Ancient Rome, in Aries, P. and Bejin, A. (eds) Western Sexuality: Practices and Precepts in Past and Present Times. Oxford: Blackwell.

Walkerdine, V. (1984) Some day my prince will come, in McRobbie, A. and Nava, M. (eds) Gender and Generation. Basingstoke: Macmillan.

Willis, P. (1977) Learning to Labour: How Working-Class Kids Get Working-Class Jobs. Farnborough: Saxon House.

8

What's in a Ban? The Popular Media, *Romeo and Juliet* and Compulsory Heterosexuality*

Debbie Epstein

Most of the chapters in this book trace the ways in which hetero-sexuality is constantly recuperated (though not always in the same form). Challenges to normative versions of heterosexuality are frequently incorporated within changing versions of what it means to be heterosexual. For example, notwithstanding efforts by the Moral Right to revert to earlier views of such relationships, non-marriage of heterosexual couples who live together is no longer scandalous but a recognized and, for the most part, respectable variant of dominant heterosexual lifestyles. However, there are times when particular events around sexuality become *causes célèbres,* the subjects of intensive discussion and even moral panic in the popular media. These cases may involve a direct challenge to normative versions of heterosexuality (like the extensive coverage of so-called 'virgin births' in the popular press and on television in 1991) or the 'shock–horror' of events which seem to present wider challenges to the institution of heterosexuality itself (as in some of the actions of OutRage in the UK or Queer Nation in the USA). The story of Jane Brown and the tickets for the ballet of *Romeo and Juliet* is one such case.

'Head bans Romeo and Juliet' ran a front page headline in London's largest 'local' paper, the *Evening Standard* on 19 January 1994.

---

* A slightly shorter version of this chapter appeared in *Curriculum Studies: Special Issue on Sexuality* (1996).

According to this story Jane Brown, the head of Kingsmead Primary School in Hackney, one of London's poorest boroughs, had turned down the offer of tickets for a performance of the ballet of *Romeo and Juliet* at the Royal Opera House. Over the next few weeks there was coverage of this issue in every national daily paper and in the Sundays. There was also a certain amount of international coverage with articles appearing in US, Australian and New Zealand newspapers. With some significant exceptions, Jane Brown was excoriated for what Pat Corrigan, at that time chair of Hackney's Education Committee, was quoted as calling an act of 'ideological idiocy and cultural philistinism' (*Evening Standard* 19 January 1994). This chapter is not primarily about the 'facts' of the case, which are, as one would expect, contested, but rather about the way in which it was used by the popular press to (re)produce a range of (sometimes contradictory) discourses around sexuality, 'race' and 'political correctness', with implications for the formation of policy, particularly around sexuality and education. This chapter will also explore some of the ways in which Jane Brown was seen to embody certain discourses around sexuality and education, while Gus John, the African–Caribbean Director of Education in Hackney carried discourses around 'race'. As I shall show, the division, indeed contest, between them and their respective 'supporters' bespoke ways of understanding Blackness and being lesbian and gay as mutually exclusive, though both are also seen as signifying that other demon of the 1990s, 'political correctness'.[1]

Ordering events

Trying to sort out an account of 'what actually happened' in this case is difficult as one would, perhaps, expect in any moral panic. However, it is clear that there is a progression in terms of what the main issue was seen to be in the popular press. The first reports (*Evening Standard* 19 January 1994, 20 January 1994, *Daily Mail* 20 January 1994) focused their attention on the 'fact' that Jane Brown had turned down the tickets on offer from the Hamlyn Foundation for the ballet of *Romeo and Juliet* on the grounds that she considered it 'a blatantly heterosexual love story' (*Daily Mail* 20 January 1994). However, by the next day it was becoming clear in some of the press coverage that the main issue was not going to stay with the question of *Romeo and Juliet* but would revolve around Jane Brown's sexuality. Thus we see a progression of attacks on Jane Brown for being 'politically correct' (bad) to being a lesbian (worse) to being a PC lesbian (worst). For example, the Secretary of State for Education (John Patten) is quoted as saying that '[refusing the tickets was] another example of the dangerous effect of creeping political correctness and the damage it can do to our children' (*Daily Mail* 20 January 1994). The same day, the *Evening Standard* carried a story which claimed that 'angry parents called today for the immediate sacking of the headmistress who banned their children from seeing *Romeo and Juliet* because it was "blatantly heterosexual"' (*Evening Standard* 20 January 1994).

This story ended with the information that Jane Brown had been appointed as deputy head of Kingsmead School by the former Inner London Education Authority (ILEA). This seemingly irrelevant piece of information is significant for the connotation it carries with it of widespread accusations made in the media and the Conservative campaign against ILEA in the popular press during the mid- to late-1980s. These accusations that ILEA was controlled by the so-called 'loony left' (the 1980s precursor to 1990s accusations of 'political correctness') constituted a significant plank in the justification of the abolition of both the Greater London Council and of ILEA itself.[2]

On 21 January 1994 we see the first intimation of the turn the press coverage would take over the next weeks when the *Evening Standard* revealed that 'according to the electoral roll, she shares a Clapton house with another woman, Nicki Thorogood, who stood down as chair of Kingsmead primary's governing body last year' (*Evening Standard* 21 January 1994).

The same day, the *Daily Mail* ran five full pages about lesbian and gay issues, which I shall consider in more detail below. One of these pages carried a photograph of Jane Brown, taken from very low down, with nothing else in the picture which would serve to provide a comparison of size or stature. The effect is that she appears to be very tall and 'butch'-looking.[3] She is described as 'wearing a blue donkey jacket, red jeans and boots – her customary school attire' (*Daily Mail*, 21 January 1994). This coding of Jane Brown as being a rather 'butch' lesbian ushered in a series of attacks on her primarily for her sexuality which rapidly became irretrievably intertwined with her other 'crime' – that of being 'politically correct'. By this point, the main focus had shifted to the person of Jane

Brown herself, as is graphically illustrated in the *Sun*'s headline 'I watched as the Romeo ban head kissed woman pal in garden' (22 January 1994). This article was accompanied by a photograph so similar to that which had been used in the *Daily Mail* that it is hard to tell them apart. Throughout the whole treatment of the story in the press, these are the most common visual representations of Jane Brown to have appeared, though head and shoulders versions were also used. The other visual representation of her appeared in the *Evening Standard* (26 January 1994) and showed Jane Brown bent over with a scarf around her face. The caption read 'Hiding: head teacher Jane Brown shields her face from photographers last night.' The connotation here was clearly one of criminality. This view of people apparently rushing past cameras with their faces hidden is one more often seen as those accused of (usually serious) crimes rush past the cameras into court.

In considering the events that took place around the *Romeo and Juliet* scandal, it is worth noting not only the order in which events took place, but also the timing of these events and of the press coverage of them. The original telephone conversation between Jane Brown and Ingrid Haitink, of the Paul Hamlyn Foundation, took place early in September 1993. This discussion was about the possibility of some of the children from Kingsmead School attending a ballet performance at the Royal Opera House. During the course of this conversation, Jane Brown is said to have made the statement about *Romeo and Juliet* being 'blatantly heterosexual'. During October 1993 the Hamlyn Foundation sent a letter to Hackney Council about their subsidized ticket scheme, in which Jane Brown's refusal of the tickets was noted with 'a little surprise' (John, 1994, p. 9). This was not reported in the press until some three months later, when the first press article appeared in the *Evening Standard* on 19 January 1994. This gap in time raises some questions about why an event should become newsworthy (and, indeed, worth extensive and often front page reporting in all the national dailies as well as in many of the Sunday papers) some three months after it had actually happened. Below I shall discuss some of the immediate political context for the publication of the three-month-old 'news' about Jane Brown and *Romeo and Juliet*, suggesting that it was the context, rather than the event itself which made it newsworthy. Neither was Jane Brown's action considered to be a matter for disciplinary action by the Council in September/October 1993. Indeed, we see a progression here too. In October the adviser concerned thought that Jane Brown's decision was 'rather unfortunate' but not a matter for disciplinary action against her (John, 1994, p. 9). However, in the context of the publicity of January 1994, the *Daily Mail* reported that 'Now headmistress Jane Brown faces disciplinary action or even the sack after her action was condemned by parents, her bosses and Education Secretary, John Patten' (20 January 1994).

In this respect, Gus John's (1994) account of the affair is somewhat confusing. On the one hand, he says that he found her to have made 'a gross error of judgement' with regard to the manner in which she had declined the tickets for *Romeo and Juliet*. On the other, the accusation which he laid before the governors of the school was not one of a 'gross error of judgement', but one of 'gross misconduct' – an altogether more serious offence. Furthermore, there was been a shift of what constituted the 'gross misconduct'. In the first instance it appears to have been Jane Brown's action in refusing the tickets in the manner in which she did; then it seems to have become the way in which she dealt with Gus John's *investigation* of the affair (John, 1994). But by 26 January 1994, the charge of 'gross misconduct' seems to have been to do with Jane Brown's appointment as head and the fact that she lived with the ex-chair of the governors of the Kingsmead School (a relationship which, she says, developed after her appointment and which led directly to the resignation of her now-partner from the position of chair of governors). Again, reports about how this happened seem rather confusing:

> After listening to [Jane Brown's] explanation [of the timing of her relationship] John said he was satisfied with her explanation and added that he planned to issue a statement to 'kill the speculation about the propriety of her appointment at the earliest possible opportunity'. He went immediately into a meeting with the school's governors where he repeated what he had told Brown and Richard Rieser, her union representative.
>
> But by the time the *Guardian* published a report of John's comments on Monday morning, the situation had changed. As soon as the first edition of the *Guardian* was printed, a Hackney Council spokesperson vehemently denied that John had been satisfied by Brown's account and stressed that the investigation was far from over. (*Guardian*, 27 January 1994)

Whatever the actual course of events, and despite the carefully measured coverage of the *Guardian* article quoted above, representations of the affair in the tabloid press appear to have made the assumption that Jane Brown's lesbian relationship was, in and of itself, and regardless of Nicki Thorogood's position as ex-chair of governors of the school, evidence of impropriety and a conflict of interests.

Competing cultures

In this section of this chapter I will trace a number of different ways in which the affair of Jane Brown and *Romeo and Juliet* can be seen in terms of representations of different versions of (popular) 'culture' and (high) 'Culture'. In this context I have identified four different ways in which clashes of culture/Culture are involved: between political correctness and 'proper culture/Culture'; between lesbian and gay culture and 'proper culture/Culture'; between the Kingsmead parents and 'proper culture/Culture'; and between the cultures of some of the more liberal broadsheets on the one hand and of the tabloids on the other.

Can this be culture? 'political correctness', the working class and the nation

The first accusation made against Jane Brown was that she 'banned' her pupils from seeing the ballet of *Romeo and Juliet*. Here she is seen as having deprived her pupils, by implication uncultured working-class children, from being inducted into the glories of Shakespeare and, therefore, 'British' (i.e. English) Culture. It is interesting to note, in this context, that the difference between the play and the ballet disappeared from the news coverage almost instantly. This elision of the play and the ballet is, perhaps, significant in that Shakespeare as playwright is, in popular common sense, an undisputed (indisputable) part of the canon of Englishness as expressed in 'high Culture' while ballet is much more problematic in that it is often categorized as 'effeminate' (and therefore dangerous to the masculinity of boys) and much less central to concerns about Englishness/Britishness.

The accusation that Jane Brown had thus deprived her pupils of their English heritage in some way was, thus, represented as a clash between being PC and, therefore, 'trendy' on the one hand and inducting her pupils into proper Englishness, via High Culture, on the other. This representation feeds directly from and into what Stephen Ball (following Kenway) has identified as 'discourses of derision' against teachers in general (Ball, 1990, pp. 31–42). As Ball comments:

> The social subject of neo-conservatism is the loyal, law-abiding family man (or housewife/mother), holder of and believer in traditional values and sober virtues. Over and against this ideal citizen/parent is set an alternative subject: the carrier of alien values or alien culture, the agitator/trade unionist, sexual deviant, or working, single-parent mother, permissive/liberal, and progressive teacher – in other words 'the enemy within', the traitor. (p. 40)

'Political correctness' (whatever that means) is, then, represented as an attack on Englishness/Britishness both of the working-class cultures of the pupils of Kingsmead School and of English/British canonical culture as represented by Shakespeare. In this context, being (seen as) PC is illegitimate, especially for school teachers. This is borne out by the full page attack on 'political correctness' carried by the *Daily Mail* (21 January 1994). Here, under the headline 'To PC, or not PC? What political correctness would mean to Shakespeare', the paper's drama critic, Jack Tinker, speculates on what Shakespeare's plots might have been like had they been written in supposedly PC form. The implication, here (which is brought out more overtly in leading articles and quotes from various notables such as John Patten, then Secretary of State for Education), is that political correctness and its concomitant, 'trendy teachers', are inherently a danger to children.

In this context, children are represented as innocent and likely to be easily led astray. Thus the *Daily Mail* (20 January 1994) described the affair as a '*pas de deux* between political correctness and the innocence of childhood'. This is reminiscent of the attacks made by Tory politicians and the popular press on the 'loony left' in the mid-1980s. Mrs Thatcher, for example, in her speech to the Conservative party conference in 1987 claimed that:

> Children who need to be able to count and multiply are learning anti-racist mathematics – whatever that may be. Children who need to be able to express themselves in clear English are being taught political slogans. Children who need to be taught to

respect traditional moral values are being taught that they have an inalienable right to be gay.

In this speech, there is a clear statement that teaching and oppositional politics (whether categorized as 'PC' or 'trendy') are in some fundamental way, incompatible.

Queer fear: lesbian and gay teachers as a danger to children

There is, implicit in much of the coverage of the 'Romeo and Juliet affair', the notion that identifying as lesbian or gay is incompatible with being a teacher. The visual representation of Jane Brown mentioned above, taken together with the description of her clothes in the *Daily Mail* (21 January 1994) in terms which make it clear that 'her customary school attire' is unacceptable for a 'respectable' head teacher, produce the impression that there is something intrinsically dangerous about the existence of lesbian (and gay) teachers *per se*. The particularly derogatory tone adopted about her clothing by Ann Leslie in the same paper adds to this notion. Indeed it is clear, from this coverage, that the very possibility that children might learn to consider non-heterosexuality a thinkable (if not viable) option through the example of lesbian and gay teachers is regarded as a cause for extreme concern. This is reminiscent of much of the coverage of 'positive images' of lesbians and gays in Haringey and ILEA during 1986 and leading up to the passage of Section 28 of the Local Government Act 1988.[4] During that period *Today* (2 September 1986), for example, wrote about 'positive images' in the following terms:

> There was a time, in the dawn of the permissive society, when enlightened liberals campaigned for an end to the laws which made homosexuality illegal – on the grounds that they were a vicious discrimination against a minority. But by a law of human nature, once this reasonable concession was granted, some homosexuals could not stop there. Next they wanted homosexuality to be regarded as socially quite acceptable. Then they wanted actually to crusade for it, by having it taught in schools and written about in books for children as something quite admirable.

Here we see a number of discourses in play, all of which point to the unacceptability both of lesbians and gays as teachers and of the possibilities of lesbian or gay sexuality being visible within the schooling system. On the one hand the 'reasonableness' of the concession of decriminalizing (but not legalizing) gay male sexuality is set against the inherent unreasonableness of those 'homosexuals' who 'could not stop there' but had the temerity to demand that their sexuality should be 'regarded as socially quite acceptable' – clearly, in the context of this piece, an unacceptable demand. The subtext of the following sentence seems to be that having homosexuality (sic) 'written about in books for children' and 'taught in schools' inevitably compromises the supposed innocence of children. This subtext, both feeds and derives from popular mythologies about the predatory nature of lesbian and, even more so, gay sexuality and the particular common senses surrounding their supposed predatory nature and danger to children (common senses which fly in the face of the statistical profile of abusers of both girl and boy children as being overwhelmingly heterosexual and male).[5] Lesbian and gay teachers are, therefore, represented as inherently dangerous to children

At the same time, there is some suggestion, especially in the coverage by the *Daily Mail* and the *Sun* that Jane Brown's lesbianism was part of her being middle class and therefore alien to the working-class children in her school. We see, for example, the *Daily Mail* reporting that she had changed her name from the double-barrelled (and therefore inevitably middle class) 'Jane Hardman-Brown' to 'Jane H. Brown' (21 January 1994). Additionally, both papers feature a picture of the house occupied by Jane Brown and Nicki Thorogood with the (contradictory) information that it cost £100,000 (*Daily Mail*) and £80,000 (*Sun*). There is a connotation of ill-gotten gains here. Although not explicitly stated, the question is raised of how these two women could manage to afford such a house. By allusion, then, the 'gross misconduct' of which Jane Brown was accused by Gus John and Hackney Council could be construed as including financial corruption or, at the very least, somewhat suspect management.

'Proper' parents and 'proper' culture

On the one hand, then, Jane Brown was represented as being hostile to the working class values of the parents of her pupils. Every tabloid report in the first few days of the 'scandal' claimed that parents were 'outraged' by Jane Brown's decision not to take up the offer of seats for the ballet of *Romeo and Juliet*. These articles also contained reports of (assumed white and Christian) parents' upset and anger at the fact that the school had abandoned the practice of having 'Father Christmas' visit to bring the children Christmas presents. For example the *Evening Standard* (20 January 1994) reported that 'she had already upset parents by banning nativity plays, Santa Claus and Christmas presents at Hackney's Kingsmead Primary School because there were too many ethnic groups'.

Apparently neither the *Evening Standard* nor the other tabloids taking the same line at this point (including the *Daily Mail*, the *Daily Mirror* and the *Sun*) were able to entertain the idea that some parents might be upset by the conventional focus on Christian festivals in British primary schools. Or if they could conceive that this might be the case, then these presumably deviant parents (be they agnostic, atheist, Hindu, Jewish, Muslim, Sikh or of another religion) did not count in the scales measuring parental 'upset' and/ or 'anger'. Furthermore, the widely report 'fact' that the parents at Kingsmead were angry with Jane Brown immediately became untenable when, at a well-attended meeting with the governors of the school, they voted, virtually unanimously, to support her against the charges laid by Gus John in his capacity as Director of Education for Hackney. The demand to suspend Jane Brown pending investigation was comprehensively defeated at this meeting and, indeed, it was only after this vote that the main focus of media attention shifted from Jane Brown's refusal of the tickets to see the ballet of *Romeo and Juliet* to her personal conduct and her lesbian relationship.

It is important to note here that, within New Right discourses of choice and the market, 'parent power' has been seen as part of package of 'back to basics' and a 'return to standards'. 'Proper' parents are supposed to want English/British Culture (and not multicultural or anti-racist education), to welcome tests and league tables, to want their children's schools to opt out of the control of (politically correct) local authorities and so on. In this context, John Patten's weapon of 'parental choice' had backfired. As the *Evening Standard* made clear in its leading article following the vote to support Jane Brown, for parents to deserve to have choices, they should make the Right choices.[6]

It is parents who have no wish to set up an inquisition into Ms Brown's private life. It is parents who are impressed by the school's educational standards . . . The Government wants to take power from local education authorities to school governors – because parent power is what counts, and parents know best. The *Romeo and Juliet* case turns the stereotypes on their heads. Mr John Patten, the Education Secretary, has the power to overrule the governors here. *He must act to ensure that pupils are not prevented by PC nonsense from getting a good education.* But he, and his successors, must steer clear of simplistic 'parent power' in future. (26 January 1994 [my emphasis]).

In this comment several things become clear. The implication of the first sentence is that the parents are, quite obviously, wrong to resist setting up such an inquisition. Parental judgements about what constitutes a 'good education' are clearly invalid if they resist the common sense view that 'PC' is inherently the enemy of good education. The only right choice, in this context, is the Right one and if parents do not make it they should be over-ruled by the government.

Broadsheet narratives
Among the hostile reporting of the affair in the tabloid press there can be found some significantly favourable coverage in some of the more liberal broadsheets. Suzanne Moore, for example, writing in the *Guardian* (28 January 1994) under the headline 'Hackneyed words from PC bashers' comments:

Can it really be true that the fabric of our nation is being undone not by poverty, unemployment and deprivation but by a mere idea . . . The virus of political correctness is out to get all of us. And if it can't get to us, well, then it will get to our children. They will, after endless multicultural school assemblies, no longer be the right-thinking British children we want them to be. . . .

Deprived of decent nativity plays and the odd ballet, they could grow up thinking that differences of race or sexuality should not automatically mean disadvantage. My god, what is the world coming to. Let's deprive our children of books, of school buildings, let's give teachers less teaching time and more forms to fill in, let's refuse to teach them modern history, but whatever happens we must never ever deprive them of an outing to see a ballet of *Romeo and Juliet.*

The irony deployed by Moore here is, perhaps, expressive of an alternative set of liberal common senses. Moore is well-known within British journalism as overtly feminist and interested in questions of media representation.

Similarly, Barry Hugill in the *Observer* (30 January 1994) and Ruth Picardie in the *Independent* (3 February 1994) both wrote sympathetically of Jane Brown, not only as a 'good teacher' but as a kind of corrective to the oppressive forces of mainstream popular (tabloid) culture, teaching children the 'basics' of 'tolerance' as well as of reading, writing and arithmetic. This clash of cultures between tabloids and broadsheets reveals itself in the somewhat different chronology of coverage in the broadsheets to that which I have drawn attention to in the tabloids. In the 'quality' press, coverage started with unfavourable comment on Jane Brown's refusal of the tickets for the ballet of *Romeo and Juliet*, shifting to a focus on her lesbian relationship, but resolving itself into a certain sympathy with her as a 'tabloid victim' (*Times Educational Supplement*, 4 February 1994).

Reading between the lines

In exploring media representations of the *Romeo and Juliet* affair, it is important to consider what the political and other contexts of this particular moral panic were. I have pointed out above that questions arise from the delay between the initial events happening and the outcry in the popular press. Here I will explore some of the specific events and debates framing the affair.

Equalizing the age of consent

The entire affair took place in the run-up to the vote in the House of Commons on whether the age of consent for gay men should be equalized with that of heterosexuals in the UK at sixteen. While the *Guardian*, *Independent* and *Observer* all supported this move, the tabloid press (and the right-wing broadsheets) lined up against it. It is, surely, significant that the massive coverage of the affair in the *Daily Mail* took place within the context of that paper's vigorous campaign against the reduction of the age of consent for gay men. As part of this campaign, the *Daily Mail* carried five full pages on issues related to lesbian and gay sexuality on one day (21 January 1994). What these pages amounted to were a set of reasons why gay men and lesbians are not and should not be equal with heterosexuals. The front page of the paper carried a banner headline 'The gay myth and the truth' over a two-page article about (somewhat suspect methodologically speaking) findings that there are far fewer gay men in the population than had previous been thought. These two pages were accompanied by two pages about political correctness and Jane Brown and another full page article by Mary Kenny entitled 'The making of a very vocal minority'. The substantive argument of this article and of 'The gay myth and the truth' was that: if there were fewer gays than previously thought then this must mean that their claims to equality would, automatically, be illegitimate; and that the 'gay lobby' (and implicitly gays and lesbians in general) represented a substantial threat to the common good (out of all proportion to their numbers).

These arguments are particularly interesting in that it is unlikely that even the most right-wing popular dailies would argue that Jews (with a proportional population in the UK similar to those suggested, in the pages of this issue of the *Daily Mail*, to be the case for gays) should have fewer civil rights than other (white) citizens. At the same time, the argument about the disproportionate influence of lesbians and gays is quite similar to the arguments produced by Nazis and neo-Nazis about the damage inflicted by Jews on the population at large. Indeed, there is evidence of both fear and projection similar to that associated with some forms of expression of racism and anti-semitism in much of the tabloid coverage of both the issue of the gay age of consent and of the *Romeo and Juliet* affair.[7]

Turning back the clock: the government's 'Back to Basics' campaign

The moral panic surrounding Jane Brown's refusal of tickets for her pupils to see the ballet of *Romeo and Juliet* took place in the wake of a series of scandals about sexual morality among Conservative ministers which had rocked the Government's 'Back to Basics' campaign. This campaign was heavily dependent on discourses of some kind of 'Golden Age' when we enjoyed 'basic' standards of behaviour and which Britain (England) was supposed to have enjoyed at some time in the past when sexual scandals did not happen, young single mothers did not threaten the good of the nation and everyone knew how they were supposed to behave. Ruth Picardie's article in the *Independent* (3 February 1994) was concerned specifically to draw a contrast between the experience of Jane Brown, as a lesbian head teacher, and that of Julia Stent, the mother of Tory Minister Tim Yeo's 'love child'. Indeed, the article was headed 'Two women of Hackney' with the subheading 'In one London borough, contrasting lives that have set the nation attitudinizing. The moral: better a Tory mistress than a lesbian headmistress.' The question raised by this displacement of scandals about the heterosexual (bad) behaviours of Tory ministers is whether it seems safer to the producers of the tabloids to focus on a lesbian scandal than on a heterosexual one. If lesbianism becomes the focus, in other words, does this help to recoup some safety within heterosexual boundaries?

Westminster Council, the Audit Commission and suspect finances
The Kingsmead Support Group (in a leaflet advertising a lobby of Hackney Council on 8 February 1994) have suggested that the affair was, in part, a distraction from the impending scandal about corruption and financial mismanagement in Westminster Council under the leadership of Dame Shirley Porter – often labelled (along with Wandsworth) the Conservative Party's 'flagship council':

> The ticket offer was jointly subsidized by the Paul Hamlyn Foundation and Westminster Council. The weekend before the story broke out Westminster Council was in big trouble and receiving bad publicity for alleged housing fraud of over £20 million. (Kingsmead Support Group, 1994a)

While there is no internal evidence of this from the actual coverage in either the *Evening Standard* or the national press, there *is* clear evidence that the affair was used as a club with which to beat a Labour council around the head. For example, the *Daily Mail* carried a half-page article entitled 'Hackney, hypocrisy and a head who only obeyed orders' (26 January 1994) which raised questions about 'corruption' in left wing councils.[8] The connotation of being someone who 'only obeyed orders' is clearly that this was the defence used by Nazi war criminals in the Nuremberg trials (and, indeed, by others in defence of their activities as torturers for oppressive regimes around the world). This is reminiscent of coverage of both anti-racist and lesbian and gay activism in 1986 and 1987 when Brent Council and Haringey Council were compared, in the popular press, with both Stalin and Hitler (see Cooper 1989, 1994; Epstein 1995).

Making Labour 'safe'

In the light of attacks like these on Hackney Council, it is, perhaps, possible to understand the reaction of both councillors and officers of the Council as part of an attempt to 'live down' the epithet of 'loony left' – an endeavour which has also occupied the Labour Party nationally for several years. This could possibly be one explanation of why Jane Brown's refusal of the subsidized tickets was not seen as significantly problematic by the local authority in September 1993, but was seen as 'gross misconduct' in January and February 1994. In other words, it could be argued that it was publicity that made Jane Brown a problem for Hackney Council rather than her putative actions. It is certainly the case that, there was an apparent rush to dissociate the Council and its officers and councillors from Jane Brown's actions as soon as the story broke and certainly before there could have been time for a full investigation of what had happened to take place (given that no investigation had taken place when the tickets were first refused).

Interpellating racism

One of the most complex aspects of this affair has been the way in which racism and homophobia have been linked. Gus John and Jane Brown have, it seems, both received a considerable amount of hate-mail including death threats. Some of the hate mail received by Gus John has been explicitly racist and it seems that at least some of the support received by Jane Brown came from a racist dynamic. John suggests that:

> The defence of the headteacher of Kingsmead School . . . had become a matter of black and white.
> In other words, as some of the Kingsmead parents put it, it was a matter of not standing by and allowing 'some bloody nigger' to mess with Jane Brown and tell us what to do (1994, p. 2).

I would suggest that, in this affair, as in earlier moral panics around the activities of 'loony left councils', anti-racism and lesbian and gay activism were tied together in conflict by the popular media in ways which are both racist and homophobic. For example, in the article by Jack Tinker (*Daily Mail* 21 January 1994) about political correctness, he describes a possible 'PC' version of *Othello* in the following terms:

> Iago, being *white,* lower middle class and in full-time employ-
> ment, will, of course, be sentenced to life imprisonment, there
> being no excuse for his behaviour. Otherwise he would have got
> away with 100 hours community service [my emphasis].

Here (and in some of the other coverage) we see the interpellation of 'normal' black parents as being anti-gay and anti-PC taking place simultaneously with attacks on the those who are seen as 'politically correct' for being both pro-gay and anti-racist. This is reminiscent of much of the campaign against the 'loony left' in the mid- to late-1980s when a similar process took place. Gus John (1994), in his account of the affair and in the interview he gave to the African–Caribbean weekly the *Voice* says that the affair is complex. However the article based on his interview seems to offer a simple version of the affair as a black versus white conflict, talking about 'the gay community and racists alike' as if the two categories were identical. John is quoted, in the interview, as saying that 'Equal opportunities are about equality, not about special treatment for lesbians or anyone else'. In this he echoes attacks on anti-racism in the mid-1980s in which attempts by Labour-controlled local education authorities to develop anti-racist policies and practices were derogated in precisely similar terms (see Cooper, 1989; 1994; Epstein, 1995).

One of the major ironies here is that the earliest attacks on Jane Brown in the popular media were precisely on her record on anti-racism. What is apparent, in this regard, is that it is easy to over-simplify and difficult to analyse in complex ways the interplay of racism, homophobia and sexism in situations like this. However, they are intertwined partly through the racialized and sexed bodies of the main actors in the affair and partly because racist and hetero/sexist discourses are usually inseparable in popular culture.

On the impossibility of questioning Shakespeare
It is clear from the coverage of this affair in the popular press that any critique of Shakespeare constitutes some kind of violation of

Englishness/ Britishness and of English/British (high) Culture. There is no room given, in any of the papers, however sympathetic in other ways to Jane Brown, to the possibility that there might be an element of justified critique in her remark that a performance of *Romeo and Juliet* might be read as heterosexist. Indeed, the assumption, without question, that her statement was wrong, ill-judged and foolish could itself be read as a form of heterosexism. It seems to me that *Romeo and Juliet* is not a 'simple' heterosexual tale, given that their affair ends in death, that Romeo's relationship with Mercutio can be read as, in some ways, homoerotic, and that in Shakespeare's time part of the tension of such a performance surely came from the fact that Juliet would have been played by a young man/boy. Nevertheless, there are specific questions about dance which are more complicated than a simple dismissal of Jane Brown's comment might suggest. It is, surely, significant that the fact that the tickets on offer were for a ballet and not for the play has been all but erased in the media coverage. There is a great deal of energy expended, in popular common sense, on keeping dance uncomplicatedly heterosexual simultaneously with a stigmatization of dance for men as something not quite manly but 'soft' or, indeed, 'pansy', something which black people and gay men are supposedly good at, but not uncomplicatedly white heterosexual masculine men (Bennett, 1994).

The affair can also be read as a particular kind of 'queerbashing' in terms of the saturation of the tabloid press with homophobic reporting and comment both on the *Romeo and Juliet* affair and of the age of consent debates. Furthermore, the personal abuse heaped on Jane Brown can, itself, be interpreted as a kind of 'queerbashing'. Certainly, her future career has almost certainly been irretrievably damaged by the affair (who would appoint/promote the '*Romeo and Juliet* head'?) and her life has been threatened in very literal terms. Additionally, her partner has been 'outed' publicly and at work and has, together with her children and her ex-partner, been the target of media harassment. Finally, the moral panic induced can be seen as a form of queerbashing in terms of the encouragement it has given to children to use abusive epithets to other children, particularly at Kingsmead (as reported in the *Independent* (3 February 1994).

Filling in the gaps

There have been some significant absences in the reporting, by both tabloid and broadsheet press of the affair. The role of the Hamlyn Foundation was never made clear: how did a private conversation become the subject of media surveillance in this way? Neither was the cost of the tickets – a substantial part of Jane Brown's reasons for refusing them (Kingsmead Support Group, 1994b). According to all the press reporting in the first few days of the 'scandal', Jane Brown had turned down free tickets to the ballet on behalf of her pupils. It was only at the end of the first week that some of the broadsheets reported that the tickets would have cost the children (or their parents) £7 apiece, a price which, together with the cost of hiring a coach was considered by Jane Brown to be too high for many of her parents.

Another significant absence has been that of Jane Brown's own perspectives on the issue. Along with most other local authorities, Hackney Council has a blanket policy forbidding its employees to speak to the press. The *Observer* (26 January 1994) reported Gus John as saying that she was free to speak to reporters, but no discussion of the limitations of what it would mean for someone in her position (as the focus of intensive attack by the popular media) to do so and what the potential results might have been for her given this situation and the undoubted hostility with which any remarks Jane Brown might have made would have been received.

A final significant absence from press reporting was that of other work being done in the school around ballet and drama on an on-going basis. Indeed, the information that there was any such work appeared only in the *Guardian* (and that was in a reader's letter) (26 January 1994) and in the small circulation journal *New Statesman and Society* (28 January 1994). Presumably reporting such work elsewhere would have compromised the allegation that Jane Brown was (deliberately) depriving pupils at her school of a chance to partake in these aspects of (high) Culture.

Conclusion

As I complete this article (in December 1995) the Kingsmead governors' investigating committee have found in favour of Jane Brown and the school has had an excellent report from their OFSTED (Office for Standards in Education) inspection, a report which commented particularly on the strong 'cultural work' being carried out in the school. However, Gus John has taken out grievance proceedings against Hackney Council for their alleged racist failure to support him through the affair and a Black teacher from the school who had been suspended by its governors for alleged incompetence has taken them to an industrial tribunal, also for alleged racism. The affair is significant, not only as an example of the ways in which moral panics (re)construct popular common senses, but also as a means by which heterosexuality is kept in place. It exemplifies the ways in which issues around sexuality and 'race' are intertwined. The extreme punishment of Jane Brown for being a lesbian through the moral panic in the tabloid press serves as a warning to lesbian and gay teachers that coming out of the closet is, at the very least, risky. It also serves as an illustration of the energy which is devoted to the policing of heterosexuality, particularly in the context of schooling.

Notes

1. See Cameron (1995) for an excellent discussion of 'political correctness'.
2. For further discussion of this campaign, see Cooper (1989, 1994), Epstein (1995), Sanders and Spraggs (1989).
3. Jane Brown is, in fact, a small woman, not much over 5 feet tall and quite slim. It is important to note, here, that I do not regard being 'butch' as a problem and recognize that this is a choice for many lesbians. What is at stake here is the connotation of this image in popular common sense.
4. See Cooper (1989 and 1994) for more detailed discussions of both lesbian and gay activist politics and attacks from government and popular press on them in relation to positive images in Haringey and ILEA and to the formations of the politics around the introduction of Section 28 of the Local Government Act 1988.
5. See Kelly *et al.* (1991) on prevalence of child abuse and the profile of abusers
6. See also Epstein (1993) for further discussion of this point
7. See Cohen (1988) for a discussion of forms of anti-semitism and racism in Britain.
8. It is, perhaps, worth noting that the author of this article, Cornelius McAfee, also appeared on Central Television's *Friday Night Live* on 28 January 1994, offering the same explanation of the affair as that which appeared in the *Mail*.

References

Ball, S. J. (1990) *Politics and Policy Making in Education: Explorations in Policy Sociology*. London: Routledge

Bennett, B. (1994) Personal communication.

Cameron, D. (1995) *Verbal Hygiene: The Politics of Language*. London: Routledge.

Cohen, P. (1998) The perversions of inheritance: studies in the making of multi-racist Britain in Cohen, P. and Bains, H. S. (eds) *Multi-Racist Britain*. London: Macmillan.

Cooper, D. (1989) Positive images in Haringey: a struggle of identity, in Jones, C. and Mahony, P. (eds) *Learning Our Lines: Sexuality and Social Control in Education*. London: Women's Press.

Cooper, D. (1994) *Sexing the City: Lesbian and Gay Politics Within the Activist State*. London: Rivers Oram Press.

Epstein, D. (1993) Defining accountability in education, *British Educational Research Journal. Special Issue: Equal Opportunities, Research and Educational Reform.* 19, 3: 243–57

Epstein, D. (1995) In our (New) Right minds: the hidden curriculum and the academy, in Morley, L. and Walsh, V. (eds) *Feminist Academics: Creative Agents for Change*. London: Taylor & Francis

John, G. (1994) Victims and demons: facts and fiction in the Kingsmead Affair (mimeograph). London: Education and Leisure Services, Hackney Council.

Kelly, L., Regan, L. and Burton, S. (1991) Short summary of findings from: an exploratory study of the prevalence of sexual abuse in a sample of 16–18 year olds, (mimeograph). London: North London Polytechnic (now North London University).

Kingsmead Support Group (1994a) 'Support Jane Brown and Kingsmead School', leaflet advertising a lobby of Hackney Council on 8 February 1994.

Kingsmead Support Group (1994b) 'Why refuse the offer of a subsidized trip to the ballet?' Newsletter No. 1, February 1994.

Sanders, S. and Spraggs, G. (1989) Section 28 and education, in Jones, C. and Mahony, P. (eds) *Learning Our Lines: Sexuality and Social Control in Education*. London: Women's Press.

Thatcher, M. (1987) Speech to Conservative Party Conference.

Newspaper articles in:

Capital Gay: 4 February 1994

Daily Mail: 20 January 1994, 21 January 1994, 26 January 1994

Evening Standard: 19 January 1994, 21 January 1994, 24 January 1994, 26 January 1994, 27 January 1994, 28 January 1994, 31 January 1994, 18 March 1994

Guardian: 21 January 1994, 24 January 1994, 25 January 1994, 26 January 1994, 27 January 1994, 28 January 1994, 4 February 1994

Hackney Gazette: 21 January 1994

Independent: 3 February 1994

New Statesman and Society: 28 January 1994, 18 February 1994

Observer: 23 January 1994, 30 January 1994

Pink Paper: 4 February 1994

Sun: 22 January 1994, 28 January 1994

Sunday Times: 30 January 1994

Times Educational Supplement: 4 February 1994, 11 February 1994

Today: 2 September 1986

Voice: 15 February 1994

9

GRIEVOUS RECOGNITIONS 1:
Poems of Love, Loss and Reparation

Richard Johnson

Your Self Not Mine

Seaside sister
Barefoot tomboy
Searching the shingle
On your southern coves
Curiously seeking sea creatures
Rockveins, pebbles, plants,
Natural facts and things
To exclaim and name,
And all the while
Dreaming for your wild self
Singular travels over seas
One day.

Sometimes you stood
Before the mirror
Slender in some new skirt, dress, top,
Glancing sidelong appraisal,
Turning, swinging cloth, hair
Glimpsing elegant possibilities
Or that vividness of yours,
Kissing the air
In deprecation or despair
So I wish I'd said -
How I wish I could say -
'How beautiful you are!'

Long-time lover
You had power
To charge my finger tips
To comfort and to heal you,
Still terror even, soothe pain
(Some I had inflicted)

Rouse yearnings,
Flood our surfaces,
So I could find
In your strong, slow encoiling of me
And in the crying of my name
Your gifts to me.

Selves you grew
Turned away from me
And my abuses,
Strong strangers striding home boldly
Eating and sleeping, with me unseeing,
Till they left creations
Hidden, some hoarded,
Fine pottery, paintings,
Close friends, political and charitable traces
And letters to me you did not send
And stories you never told me.

This last Jill,
Unmanageable she,
So strongly grown against me,
Rightful claimant
Of respect withheld,
Equal at least,
Who conjured communion
From disappointments,
Who lifted qualifications
From our loving,
This self – Your Self not Mine
I mourn most helplessly.

For after we had shared
The loss of our fathers
And of our many unrealizable desires,
You grafted your independence so close
You made such peace with me
That your last wave
Your 'Good-bye Gran!'
Your acceleration beyond
Familar streets at dawn
Your instant blue-lit extinction
Tore from out my chest as well
A ragged, pumping, bleeding part of me.

(April–July 1992 Revised November 1992)

4.30 a.m.

These creatures scent my waking.
Anxious marauders
They chase my shredded sleep away
Nip lazy dream-thoughts
Skitter and snarl
Till I flinch
And tremble as they do
And scan the day's horizon
For some thing
To fear.

Some creatures crouch outside,
Raising cacophonies
Of household duties,
Drowning out the dominant notes of loss
With different things to do;
Others work sharp teeth inside of me
Pick and gnaw
Would puncture a heartbeat
If I took breath
To let them in.

Memories
Expel them first
And make me cry.
I call on
Her proud loving
Vibrant living
Unfinished creations
The shock-stopped
Stillness
Of her death.

The later tears are
Hard-squeezed
By guilt
From my conviction sure
That my love died
Of my excessive wishes
Strapped
To torsions
She might have fled
If freed.

Sometimes, though,
It's easy
As though pain
Prepared the flood
And only circumstance withheld it.
This general sorrow
Gracious somehow
Drowns out the devils
Honours her as source
And gives me sleep and peace.

(22 December 1992–12 January 1993)

Safe As Houses

I'm the house
Our home
Exploding from inside
Precipitating earthwards
In arbitrary piles
Reassembling then
As bricks
With no mortar.

I'm the garden
Made around a tree
In sweet work
And companionable choices
Hacked down
Grubbed up
To be a grave.

I'm the leafy streets
Soothing sights
And easy routes
Remembered in our family
Despoiled
Reduced to ash
And blown away.

(June–July 1993 Revised January 1996)

Portraits of 1959

He drew himself
Long-faced
And melancholy
In a charcoaled world
Of cliffs, pools and churches
Land of diminished monochrome.
He wrote himself
As pilgrim not progressed
Ways barred
To ordinary adventures
And a painter's glories
Choked up on his own desires
Curved back to childhood's size and places
Where abandonments
Forgotten not forgiven
Stored up the crooked energies
For harm.

Grown woman she
Skill-sure capable
Moved confidently
Through jokes and laughter
And class-room complications
Coloured this scene
Emerald and turquoise
And electric blues
Warmed it
With long brown arms
And summer-sandalled feet
Lit it
With jet-black hair shine
And grey-green eye tease

Looking
Hard at him
Many times
Before he dare.

I wish I could remember
More of the meanings
Of the love we made
In my twentieth year
How I knew you
As redeemer when
We kissed
In your car
Afterwards
And you said
How beautifully I did it
And how we hid in
Waving-grass green
And down-flower gold
And shadowed a way
Past sleeping boys
To be in your bed
By midnight.

Now you see
He portrays her
As glowingly his equal
Or vividly superior
But she is voiceless
And figures only
In his man-made design
Her wife-time began
In this wonder-love
When she must desire
To attend his many needs
Or pay.

Supply his many incompetences
Lighten his world, he says
Feeding him already
A 'strong' woman
A 'weak' man
It's the perfect arrangement.

But how could this sad boy
Abuse
So powerful a lover?
And does this
Other voice of yours belittle her
Who mirror-met your greed
With urgent pleasures of her own
Could mock your thinking self, remember,
Before the academic reinforcements
And even after.
Joke you from self-importance
(Well, temporarily at least)
And knowing no other way
Of strong loving
And no victim either
Chose to be
Your wife?

It's you
I wish
Could tell me
More of the meanings
Of the love
You made
In your twenty-fourth year.
What
In your life

Made you hold me?
How did your eye
Picture me?
And how
Compelled
To love
Were you
In the Age of
Marriages?

(1 January 1993–8 February 1993 Revised January 1996)

Wedding Album:
Chapter and Verse (1963)

I look
In the book
Where you wrote
Our full names
The bride
And the groom
And the time
And the place
Where your darkness glows
In the wedding-cake clothes
You make masquerade
To the camera's gaze
And your eyes
Take a fire
Give a nudge
To desire
I can feel
To this hour.

When I look
In the book
In the night
When I wake
The words
Are in gold
And I ache
At the sight
For I see stiff-iced form
Hold you tight by the arm
And the work of the show
Take your mischief away

Your unruliness lost
In the rules
Of the day
Your saltiness
Sweetened
Somehow.

The boy
In the book
Clasps your hand
To be real.
Does the grin
On his face
Hide the pain
He can't feel
For rites that didn't really say
What it was he felt that day?
For incongruities
He couldn't name?
For unholy doubts
On holy oaths?
For generalities
of promises
impossible
or dangerous
to keep?

Did I really want
To have you
Hold you
In unsought bitter
Possession
For ever more?
Did I want
To fill our bed
With metal edges?

I wish I'd seen
The swallowed anger
Of the bride
The straining will
To be the best girl
You had to be.
I wish I'd eased you
From compulsions
And been strong enough myself
To let you go.

I will not make
A second book
At all like this
Or bind a wife
In gold on white
With goods
Or honour
Or sacrifice.
I will love again
But not alone
I will live with you
But not as one
We'll join us
In an open weave
A light resilience
Fabricate
And she and I
Will walk aside
In memory's meetings
Intimate.

(21 July 1993–21 October 1993 Revised January 1996)

A Hateful Dialogue
in One Voice Only

Remember
how I hated
lousy father
useless husband
You
And how you
wouldn't listen
or support
my stumbled speech,
Or nurture
my thinking
as you did for others
everyday,
Or talked
pretentiously
and did so little
left it all to me.
Self-deluding dreamer
Convenient idealist
How I hated this
hated this
in you.

When I couldn't hide
my strangeness
in the world
you made,
Was famished
for another home
for lovers
I never had
you stopped me having

For dreams and words
the same as mine
And couldn't stand
the speechless greedy pleasure
I curled up with
as I turned
away from you,
I had to start
To tell you this
I had to talk
away
the love we had
in hope of new.

When
my anger
roamed our rooms
you stuck around
for the hand-to-hand combat.
We talked
grit-eyed
early hours through.
You spouted
impossibilities
about love shared
all ways.
I thought, I should have left
and saved my life
but you held me there
through all the pain
you caused.
You made contrition
Through domestic contribution
So I could suppose

here was constancy
of a kind.

Your anger
was nothing
to the monsters
I share
my body with
today
bursting ribcage
to consciousness.
Of these I name
the uncompletion
Of my reparation
For the secondness
I forced on you
To work
To causes
To socialism
To feminism,
Oh my secondary lover
Living secondarily
With so much constancy.

So now you know
the secret
of the smile I
died with?
And of the lip-twisted
cynicism
you seemed to see
when you visited
my coldness
a second time

when you caressed
refrigerated flesh
pressed down hard
and hopelessly
on my belly
and howled
denial?

Don't worry.
I know
you did not wish
for me
to die.

(March–July 1993)

Fragments from 'Loving Two Women'

The bass notes
minor key
accompanied me
all down the sound
of children singing
inside the strongest ring
of your absorption
Would interrupt our best tunes
Disharmonise the melody on
our only days
Warn of the fall
the self-despising
My base note.

That's when I put on you
an old disinheritance
living away in our home
as a stranger
And came to ascribe
all sad soundings
to our marrying
Blame you for asymmetries
I made as much
or more
than you.

And this was when
I wouldn't talk
as we had always talked
Wouldn't change
as I had tried to change

When the part of me
so strange
A part of me
that wasn't what
you knew of me
A part of me
I had to own
sought to love elsewhere

***

This life, too far
beyond the dutiful
I bring as death to you.
I am killer coming home
with steel-sharp secret
must unsheathe
to cut so deep
your flesh gapes, bleeds
from my own needs.

The threat you feel
To life itself
I must disguise
from my own eyes
with principles
appropriate
approximate
so many reasons why.

Soon I learn
the every consequence
of choices made
compellingly
without you.
But chose

no decent
vicious distance
of the murder man
Attend
to all the pain
through frightened nights
and panic days
See your heart's
irruptions into working hours
Watch your best face forward
crumple into tearful talk
Find the strength you owed
to confidence in love
erode to desperation's frailty
so frightening to us both.

And count out each
divided week
by itemizing
allocating
bits of
you and me
And offer up
amendments every one
if only I could keep
the hope ashamed
I'd ripped away from you.

I blank out all the feelings
from the warm hours
for my hard night drive
at the western city's glare.
Sometimes as I go
I wrap defences
round the stone

that dread drops down
my centre line
And midway hold
both dearest faces' features
in my mind:
not in harmony
but differently loved
and equally so
and not split either
but together
and possible
and in my same place.

* * *

I pray you won't be waiting
with the sleepless shaken anger
for the bitter day you had
Nor with back-turned silence
and pretending sleep
that ends the same.

This prayer to undiscover
what I knew
I had exacted
couldn't wish away
the storm.

It was best instead
to travel turbulent
the place of calm
we reached;
And holiday
where trust grew back
in smaller things
as tiny stitches

new patterns make
on old materials –
worn and spare and taut
but looking good
and beautiful
and tough enough
to hold.

* * *

If you had lived
I might have pride
For loving both
in constant obstinacy.

Now driving east
no force field's
there for me to break.
For you are nowhere
or are every where with me
and I must live your absence
and its meanings
every day.

(Taken from a longer poem sequence – 'Loving Two Women' –
first written December 1993–July 1994)

Last Walk in the Forest

From here, upon this bank, you'll see
The cherry and the apple trees
Invent again the colour green
Turn pink cups up to sun and bee
Hang white bells down to welcome you;
And when their touches circle down
To pattern places you have been
And when their richness glows and falls
To nourish you sweetly seasons round
And when the evenings blank and freeze
Signifying sorrow in tapestries of leaves
And when the walkers beat the track
And crack the stretched-out skin of earth,
And in the negative of night
When I'm asleep in city light
And you are so alive
On your bright woodside
I pray you'll find in oak or stone
Or in the presence of this place
Companions, of long standing.

You loved the forest settlements
Smooth fertility of sudden fields
Tamed from tangle and fecundity
By the round grindings of the sheep;
Snuggled cottage to covet
In easy passing talk
On rural bliss and major inconvenience.
But now in borderland again
On a day more obscure by far
When yew's black smoke
Spreads doubt across the path, my task

I pray for Evergreen
To take your substance up
To pinkest perfect fruits,
Take flight through oakland skies
To further generation,
And that a tree of graves
Give life to you again.

Finer days than this
Put tree tops in the pool
And black birds passing,
Mauve mouths in glossy green
When rhododendrons open.
But January mists press
The pool so unreflective flat
The mirror's vacant day
Shows drowned limbs only
Raised to the stultified sky:
No room for a warm return of you
No image food for crying
Only great gasps
Thrust down my throat again
Tasting of a burned-out metal,
Of the ashes.

Forest to field, field to forest
My fourth choice plays back
The global depredation,
Makes intricate connection
With plants and warm creations,
Congregates swift wings
To roll over berried hedges,
Vegetates fleshy species on wet margins:
Primrose, cowslip spread, seed, cross;

Turf turns to tussock
From the rough nosing of moles
Raising round refuge for eyebright
Milkwort, thyme,
While beetle and woodpecker
And the fungal subversion
Degenerate a whole orchard
To knobbled, knarled and pitted woods
Leaved in cancerous clusters
Bearing spiteful fruit of
Crabs and prickly pears.

I came here so heavy
And it lightened me.
I claimed it
In your name
Imperially.
In time I learned
To read a poem here
So you could rest
In such a kinder pattern
Of remaining
Vulnerable too.

Alone, our older pleasures
Reached me through the bar of winter cold
To warm my wish and will
For the hardest task at last
Of loving you;
And I could cross the bridges now,
Brush aside a rose's warning glow,
Find a line
That tunnels through the birches,
Overlooks the forest tracks
And slightest paths of deer,

Underpasses pine groves' high solemnities
And plunges down the river cliff,
Descends again through root and rock
To touch the forest's deepest vein
The brook.

This is the brook
Too full to overwhelming
Where our children played
For sealess midland summers;
Where we found
The hellebore besides
We could not find in any book.
We used to walk-wade
Looking for the creatures under stones,
Curl up like questions
On the sun-soaked bank,
Flow together or apart
Or not at all
As the stream they dammed,
Till it broke through
To carry all our memories away.
So now I carve
Upon this split, divided oak
A 'J' to hold you here
To make the time
We did not have
To grow it up again.

The brook is wild
It takes you to the sea,
But I shall seek a place somewhere
We didn't go,
A wildness that would never show
Upon the maps we used;

Higher where the trees grow thin
And beech and bilberry mixes in
With dominant oak, occasional yew,
Higher where the deer cries
Stops to turn, engage strange eyes
Delicate, curious, satisfied,
Pointing me to a glade he grazes
Ringed around by mist at dusk,
A space to trust
A circle with,
To lay anemones from the wreath,
To crouch, to cry, to say good bye
To turn to go
To leave alone
To hear you say
'Scatter me
In a wild place',
Shout and sigh
I did, my love
I did!

I think your death became
A little life for me.
I was so closely homed on you
To show your worth
To all the people,
To have to do
The things you had to do,
Remembering wishes
Not last, because you had no last,
To see you to the earth,
That once accomplished
I had no line,
No skill of yours to read
The faintest trace

Of what I now
Might be,
Of how
I came to be

Here

In
A forest

On
A dark night

In
the winter

On
my
own.

(October–December 1993)

Grievous Recognitions 2:
The Grieving Process
and Sexual Boundaries

When it was first suggested that I should write a commentary on the poems, I resisted the idea. I did not wish to clarify the author's meaning, or provide a 'reading'. Writing a commentary ran against our insistence that the poems had the same intellectual/analytic status as more recognizably academic pieces. If this was so, why was it necessary to frame poetry in a more academic voice? In learning to write poetry, I enjoyed the experience of ambiguity, so different from my usual academic practice of closing meanings down, of 'being clear'.

The actual writing, however, suggested a more positive role for some kind of authorial comment. The poems themselves arose in the course of dialogues of different kinds, often across or around major social boundaries. They were extensively commented on and revised.[1] Sometimes this process is embodied in the 'dialogue' form in which they are written. Moreover, just as their first production (my 'authorship') was influenced by other people's stories, so their second and subsequent productions (many different readings) must be influenced by readers' lives, ideas and feelings.

All this suggested a different way to think about a 'commentary'. It could be a way of having further conversations in a different voice. Commentary and poems could be separate but related practices, neither dependent on the other, though sharing a similar autobiographical base. This way, I did not have to comment on the poems themselves, or not directly. I could focus on the circumstances from which the texts arose, including the conversations.

It is partly for this reason that I take other people's comments as my starting point here. There were many, especially from the authors, editors and publishers of this volume. In addition, the poems themselves, in their first, second or subsequent versions figured in the dialogues within the Politics of Sexuality Group which I have sketched in Chapter 1. As I note there, the second phase of the group's work, focusing on our book plans and individual contributions, occupied much of the academic year 1992–93; this was also the period during which most of the poems were written.

What's left of my original resistance is the hope that the poems will be read first, and the 'commentary' after, and that the two will be read as relatively independent statements, the second a further reflection on the circumstances which produced the first. Of course, there are larger reservations about the whole process, not so much about the writing of the poems, as about the making of them public. I discuss some of my doubts, fears and counter-narratives about this, later in this piece.

Grieving, sexuality and identity

One of the strangest comments I received, but also one of the most generative, was that the poems were not about sexuality, but about grieving. I have thought a lot about this. There is an obvious truth in it, which I detail below. But there are several reasons why I do not think that such a split can be sustained.

First, to make such a division we must construe sexuality very narrowly. By 'sexuality', I do not mean a discrete set of physical acts (procreative or otherwise), still less some patterned sequence of biological 'arousal'. I mean sexuality as it is understood in this book as a whole: a set of discourses, structures of feeling, social and personal identities, and material and social practices which are routed through bodily possibilities of pleasure and desire. Obviously, in the context, I find it hard to disassociate sexuality from narratives and feelings of heterosexual love and romance. From this point of view, how can grieving for a lover *not* be about sexuality?

Second, in its lived relations, even perhaps in its official discourses, sexuality is not a discrete domain, but intersects with many different processes. There are certainly forms of power which play around the sexual categories themselves as lived positions – around the hetero/homo binary for instance, or within heterosexual relations on gender and other lines. Sexuality seems to be a kind of junction point of power, where other social relationships conjoin and are condensed. Sexual relationships are deeply shaped by other forms of power; similarly sexuality or some erotic trace enters into relations of many different kinds. In other words, sexuality, like other points of condensation (teacher/taught relationships for example) often works precisely through its intersections with other discourses and practices. I will try to make this more concrete later, but clearly grieving may be 'sexualized' too.

Indeed to separate sexuality from dying and grieving would be to rip apart a tangle of interlacing connections in contemporary cultural formations. The most striking instances are amongst the links forged in the process of living, dying and mourning in the midst of the AIDS epidemic. Death and sexuality are linked in many other ways: through the sexualization of death and the association of sexual abandon with dying, through the fact that both sex and dying are domains of bodily possibility and impossibility, and through the elaborated metaphorical significances of both domains in our culture.

Re-reading the poems, in the light of our (nearly) finished book, it seems to me that death is another kind of 'border' and that grieving and its accompanying activities are another kind of 'patrol'. Like all 'border patrols' grieving rituals and practices are there to police the boundaries. At the same time, even the best defended frontier guards may tremble at the perils of dwelling in the borderlands. They are dangerous places, where new identities – neither One nor the Other – may arise. This movement or ambivalence (firm policing on shaky ground) can be traced everywhere in this volume, even where the writers choose to stress one side or the other. The necessity of defences and the dangers of the borderline – of 'liminality' in the current theoretical language – are sides of the same spatial and psychic economy.[2] This is clear whether we are looking at the homophobic behaviour of young men (Chapter 6), the origins of a 'muscular intellectualness' which is articulated to heterosexual identity (Chapter 7), the social expulsion of the AIDS carrier as a 'monstrous' threat (Chapter 4), or the grief of a heterosexual man on the death of his lover. In each case acts of policing or recomposition – often the very same acts – double also as the breaking in of vulnerabilities and uncertainties, themselves often fuelling the drive to be secure.

In an important book on grieving and loss (especially about parents who have lost children and children who have lost parents) Louise J.

Kaplan captures the double movement: both the conventional 'patrols' and the subjective disarray around them

> Mourning rituals and conventional behaviours of the bereaved are designed to give a semblance of order and rationality to the unruly passions of bereavement. Convention tells us something important about the state of mind of the bereaved, but I am more interested in the latent madness that goes on behind the veils of custom – the rediscovery of the lost beloved in the restoration and resurrection of lost dialogues. (1995, p. 9)

From one point of view, mourning is a work of reassurance and boundary-maintenance against the shock of death and loss. But the reassurance is necessary – even though it may not succeed – because the death of someone close to us produces a 'madness': overwhelming emotions, that throw into giddy, vulnerable, high relief *all* our own identities. This madness is as social and socially-produced as the routines of patrollers – which may also be very mad. (There is a hint of a natural/social opposition which I do not altogether accept, in the Kaplan quotation.) Grieving might be best understood as a desperate work of personal recomposition. In particular the death of a lover must disturb the sexual identities of the survivor(s).

Early mo(u)rning activity . . .

The poems were written as part of the work of grieving for Jill, my wife and lover, who died suddenly in the early morning of Saturday, 25 January 1992 after a relationship of 33 years. Jill awoke with a pain in her chest at six in the morning. After some fatal delays, an ambulance arrived around 8.00 a.m. I hadn't registered the fact that she was so ill. I thought she'd have some tests at the hospital and then we'd come home. So I didn't go in the ambulance with her. I was following in our car when suddenly the blue lights were switched on and the ambulance raced away. When I arrived at the local hospital, I was asked to wait in a small room with someone to keep me company. After about half an hour, and what I now recognize as some warnings, a doctor and nurse came in and said that Jill had died in the ambulance. They had tried to resuscitate her but had failed.

During the years that followed – and often today – some unconscious alarm wakes me regularly at 4.30 a.m. I am still not clear whether it is the fear of dying myself that wakes me up at this particular time or the hope of saving Jill. I can only assume my unconscious tells me that waking up at 4.30 a.m. is soon enough to make a difference. Anyway, writing poetry, in bed, was something I started to do in the hours when sleeping was too dangerous. It went along with other activities which seemed at first to help and then became essential. They included writing a diary which recorded wild, productive bouts of dreaming and attempts to find some directions in a radically disordered life. I also started looking through a large collection of photographs of Jill and our children, friends and families, including our wedding photos. This activity led to compiling a new album – a 'photo-life' of Jill with letters, public and private documents, and images of the walks we took, the things she made and of the places where I left her ashes.

Later, though not intending to write about it in any way, I started to read about the grieving process, first books given to me by friends, then texts I found myself, often because I knew them in other contexts. Melanie Klein's discussions of mourning as involving 'inner chaos', intense activity and a reliving of infantile feelings was very important in coming to terms with the process. (Mitchell, 1986, pp. 146–74). Klein understands this chaos or disruption in terms of a loss of identity – more strictly 'the loss of *internal* "good" objects'. Especially important for me was her argument that grieving involves the bereaved in trying to recreate and to re-embody the lost loved one – 'setting up the lost loved object inside himself'. Later I read other accounts – including Adrian Kear's article in this volume (Chapter 10) – that argued a similar case in different terms, in Kaplan's book, for instance, in terms of 'lost dialogues'.

This analysis, which depends on the basic psychoanalytic idea that we build or introject strongly imaginary versions of Others inside ourselves, helped me to understand my early mo(u)rning activities. I was trying to re-create Jill (a version of her of course) inside myself. I was restoring or imagining the talks which I couldn't have with her anymore. This analysis corresponds to my feelings and practices at the time.

The feelings associated with trying to embody Jill were very physical, often sexual and tender. They involved trying to grasp or recreate her looks, gestures, the feel of her skin, the way she physically touched you (a quick hand on the arm) when she engaged with what you said, the sound of her voice, her vehement expostulations and favourite sayings, her Otherness, her persona, her very vital presence in the world. It also seemed to demand a lot of activity. To make Jill's book, for instance, I had to look through photos, make choices, track down negatives and have new prints made, compose pages of images. It was exciting to discover images I hadn't seen before, or had forgotten, in the collections of family or friends. Some of these, some of her typical gestures (delicate fingers stretched to balance) went back to her toddlerhood. I also found I could enlarge all or parts of especially important images (a clear-eyed, sceptical stare straight back at my camera's eye – I took most family photos). Then, when the whole was composed, I could turn the pages and follow the sequence of her life, especially, but not only, her life with me.

In a way, these activities were reassuring. I felt I was taking control over overwhelming feelings, producing them when I had time and space to do justice to the memories and to our relationship. At another level, grieving added further disturbance and a loss of control. Many of my activities were fiercely concentrated and wholly preoccupying. I knew they were 'mad'. In psychoanalytic terms, they were 'obsessive'. And worse, perhaps, I craved and loved this madness. I *wanted* to wake up in the morning to pursue these activities madly. I am deeply thankful to all the wise people who told me that the most bizarre of grieving activities were OK.[3]

Of course, this was also precious time – with Jill, with Jill in me. Intense pleasure, deep disturbance, appropriative impulses and that desperate sense of in-completion which accompanies loss were all combined. Some of the impulses which seemed at the time inappropriately sexual, make sense within the psychoanalytic arguments. At night I slept not only in 'our' bed, often hugging a pillow, but with or in Jill's clothes. During the day I took on many of her roles. I occupied her spaces in the house. I searched for and appropriated her possessions and creations. I became miserly about our (her?) money, for example; I spent strangely pleasurable hours, sitting at Jill's desk in our bedroom, calculating savings (especially important now) and income and expenditures. I had never managed the household money in detail before – now I was copying, or parodying, her 'carefulness'. I tried hard, often with desperate feelings of helplessness, to be a good 'single parent' and to care for my recently widowed mother. I took over 'feminine' roles and identities, rather self-consciously I fear. I got tidier (cf. Mitchell, 1986, p. 158). I looked after the house, 'husbanded' it, and, before we sold it, made many improvements.

Consciously, I used to think that I was keeping Jill alive by installing her, very securely, in my memory. This was linked to my and her disbelief in any other kind of afterlife. Much later when reading the final version of Adrian Kear's article in this book (Chapter 10) in order to write Chapter 1, I was struck by the similarities between the grieving process and Adrian's account of introjection and ingestion/ incorporation. Following an analysis of Nicholas Abraham and Maria Torok, he distinguishes between introjective and incorporative modes of appropriating of the Other into the self. In introjective modes, the subject takes in the Other by verbal means. The Other is embodied in the self imaginarily, through practices like the writing of poems. While introjection is a more or less conscious process, incorporation works secretly through unconscious means. It involves the ingestion of objects – literally things – rather than the embodiment of the Other through words or images. These forms of 'eating the other' are more or less transformed or verbalized, more or less metaphorical. In Adrian's readings, as in Klein's psychoanalysis, these forms of ingestion/ incorporation are strongly associated with melancholy and mourning.

It is clear to me that many of my early forms of grieving were incorporative in this second sense, ways of appropriating Jill – her things, her clothes, her spaces, her actions, her money, her roles. Other forms – the poetry, Jill's book, the diary – were more 'introjective'. There was no simple transition from the one to the other, no clear model of stages, but there was perhaps a progress towards the symbolic articulation of feelings which could not be at first expressed in more verbal ways.

Beyond this, I also came to recognize the appropriative or possessive nature of the activities themselves. This sense was reinforced in a very disturbing way both when Adrian and I talked about earlier versions of his thinking and, finally, when I read the very sharp final version. Here appropriative modes are clearly related to the power of men in heterosexual relations. This made me think – makes me think – that my unequal relations with Jill were being reproduced even in the grieving process.

On the whole these activities were not shared, though I showed some of the poems as I wrote them to Becky and Paul, our children; to my mother Iris, who lived with us; and all of them later to Jill's brother John. The poems – or some of them – were also discussed, in the Politics of Sexuality Group, which included several personal friends. Group discussions were, as we shall see, one powerful influence on the poems themselves, and thence on the grieving process. It was also in the course of discussing the poems in the group that the idea of doing a sequence of poems, and publishing them, arose. Even so, the primary relationship from which the poems arose was that between Jill and me. Like other activities, writing the poems was a way of trying to continue the intimacy – all the talk and the touching and patience with each other which had been an especially strong feature of our relationship in the last years. Many of my acts can also be read – in a Kleinian and, as we shall see, in a more 'political' framework – as acts of attempted reparation (cf. Mitchell, 1986, p. 154). As is clear in the poetry, they involved guilt, sometimes an idealization of Jill and a strong and desperate sense that I was only really doing her justice, after she had died, when it was too late. On the one hand, this did restore Jill as a 'good object' in my memory and psyche. On the other hand, a kind of active guilt or better perhaps, a sense of responsibility was (and is) one of the strongest emotions in my grieving. It re-emerges again and again, whether as a kind of dread or sickening realization, or as an impulse that works through to the level of conscious intentions. It was this inner sequence that gave a personal bite to the Politics of Sexuality Group's discussions about sexual abuse and heterosexuality, and, again, to my reading of the finished articles in writing this commentary and Chapter 1. I will return to these connections later.

Yes, the poems are 'about' grieving – they were part of the grieving process itself.

Conditions of dying and the hetero/homo border

One thing I came to realize in talking to friends and reading about grieving, is that the exact circumstances of a person's death decisively shape the forms of grief.[4] While there are conventions, certainly, there is no 'standard' pattern for grief. Nor, it seems to me, is there a 'normal' pattern of development, though much of the literature constructs such a norm. My own grief seems to have followed a cyclical rather than an developmental pattern. Even now, four years later, I can still shake my head in disbelief at Jill's dying or find it strange that I have written all of this, in alien languages, about such impossible feelings and events. In some of the literature, this disbelief is supposed to be a very early 'stage'. The suddenness of Jill's death seemed to determine many of the responses of those who loved her and were loved by her. In addition to (and not separate from) the psychic processes we have already noted in grieving, death also poses specific questions about memory and about interpretation. Dying has a profound effect, for the survivors, on memory and on cognition. The suddenness of Jill's death put a desperate premium on remembering and at the same time seemed fatally to weaken this vital faculty, both individually and in the deeply wounded little collectivity of our family. The loss of that aspect of memory, where you bounce stories off the other to check them out or amplify them was especially shocking. The burden of having to remember for both of us, sometimes for all of us, was, therefore particularly heavy.

The cognitive burden, the burden of explanation, is equally important. All mourners must ask: why did she/he die? Again, if dying is a gradual process, there is time to check out the meanings with the person. The suddenness of Jill's death meant that she had no time to reflect on her own life and death. Selfishly, she could not tell me all the things I needed to know. The poems specify several of these unanswered questions, but what I most needed to know was whether she held me responsible for her death and, behind this, whether I was in fact responsible.

I am sure (partly from discussions with other grievers) that a similar individual shaping can be given for all the particularities of loss by death: suicides, accidents, murders, disappearances, long or short illnesses, and 'dying of old age'. But the shaping isn't individual or contingent alone. Grieving is a socially-prescribed ritual and death has no one meaning. Nor is there equality of access, or equality of applicability for everyone to the conventional or dominant forms and meanings themselves. Some forms and conditions of loss are much more readily recognized than others. It is quite wrong to understand dying as only a natural catastrophe that breaks into the social world: it also has its own social character. The rest of this commentary, without ceasing to be autobiographical, is concerned with the larger social determinations of grieving, and especially the connections with the social categories of sexuality, gender and power.

I know that painful and perilous though it seemed, my grieving would have been different, and more difficult, if my lover had been a man. There are terms and forms enough for the public recognition of a grieving husband or wife, even, though already more borderline, for a heterosexual lover. Writing 'widower' on a form or ticking a box marked 'widowed' or applying for a single parent's allowance was strange enough, but what if there are no publicly acceptable categories at all against which to gauge your feelings, no public markers or only very derogatory ones? In relation to sexual categories, the gay/straight boundary is crucial here. The process of grieving and dying in gay experience is explored in a series of stories by Adam Mars-Jones and Edmund White published as *The Darker Proof: Stories from a Crisis*. I found the bleak sense of neglect, the impermanence of memory and therefore of 'life after death' unbearable in some of these stories.

> Everyone else, after all, had memories of Charles that antedated the illness. They at least had good years to set against the bad, and a mellow auditing of accounts to hope for.
>
> In practice, he knew that things didn't work like that, not for anybody. With the person gone, the memories attached to the person died their own small sort of death. They had no independent existence, any more than Christmas tree lights had a function when the Christmas tree was gone. Sooner or later they had to be tidied away (Mars-Jones and White, 1988, p. 53).

Very reluctantly because this is one of the hardest things for a griever to say, I know that Mars-Jones is right that 'the memories attached to the person die their own small sort of death'. I'm just hoping that some of this will be reversed as I grow older and my longer-term memory improves. Yet there is, of course, a *social,* a more than individual, relativity about this process. As AIDS and gay activists know well (have taught a wider public indeed) it also matters – for the private remembering – how and how far those who die are publicly remembered.[5] Even personal memory depends on public supports, the witness of others and social networks – at best a 'community' of rememberers, who are also of course, partly constituted through their shared grief and memories. The grieving practices within gay publics, especially in relation to AIDS, are of central contemporary significance in the sexual borderlands of dying. The grieving rituals of the mainstream heterosexual public have a predominantly religious pattern which usually presumes a familial group of mourners linked through the heterosexual matrixes of marriage and inheritance. Gay activists, sometimes for their own funerals, have invented new, more appropriate forms for grieving which also celebrate the lives of those who have died. They have thereby, and in other ways, produced 'alternative families' and different forms of kin. The alternative forms of celebrating a life have acquired considerable publicity, sometimes because of the fame of those who have died, but also because of the visibility of gay styles, stars and practices within mainstream media and popular culture. As in so many other matters, gay creativity has influenced those who do not identity as gay, or who do not identify as gay sexually, though they may identify with gay in different ways. I know that my choice of an independent non-religious 'celebration' of Jill's life, with lots of personal witness, was made easier by these breaks from orthodox rituals, by the support of friends (lesbian, gay and straight) as well as by the knowledge of Jill's own attitudes to funerals and burial. Both her father and mine had just died, mine in November 1991, hers early in January. She had spoken about her unease that so resolutely and quietly sceptical a man as her father had been buried with full Christian honours. This was how I knew some of what to do, even though Jill had left no will or instructions.

Heterosexuality and gender inequalities as 'abuse'

Heterosexual relations and the associated cluster of gender relations were central in my and Jill's relationship. So of all the borders and identities that were disturbed by her death, those of gender and heterosexuality were the most significant, at least for me. I hope that this preoccupation with heterosexual relations of power comes through in the poetry and that it is clear to the reader that grieving is all the time interwoven with other themes: with recognizing the abuses that enter into gender inequalities, with the contradictions of marriage, with the problem of 'possession' in struggling over dependence and autonomy, with the ambivalences of loving and hating, and with the difficulty of loving and trusting outside very rule-bound forms of relationship. These rules may involve terrible denials but, since we are invested in them anyway, the breaking of them may also do great harm.

Jill's death and my survival brought these themes into the harshest of lights. Many stories were told about the reasons for her dying including the medical story of 'myocardial infarct' (heart attack), in itself unusual in a woman of Jill's age with no predisposing factors. The nastiest and the most persistent story I tell myself is that I killed Jill. I did not kill her deliberately, but I am none the less responsible for her death.

This story has acquired many different contents over the four years since her death. It is a very convincing story. Throughout our marriage, at least until the last few years, I reaped the dividends of gender inequalities, especially those that prioritized my 'career' and subordinated her energies to the needs of family and husband. Often, in addition, my behaviour, based in much unacknowledged distress of my own, made her life more difficult than it should have been. I was difficult to live with, partly because of a persistent melancholy undertow in my life. And I didn't look after her properly.

In addition, I asked Jill to accept another close and sexual relationship which began in 1984, continued on this basis for four years, and remained an important friendship for me from 1988 to Jill's death in 1992. I began by believing that having two 'primary' relationships was possible. I soon learned that it was very hard for everyone. The emotional pain must have taken a physical toll of Jill's health. It seems likely that it was the stress of this period that damaged her health permanently, literally 'broke her heart'. I still scan medical reports for evidence, one way or another, for the significance of stress in the production of heart attacks. It is true that I supported her through the emotional consequences of her decision to stay with me. Our relationship did survive and it did change and deepen, and I think that it 'equalized'. But this more-than-survival is full of ambiguity, for if Jill had not stayed with me to renegotiate our relationship, perhaps she would now be alive. Even my continuing to love her may have contributed to her staying and therefore the prolongation of stress. In particular, it feels today that I did not reckon fully with the possible physical consequences for her of what I had done.

So the borderline crisis for me when Jill died was centrally around my own heterosexuality and masculinity, and around these social identities more generally. This personal crisis converged powerfully with the fact that I was already working on two projects in relation to sexuality – one with Debbie Epstein on Sexuality and Schooling and the Politics of

Sexuality Group on what was to become this book. This meant that during the crucial period of mourning, during which I continued to teach and attend group meetings, grieving was fed not only by my early morning activities, but also by group discussions and by a reading programme on heterosexuality, gender and power. In particular, we had discussions in the group about sexual abuse in childhood, and about abusiveness in relationships more generally, at just the time when I presented my first poem to the group. 'Your Self Not Mine' was revised and re-titled in the light of group discussions. Several other poems, especially 'Portraits of 1959', were strongly influenced by the dialogue on abuse.

The oppressiveness of heterosexuality is, of course, a leading theme of this book. It is central especially in the analysis of some of the exchanges reproduced and analysed in the study of the *Oprah Winfrey Show* (Chapter 2) in the analysis of professional practices around IVF (Chapter 3), in the poem sequence 'Impedimenta' (Chapter 5), in the discussion of the Jane Brown case (Chapter 8) and in 'Eating the Other' (Chapter 10). It is important to stress that though sexuality is one location of abuse or of oppression, the argument about abusiveness or about oppressive behaviour is a wider one. This is suggested by the examples in this book. There is something deeply abusive, for example, in the exchanges between the couples in the transcripts of the *Oprah Winfrey Show*, especially in the gross yet casual (that is, habitual?) refusal of recognition by the men of the words and needs of their partners – put simply their refusal or inability to listen. There is something abusive too in the systematic sanctioning of situations likely to reproduce this behaviour by the professionals involved in the programme.

There are some obvious difficulties in extending the use of 'abuse' in this way. It may blur the difference between actively violent behaviour and complicity in relations of power. Often it is better to use the more general, familiar and more 'structural' term 'oppressive'. Yet sometimes it seems important that our critical language about sexual, gendered and other forms of power should carry a stronger moral charge and imply more of agency. Directly naming behaviours, including your own, and facing their consequences for others seems to me a crucial dimension of a politics of masculinity, or of any politics addressed to more powerful positions. I am not talking about 'indulging in guilt' here, as though the guilty one was the main sufferer ('Poor Me!'). I am talking about the motives and the energies for changing in relation to others. I believe it is possible for men to change in heterosexual relationships in relation to the needs of their partners, including the need for separation, independence and agency (often counter to your own) which abusive power denies. In this process the relationships themselves can change, and though there are also massive cultural and institutional supports for conventional heterosexual relations it is also possible for men to campaign on these grounds too. It is also possible for heterosexual men to recognize the violent abuses associated with homophobia and to change also in these relations. Being fully aware (emotionally alive as well as intellectually conscious) of the abusiveness of your behaviours for others, especially for others whom you love, can be a powerful motive to change.

To adopt this wider view of abuse, however, is not to argue that sexual abuse is a model for or essence of other forms of abusiveness, nor that abusive heterosexual relationships between children and adults can be equated with abusive relationships between adults. There are specific features of child–adult relations, particularly large discrepancies of power, that have to be attended to. It is to suggest, however, that abusive forms of power may enter into heterosexual (or homosexual) relationships at many different points, not all of them 'sexual' in any useful sense. We might add that the more overt forms of erotic domination and submission (for example sado-masochistic practices between consenting adults) are not necessarily abusive at all, especially if the surrounding relations of power do not correspond to those that are acted out in sexual play.

It was important for me to go through these arguments to understand my own behaviour. I came to the conclusion that though there had been abusive moments in my sexual history, the key abuses in my relationship with Jill were mainly of another kind. In some ways directly sexual relations – 'making love' – was something we negotiated over (though not always equally) from a relatively early stage, sooner, for example, than over domestic labour, or child care, or intellectual equality and respect. (Later I want to suggest that this corresponds to a particular historical form of heterosexual coupledom.) I was most abusive I think at the points where I did not recognize, or refused to recognize the differences between my needs and hers, and so, since I became the more powerful partner, subordinated her life to mine. In this sense, abuse is about possession and dispossession, about the ownership of lives, about who or what we live for, and on whose terms. Abuse is about 'eating up the other' ('God Spoke/ ate well'), subsuming her into yourself, into your project. Abuse is being 'one more arm/of your arms' or being 'cut . . . loose to die, he said/ to kindle my fire'. Abuse is turning a confession into a ground for criticism, or never having 'to be embarrassed' of a partner, wherever you might go! In the most general sense (though it is risky to generalize) abuse is refusing or denying recognition to the other from your position of power and in the terms in which the other defines herself. It is also a refusal of her difference, her Otherness, her Self in relation to yours. Abuse is systematic misrecognition.[6]

It is because of these belated recognitions that the themes of Jill's 'own self', 'Her Self Not Mine', her 'wildness', the ways she exceeded my 'knowledge' of her, the ways she was different and separate, the ways she dreamt of something different have a presence through the poems. Because this element is strongest in the first (revised) poem of the sequence, I reckon it to be the most 'loving'.

To some extent these recognitions were already in place in our lives before Jill died. By the later 1980s Jill was literally creating a life of her own including a sort of independent interior space where neither I nor our children were the key points of reference. She had always retained her own career as a specialist teacher (she was brilliant at teaching children to read) but was increasingly involved in a wide range of other activities, networks and friendships: the Open University, CND, her women's therapy group and her work as a potter were some of the most important. Second, I was making changes in my life in relation to hers, in ways I thought of as reparative for the past. It was obvious, for example, that really substantial changes in our roles and relationships were impossible while I continued to be so committed to a leading role in the Birmingham Department of Cultural Studies. I can't do justice here to the contradictions that arose, in my own family, from the intensity of the demands of the Cultural Studies project from the mid-1970s to the late 1980s. There was something horribly contradictory about the way Jill was positioned in relation to it, not least in its explicitly feminist moments. The clearest confirmation of this was the way we were both benefitting from my withdrawal by the early 1990s. As her own project as a Special Needs primary school teacher ran up against a host of difficulties created by government policy, we planned a kind of joint retirement, which would also coincide with our children leaving home.

The loving or reparative moves that I had already made could never be enough, and also had only just begun. This gives a particular desperation to mourning – 'Grievous Recognitions' in part because too late. It is important to stress this incompletion and the unfairness beyond the grave. Unfairness extends even to the writing of the poems and this commentary. On top of the oppressions of coupledom and the limits of reparation, Jill's death added further layers of unfairness. The greatest unfairness is that of her death and my survival. But I am now also empowered to speak about our past and she is comprehensively silenced in ways that are utterly irremediable. There is no real solution to this: that it is my voice and my point(s) of view which shape this telling.

The counter-narrative I tell myself is about my own responsibilities. Chief among these is to remember and to recognize Jill as publicly as possible – 'To Show your worth/ To all the people'. I have done this, most riskily in this volume, but also in speeches and lectures on other matters. Her death is relevant, for example, to contemporary educational policy and the abusive relationships which the Conservative Government has constructed – its violent attacks on teachers and children. Jill died in the middle of a struggle to preserve the special needs work with Jane, a colleague and friend, against some of the immediate effects of the National Curriculum. The only forewarning we (could have) had of her death was a moment of exhaustion and dizziness in school the day before, faced with a class she hadn't taught before and distressed by the erosion of her small-group and individual work. Jill was not, in her school context, in any way a victim, but I am sure that government policies contributed to her dying, just as they have driven many other teachers out of the profession through illness, exhaustion and the destruction or undermining of their work.

The other story I tell myself about inequalities beyond the grave is that I can or must speak *about* Jill but not *for* her. It may seem that the poems sometimes breach this rule. It is hard to separate the process of 'speaking for . . .' from the process of 'speaking about yourself in relation to . . .' Speaking about myself in relation to Jill seemed an important thing to do. Where I do take Jill's voice rather than just wish she could speak to me as in 'A Hateful Dialogue in One Voice Only', I hope it is clearly understood that it is always me – *my* version of *her* voice in *my* head – that I am trying to represent. The poem is a version of an inner dialogue, my doubled and still troubled hating. This is most obviously so, when at the end of the poem, I make Jill's dead body speak to me.

Questions towards an historical perspective

It may be worth trying to put this individual story into a larger historical context. One difficulty with this is that it may seem like a search for exoneration, for a counter-narrative to that of responsibility or guilt. There are other counter-narratives too which are important but which I have not explored here – though they are present in some of the poems: the representation of Jill, for example, not as a victim but as a woman who made her own choices.

Understanding the larger context need not be a form of exoneration. It does seem important to understand my own actions and the intensity of Jill's pain. Contextualizing the personal in this way also allows for thinking aloud about alternative patterns and behaviours. Of course, an analysis of gender inequalities provides a lot of purchase on the events that informed 'Fragments from Loving Two Women' and the much longer poem sequence from which this version is drawn. It was I who made the break, changed the balance of power between Jill and me in my favour. I did claim the right to satisfy my own needs, if necessary at her (immediate) expense. Yet it seems important to understand why I chose this particular solution and why it was so painful for Jill. In many ways this remains another uncompleted project for me, but I can at least ask the questions.

What kind of marriage and coupledom did Jill and I enter into in 1963, in 'the Age of Marriages'? Although I have not read deeply about the surrounding sexual culture of this period[7] I have a strong sense that marriage was strongly sexualized. Sexuality was central, for both man and woman, as part of an ideal of 'companionate' marriage. Perhaps it was central primarily for the husband and the many male commentators on marriage, but women's sexuality (however subordinated) was also recognized in ways it had not been before. At the same time, there was no coherent gender critique which was easily available to us in 1963, still less a critique of heterosexuality. This meant that such couple relationships, especially if pursued rather 'seriously' without even an average sense of irony, could be very intense and all-encompassing. I am sure I produced myself at the time as this kind of 'intense' young man, deeply invested in an intimacy centred on sexuality. Another comment on the poetry sequence which made me think hard was that it presented a relationship that was not only intense, but also very individualized, with few or no other characters on the emotional scene for most of the time. Family, friends, and even children were at best on the margins. Of course, in writing the poems, as in the grieving process itself, I deliberately focused on Jill, but perhaps that was itself a very significant choice, not a necessity. The nature of our marriage on my side was certainly connected with my own class, race and ethnic background, my own particular kind of white English middle classness. A very isolated home life as a child produced a very focused set of intimacies, sharply marked off from a public world of work and school. Those familiar with contemporary Conservative ideologies of 'the family' (and who is not!) will recognize some of its impossible inner dynamics.

I believe that the emotional/sexual condensation of our relationship, or of my version of it, made solutions to unmet needs, for both of us, very difficult. Perhaps the clearest indication of this was my own madnesses and strategies around intimacy. Rather than seeking, as I would today, recognition through different forms of friendship, I sought one other relationship in which sexuality figured, for me, as a main focus of intimacy. In other words I sought two 'marriages', since 'marriage' was really the only acceptable model of intimate relations that I had or knew how to 'live'. This bigamous solution, which was not secret, was a frightening thing to face.

'Allying otherwise': negotiating gay and lesbian identities.

As I suggested in Chapter 1, discussions in the Politics of Sexuality Group focused on the critique of heterosexuality, but also on another theme: the psychic and personal viability of heterosexual masculine identity. Much of this discussion, as in the essays on school experiences in this volume, focused on the relationships between heterosexual and lesbian and gay identities. I want to end this commentary by looking at this aspect of my grieving.

What is hidden in the poems – because they do focus so much on the heterosexual couple – is that this same period of grieving saw considerable re-investments on my part in relation to lesbian and gay identifications. It's not that I came directly to question my own heterosexual orientation – or if so, only speculatively, or nostalgically perhaps. If heterosexuality was such a treacherous ground, so full of loss, so 'melancholy' in Judith Butler's terms (1993) then an intimate gay relationship seemed attractive. I did tell stories – similar to some of those told in this volume – about homoerotic moments in my life. A story about boarding-school homosexuality, for example, was the focus for discussions in the group about how homoeroticism could, under some circumstances, be articulated to the abuse of power. This promised some insights, not pursued here, about the masculinities of ruling men and the extreme homophobia of English public life.

I have not really recovered nor successfully restored this homosexual self, perhaps because it was itself so much abused at the time. Rather I found myself adopting patterns of close friendship, political alliance and intellectual comradeship with lesbians or gay men or with those who felt more ambiguously than I about their sexuality. Like the process of heterosexual reparation, this pattern predated Jill's death but it seemed to gain force afterwards. One aspect of this was that 'lesbian and gay issues' came to inform my intellectual agenda to a much greater extent than they had before. Another was that I chose eventually to live in a household that was 'mixed' in sexual (and other) terms, not organized only around the heterosexual couple, and negotiating the gay/straight boundary on a daily basis.

The offers of friendship which surrounded me in this period did constitute a re-ordering of an emotional kind. 'Friendship' was also an explicit theme in our discussions of alternative patterns of intimacy in the Politics of Sexuality Group. I related very positively to the strand in our discussion that embraced friendships, of many different kinds, and with a more or less erotic character, as an alternative to coupledom, or as some transformative accompaniment to it. My relationships with several members of the group were important at this stage, partly because they were not, or did not seem to be, strongly sexual. All this amounted, for me, to a new investment in friendship, something which I realized I had always craved but rarely achieved. It may be that friendship, expanded and more fully recognized, is the most important answer to that over-committed, impossible intimacy that is so lethal a feature of marriage and 'the family'.

Notes

1. I am grateful to all members of the Politics of Sexuality Group for contributing to the dialogues out of which this commentary arose, especially to Deborah Steinberg (additionally for her valuable comments on the first draft), Debbie Epstein, Peter Redman, Máirtín Mac an Ghaill, Libby Kerr, Adrian Kear and David Abdi. Thanks also to editors and readers at Cassell for comments on early versions of the poems. I am also grateful to Mariette Clare who engaged with different versions, wrote replies to some parts of the poetry sequence and gave support and advice on some of the most difficult bits of the commentary. Thanks, finally, to my co-editors for suggesting I write this commentary.

2. Generally, I am influenced here by those (mainly poststructuralist) approaches to identity that also draw on the contemporary cultural re-reading of different schools of psychoanalysis. Some of the most interesting writing here, often named 'Queer Theory', explore and question the hetero/homo boundary and associated cultural binaries. My own approach has been especially influenced by Sedgwick, 1985, 1994a, b; Dollimore, 1991; Butler, 1990, 1993. But important too are texts which are not centrally about sexuality, especially Stallybrass and White, 1986; Bhabha, 1994; Rutherford, 1990.

3. I am especially grateful to Joyce Canaan, Mariette Clare, Bob Bennett,

Debbie Epstein, Jennifer Johnson, Iris Johnson, Malcolm Johnson, Maureen McNeil, Peter Redman, John Risdon, Judith Ross, David Ross, Jackie Stacey, Deborah Steinberg, Bob West, June Wheeler, Bill Wheeler and Lesley Whitehouse for support over this period.

4. I am especially grateful to Bernadette Collins for a discussion around the different circumstances of our partners' deaths.

5. For discussions of AIDS and the politics of death see Michael Bronski, 'Death and the Erotic Imagination' in Carter and Watney (eds), 1989. Examples of gay or queer creativity in matters of grieving include the Quilt Project , alternative funerals or commemoration ceremonies and many forms of writing. See, for example, the obituary for Michael Lynch in Sedgwick, 1994: 252–66 and the collection of writing by Black American gay men (Hemphill, 1991); esp. the poems, letters and stories in 'Hold Tight, Gently ' 108–64. I am grateful to Bob Bennett for this reference.

6. These formulations are strongly influenced by my reading of Jessica Benjamin's discussions of recognition, domination and the erotic (See esp. Benjamin, 1990).

7. See, however, for the position of women in this period Wilson (1980) and for masculine dilemmas Ehrenreich (1983) and Segal (1990).

References

Benjamin, J. (1990) *The Bonds of Love: Psychoanalysis, Feminism and the Problem of Domination*. London: Virago.

Bhabha, H. K. (1994) *The Location of Culture*. London: Routledge.

Bronski, M. (1989) Death and the erotic imagination, in Carter, E. and Watney S. (eds), *Taking Liberties: AIDS and Cultural Politics*. London: Serpent's Tail.

Butler, J. (1990) *Gender Trouble: Feminism and the Subversion of Identity*. London: Routledge.

Butler, J. (1993) *Bodies That Matter*. London: Routledge.

Dollimore, J. (1991) *Sexual Dissidence: Augustine to Wilde, Freud to Foucault*. Oxford: Clarendon Press.

Ehrenreich, B. (1983) *The Hearts of Men*. London: Pluto Press.

Hemphill, E. (1991) *Brother to Brother: New Writings By Black Gay Men*. Boston: Alyson.

Kaplan, L. J. (1995) *Lost Children: Separation and Loss Between Children and Parents*. London: Pandora.

Mars-Jones, A. and White, E. (1988) *The Darker Proof: Stories From a Crisis*. London: Faber.

Mitchell, J. (ed.) (1986) *The Selected Melanie Klein*. London: Penguin.

Rutherford, J. (ed.) (1990) *Identity, Community, Culture, Difference*. London: Lawrence & Wishart.

Sedgwick, E. K. (1985) *Between Men: English Literature and Male Homosocial Desire*. New York: Columbia University Press.

Sedgwick, E. K. (1994a) *Epistemology of the Closet*. London: Penguin.

Sedgwick, E. K. (1994b) *Tendencies*. London: Routledge.

Segal, L. (1990) *Slow Motion: Changing Masculinities, Changing Men*. London: Virago.

Stallybrass, P. and White, A. (1986) *The Politics and Poetics of Transgression*. London: Methuen.

Wilson, E. (1980) *Only Halfway to Paradise: Women in Postwar Britain: 1945–1968*. London: Tavistock.

10

Eating the Other:
Imaging the Fantasy of Incorporation

Adrian Kear

I've always had difficulty with *consommé*. The slightest clumsiness – an over-vigorous whisk, or an impetuous hand on the heat – clouds rather than clarifies and renders inedible a dish that should be delectable. As the muslin bag filters the liquid from the froth, the essence from the remains, it isn't alone in feeling the strain. A tricky thing, *consommé*, requiring more skill than mine for it to turn out perfectly fine.

I've always had difficulty with *consommer*. What is the logic that dictates that a single word should conflate 'to consume' and 'to consummate'? Could there be a yarn to spin from this seemingly innocuous homonym?

> The first stage . . . is the *oral* or, as it might be called, *cannibalistic* pregenital sexual organization. Here sexual activity has not yet been separated from the ingestion of food; nor are opposite currents within the activity differentiated. The *object* of both activities is the same; the sexual aim consists in the *incorporation* of the object – the prototype of the process which, in the form of *identification*, is later to play such an important psychological part. (Freud, 1991 vol. 7, p. 117 [my emphasis])

The lack of differentiation between appetites would appear to be an important *entrée* to the Freudian narrative of psychosexual development. In the opening scenes of the psychoanalytic story the child is assumed to view the world as a fantastic *buffet,* its attempts to eat everything in reach being interpreted as indicative of the insatiability of the pleasure-ego. Moreover, the infant's impulse to insert objects into its mouth, to ingest and incorporate them is understood to represent the expansive imperialism of the psychic domain, with the mouth figured as an orifice of domination that devours the external and destroys its otherness. This appetitive aggression is always ameliorated by ambivalence, however, as the pleasure principle serves to regulate the internalization of the good and the expulsion of the bad.[1] Freud proposes that it is through this process that the child eventually establishes physical and psychic boundaries, with the reality principle enforcing recognition that not everything is ego because objects, even ones that give pleasure, 'are nevertheless not ego but object' (Freud, 1991, vol. 12, p. 255). Hence eating may be considered central to the psychoanalytic account of the formation of subjectivity in that it enables differentiation between inside and outside, self and other.[2] Melanie Klein has suggested that the primary expression of this is the child's relationship to its mother's breast, which it initially believes to be identical with itself. Later, at the point of recognition of its otherness, the child introjects the 'good' breast into its ego and projects the 'bad' object on to the m/other. Klein argues that introjection is a cannibalistic fantasy in which the imaging of sucking, biting, chewing and swallowing the breast comprises the child's representation of internalization (Klein, 1988, pp. 290–91). Metonymic linkage takes a frightening twist here as the fantasy literalizes the breast (and therefore the m/other) *as food*. The combined aims of sexual satisfaction and gustatory gratification are enacted in the desire to devour the object. In this formulation, 'to consume' and 'to consummate' are conspicuously conflated – they come to mean the same thing. Of course, Freud is quick to point out that this is merely a moment in the total *teleos* of identity construction – the meta-narrative of the Oedipus complex demands that orality will be substituted with genitality, hunger will be subsumed into desire, and incorporation will be succeeded by identification. These replacements augment its position as the determining structure in the psychoanalytic framework, ensuring that genitally organized sexual identity remains enshrined as the *sine qua non* of social intelligibility. Correspondingly, the Oedipus complex conserves the hegemony of heterosexuality, privileging it as author, arbiter and achievement of sexual differentiation. But if the construction of identity is dependent on the transition from, or repression of an original orality, how might its dynamics return *within* the dominant structures of heterosexuality?

The practices, processes and fantasies of the early stages of the dramatic development of subjectivity would appear to create borders precisely through transgressing them. The outside is established in the series of misrecognitions which posit it as inside; the self misrecognizes the other as self and itself as other (Lacan, 1989, p. 1–7). If the psychic system of differentiation, separation and borderization operates through the violence of splitting, its repressed remains enter the domain of fantasy. The pleasurable tastes and flavours of the undifferentiated unity of food and sexuality might be re-encountered there, alongside their accompanying aggression. And rather than being totally subsumed into overmastering identification, the fantasy of incorporation might be shown to be of continuing importance in negotiating sexual boundaries.

This chapter seeks to examine fantasies of incorporation as they are manifested in psychoanalytic, cinematic and literary texts. It will continue to explore the ways in which the relationship between consumption and consummation, food and sex, is imaged and imagined within the heterosexually determined symbolic economy. As Susan Isaacs has argued, the majority of unconscious fantasies, whether experienced as sensations or sublimated into plastic images and dramatic representations, are primarily about bodies (Isaacs, 1952, p. 112). The limits of the body are understood to be coextensive with the limits of the self, and therefore psychic crossings of the border between internal and external are invariably enacted as physical transgressions of the boundaries between self and other. The chapter will consider how psychic and physical exchanges are interconnected in the repertoire of images of incorporation, foregrounding an investigation of how cannibalistic desires are literally embodied through the bodies of actors on film.

Perhaps it is worth pointing out that common-sense comprehension of the relationship between food and sex works according to the paradigm of metaphoricity. Hunger and desire, eating and fucking are considered to be alike one another, and because of this similarity they may be substituted in figures of speech. So, to be 'good enough to eat', 'delicious' or 'sweet' is merely to recognize a correspondence between appetites, not a connection. However, the multiplicity of such phrases and images suggests discursive displacement – perhaps the perpetual talking about desire *as* hunger is not a conflation of similarity but an indication of contiguity – metonymy rather than metaphor. Such a frightening recognition would invoke an uncanny recollection of 'what is known of old and long familiar' (Freud, 1991, vol. 14, p. 340) – the inexorable connection of appetites in all-consuming cannibalistic passion. Locating men as the enunciators of this discourse and women as their 'dish' also leads to the realization that heterosexual relationships are inscribed with intransigently violent desires.

However, it would be erroneous to assume that the internalization of objects is always enacted literally. Indeed, in adopting Ferenczi's concept of introjection, Freud acknowledges that, as a psychic mechanism, it is central to the process of ego formation and character development (Freud, 1991, vol. 11. p. 368). Introjection is understood as a process through which the subject performs 'an extension to the external world of the original autoerotic interests, by including its objects in the ego' (Ferenczi, 1980, pp. 316–17). In other words, the subject's primary narcissism includes its relation to objects, and relates to objects by including them in the ego. Introjection therefore enables enlargement of the ego by producing psychic simulations of its objects, and provides a means of negotiating the transactions between conscious and unconscious desires. The subject takes possession of the object by inserting it into its body, by imitating it in its ego, by *incorporating* it. However, according to Maria Torok, introjection and incorporation cannot be seen as coterminous. She maintains that whereas introjection denotes the process of expansion of the ego through possession and imitation of the object, incorporation is a fantasy that compensates for the loss of a love object, most particularly in states of melancholia where introjection has been prevented by the premature removal of that object. Introjection introduces the unconscious, repressed libido into the ego – the drives and desires activated by and articulated to the object are internalized rather than the object itself. Whilst introjection releases repression, incorporation activates it by 'magically' resolving loss through the instant internalization of the lost object into an artificially constructed unconscious or 'tomb'. This 'secret' manoeuvre must remain hidden from the ego and the outside, recuperating the object and masking the failure of introjection. However, the incorporated object continues to testify to loss – both to the loss of the object and to the loss of desires subjected to repression. In imaging the topography of incorporation, Torok suggests that the secret and the object lies buried in an internal 'crypt'. It resides there as a monument to the desires banished from introjection and, moreover, as the site of internment of the other (Torok, 1994, pp. 110–15). Whereas the process of introjection transforms other into self, the fantasy of incorporation preserves the other *as* other in a *secretly maintained topography*. This foreign body remains foreign within the body, 'excluded from a self that thenceforth deals not with the other but only with itself' (Derrida, 1986, p. xvii). A residence of the living dead, the self may become subject to *internal hysteria*. This state, it is argued, is manifested in somatic symptoms, such as constipation, rather than in verbal symbolization (Abraham and Torok, 1986, p. 21). Indeed, resistance to representation is inevitable given that incorporation works as a denial that can never be spoken. Its mechanism is opaque to itself, miming or simulating introjection with one irreconcilable differentiation – implementing literally a procedure that is only meant figuratively. This *anti-metaphorical* activity works in contradistinction to the desire for introjection, which may be seen as a paradigm of language acquisition. In its early stage, the ego is merely the sum of the oral libido's introjections, and is dependent on the repertoire of ingestive expressions (salivating, lip-smacking, vomiting, etc.) as its key mode of communication, regardless of hunger. This rudimentary proto-language articulates emptiness of the mouth as a request for presence, but the desire for introjection is misunderstood as hunger for food. Eating thereby operates as a deceptive sublimation in which literal incorporation masquerades as an illusory introjection (Torok, 1994, p. 115). However, it is the substitutive supplementarity of words which is able to transform hunger into desire in language. The wants of the original oral void are satisfied by their translation into lexical relations and verbal relationships, and the desire for introjection is chanelled and communicated in discourse. The subject is able to negotiate a transition from food to words by recognizing that the object is not present in the mouth but absent, and that language supplements and substitutes absence by giving figurative shape to presence – in representing it (Abraham and Torok, 1994, p. 128). Introjection is therefore central the system of representation – the substitutive economy of metaphor. In resorting to the literal, incorporation acts against metaphor, threatening representation. It does not attempt restoration of the original meaning of words but destroys their capacity for figuration; 'it involves the destruction, in fantasy, of the very act that makes metaphor possible – the act of putting the oral void into words, the act of introjection' (Abraham and Torok, 1980, p. 10). When incorporation is activated in place of introjection, it is because words are unable to express the loss of the object and fail to fill the subject's void, so the unconscious reverts to inserting the imaginary object in their place, thereby denying the loss and appearing to fill the gap. In order to hide the problem, the subject swallows the object and the words associated with it. As a consequence, the experience becomes unnameable – because the words capable of acknowledging loss and expressing desire have themselves been subjected to repression. However, if, as the Lacanian mantra has it, the unconscious is structured like a language, then the meanings of the repressed words will be displaced into other associated words. This *metonymy of words* operates in the cryptic economy through the fragile contiguity of allosemes and their synonyms. The substituted words serve to continue to conceal the unspeakable ones whilst at the same time, of course, opening up the possibility of revealing their repression. Nicholas Abraham and Maria Torok have coined these *cryptonyms,* 'because of their allusion to a foreign or arcane meaning'. (1986, pp. 18–19). That the function of these words is to hide suggests that the excluded, taboo words are accredited the status of representing repressed *things.* As such, they may also become articulated to objects, external embodiments of the desire contained and maintained by language. In other words, an object of desire is a *fetish* concealing (and revealing) the objectification of the fantasy of incorporation.

Drawing on this innovative revision of the metapsychology of mourning and melancholia, Judith Butler has argued that incorporation is a key mechanism in the formation of gender identities – identities that may be understood to have profoundly melancholic structures (Butler, 1989, pp. 57–72). In seeing incorporation as an early prototype for identification, Freud refuses to recognize their continuing connectedness in negotiating the taboos against incest and homosexuality. The Oedipal drama, that meta-narrative of producing identity by means of identification, serves to repudiate primary objects of desire and to regulate future practices of desire within a matrix of compulsory heterosexuality. Its prohibitions present the ego with the loss of a love object – a loss that it attempts to recuperate by the magic of incorporation. Although the logic of the complex is already gendered and sexualized, the proposition of primary bisexuality questions the determinacy of the process. If, to continue to take the male child as the privileged subject in this scenario, the boy's object cathexis is the mother, he is forced to abandon it because of the threat of castration embodied by the rival father. The ensuing identification with the father ensures that it is merely the object and not the aim that is subjected to repression – the incorporation of the mother facilitates the direction of desire for the other. However, even Freud doubts that the cathexis is of determining significance, making it clear that the boy is not only choosing between sexual objects but between sexual *dispositions,* between masculine and feminine (heterosexual and homosexual) (Freud, 1991, vol. 11, p. 372). Identification with the father involves consolidation and adoption of the masculine, whilst the feminine is prohibited from introjection (but is also capable of consolidation in the formation of the super-ego if the subject refutes the heterosexual aim and object in a 'negative' dissolution of the complex). Moreover, if the object-cathexis is homosexual, then both the object and the aim are repudiated and repressed. In both instances the relationship between the dual procedures of internalization is clear – identification acts as an introjection into the ego and is central in the subsequent creation of the super-ego, whilst incorporation provides a means of rescuing and resuscitating the lost objects and desires in a fantasmatic 'crypt'. In this way 'gender identification is a kind of melancholia in which the sex of the prohibited object is internalized as a prohibition. This prohibition sanctions and regulates discrete gender identity and the law of heterosexual desire' (Butler, 1989, p. 63). Butler extends this argument to include the foundational dispositions that Freud appears to take for granted, pointing out that they are themselves produced by the internalization of a culturally constructed prohibitionary law. And, as Foucault has observed, this law institutes the discursive production of the repressive hypothesis both to naturalize its genealogy as teleology (especially in the fiction of pre-discursive original dispositions transformed by taboo) and to mask its positivity in reifying power as prohibition (Foucault, 1979). Therefore, in appearing to police homosexuality, the repressive dynamic effectively produces hetero-sexuality as its effect. Moreover, the range of its discursive effects include the delimiting of desire and the distinguishing of the speakable from the unspeakable (Butler, 1989, p. 65). The domain of the unspeakable might be conceived as concomitant with the 'encryptment' instigated by the fantasy of incorporation. As an antimetaphorical activity, incorporation seeks to literalize discursivity, to turn it into corporeality. The body thereby becomes the site of signification of gender difference, localizing its specificities in the body parts accorded the privilege of sexual pleasure (Butler, 1989, p. 70). Accordingly, desire is literally configured as the desire of, and for, parts of the body. For the melancholic male heterosexual, the championing of the penis as the organ of virulent masculinity continues to mask the fact that it is the locus of the lost paternal cathexis, and the displacement of desire onto the woman-as-fetish-object effectively conceals his unspeakable history of homosexuality (Butler, 1989, p. 71–2).

The foregoing analysis suggests that the fantasy of incorporation is literalized on, in and as the body. In addition, it provides an interesting inflection to the Lacanian contention that desire for the other is identification with the Other, in which identification is resolved by incorporation and desire is displaced onto an *objet petit a* ('a' object here standing in for the other [lower case 'a' – *autre*]). As a literalizing fantasy, incorporation resists representation, hiding its history in the crypt of corporeality. But where in the body does it literalize itself? Obviously in the mouth, the contradictory orifice of internalization (food) and externalization (words). Both activities are inexorably linked to the expression of desire, either through somatization or symbolization. The fantasy of incorporation may be literalized in kissing, biting, sucking, licking, chewing, etc., or, given its status *as* fantasy, emerge as literalization *within* representation. The most immediate configuration of this tension is inscribed in the staging of the body, and the interaction between bodies, as an apparently literal activity. Film form in particular privileges corporeal codes to create its illusory reality, its syntagmatic structure depending on polysemic dramatization rather than prosaic description to demonstrate its literal significance. Paradoxically, literary accommodation of the anti-metaphorical fantasy of incorporation resides in its translation into metaphor, which remains its status no matter how literally it is enacted within representation. However, this need not preclude the possibility of literary metaphors of incorporation sliding to signify the literal metonymy of incorporation. The presentation of the woman-as-sign within hegemonic heterosexual regimes of representation occupies the primary site of convergence of this rather cryptic contradiction, which could be usefully unpacked by looking at texts that encode its problematic in terms of the relationship between food and sex.

The narrative of *Tampopo* (Juzo Itami, Japan, 1990) might provide some clarification. The film follows the title character's acquisition of competence as a noodle chef, learning the arts of noodle rolling and soup steaming, as well as appreciation of the aesthetics of the eating event, conducted under the attentive tuteledge of an array of expert men. Ostensibly the story traces the trajectory of Tampopo's career after her husband's death to show the emergence of women's equality in domains of employment traditionally occupied by men. However, the narrative structure includes a series of non-diegetic scenic inserts that indirectly qualify and question the main plot. These present different configurations of food and sexuality, encouraging the reader to frame the whole film in this way. Indeed, the film opens with a gangster and his moll attending the cinema replete with a luscious feast. His direct address to the camera observes that going to the cinema is both a sexual and gastronomic event. Whilst the former has been extensively elucidated by feminist film theory, the latter only figures in the rhetoric of consumption, the implication being that the viewer pays to eat the film. This suggests that spectatorship is itself a modality of internal-ization, the projected image being introjected into the viewer's subjective domain. In devouring the film, the spectator's scopohilia mediates his incorporative desire for the object occupying the place of the other within the screen space. The edibility of the image is therefore commensurate with its desirability – which inevitably reinscribes the dominant cinematic relation of the male gaze on the female body. In other words, the gangster's invitation to eat the film is effectively an interpellation of the audience into the eating of the other represented within the film. Correspondingly, the dual pleasures of spectatorship are insistently staged in the sub-scenes of *Tampopo* as interconnected erotic practices. The first narrative intervention features the gangster couple in a hotel-room sex scene. In a rapidly cut sequence a series of oral tropes are montaged to present playful *jouissance*. The naked woman has her ear bitten, her armpit licked and her fingers fellated by the clothed man. He sprinkles her nipple with salt, squeezes lemon juice on to it and then sucks the tit tequila on to his lips. An instant cut repeats the scene with whipped cream, another breast being dipped before being licked. The subsequent image is of sticky syrup being forced through lips clenched by fingers to be licked up by a rapacious tongue. This simulation of *cunny* [*sic*] *lingus* is succeeded by more penetrative imagery as an enormous king prawn swills around in a glass bowl filled with brandy that is held inverted on the woman's stomach. Her writhing is an ambivalent mix of amusement and abhorrence. In its analogical appearance, connoting oral sex through parallel oral activities, the sequence is reminiscent of a similar scene in $9\frac{1}{2}$ *Weeks* (Adrian Lyne, USA, 1988). This stages a series of oral penetrations and liquid ingestions in which food is used as an agent of erotic domination. The Micky Rourke character instructs the woman played by Kim Bassinger to lie on the floor by the fridge and to keep her eyes closed. He proceeds to insert various foodstuffs in to her pouting, willing mouth. An olive, cherries, and a strawberry are followed by a sip of wine. Vicks VapoRub is an unappetizing prelude to pasta and jelly, but the chilli desert is too hot for her to take. She gulps down a glass of cold milk, the seminal liquid spilling out of the sides of her mouth to produce a facial cum shot. Perrier water is also ejaculated over her, but then the emissions are concentrated into a rich syrup poured into her mouth, over her skin and between her thighs. The man's lips and tongue are the final insertions into her mouth as the scene is cut away to a morning-after bed. The final shot presents syntagmatically what has previously been suggested paradigmatically – that the fridge game substitutes for and supplements sexual play. Obviously, both sequences work through a metaphorical economy, with the food imagery connoting that which cannot be directly represented: oral sex. However, whilst the scene in $9\frac{1}{2}$ *Weeks* is consistent with its narrative of male sexual domination enacted through games playing, the *Tampopo* insert encodes another set of desires. As a literal representation, the sequence suggests metonymical linkage of food and sex rather than simple metaphorical substitution. Contextualized relative to the narrative in which Tampopo is trying to satisfy men through food, the sequence exposes the contiguity connecting these appetites and pleasures. Accordingly, Tampopo attains sexual attractiveness as she achieves culinary competence. Other non-diegetic scenes develop the motif further. An old woman terrorizes a deserted supermarket by vigorously fondling fruit, cheese and pastries, her tactile transgressions evading the suspicious shop assistant. The gangster couple return in a quick clip that shows them passing an egg yolk between their mouths until it is torn by the woman's teeth, dripping down across her chin. The brief exchange expresses the fragility of fecundity and, more particularly, positions the woman as threatening castration. The trope is extremely familiar, intertextualizing with, for example, George Bataille's novella *Story of the Eye,* in which an equivalence emerges between eggs, eyes and bollocks as they all become subject to the heroine's incorporative desires. The episode entitled 'Granero's Eye' takes place at a bullfight in which Simone has been promised the delicacy of the slaughtered animal's *huevos:*[3]

> In just a few seconds: first, Simone bit into one of the raw balls, to my dismay; then Granero advanced towards the bull, waving his scarlet cloth; finally, almost at once, Simone, with a blood-red face and a suffocating lewdness, uncovered her long white thighs up to her moist vulva, into which she slowly and surely fitted the second pale globule – Granero was thrown back by the bull and wedged against the balustrade; the horns struck the balustrade three times at full speed; at the third blow, one horn plunged into the right eye and through the head. A shriek of unmeasured horror coincided with a brief orgasm from Simone, who was lifted up from the stone seat only to be flung back with a bleeding nose, under a blinding sun; men instantly rushed over to haul away Granero's body, the right eye dangling from the head (Bataille, 1982, p. 53).

The removal of the eye as a metaphor of castration is consolidated in the text when Simone removes the eye of the priest she has throttled whilst fucking and inserts it into her vagina. Bataille's text is clearly cognisant of Freud's claim that eyes substitute for testes in castration anxiety (Freud, 1991, vol. 14, p. 352), and his contention that all fetishes are a displacement of this fundamental complex (Freud, 1991, vol. 7, pp. 352–7). The image of the *vagina dentata* in *Tampopo* again features the gangster. He meets a beautiful young oyster diver with a fresh catch. She opens a shell for him but in attempting to swallow the meat he cuts himself on the sharp edges. To ameliorate the danger she places the contents in her hands and, holding them waist high, allows him to drink from the cup. The metonymy of food and sex represents the woman as an edible fetish, with the man's fear of incorporation and castration being projected onto the object and generating his desire to consume it. Correlatively, Tampopo's credibility is linked to her edibility – and the representation of woman as food is confirmed in the final image of primary satisfaction, a baby boy sucking his mother's breast.

This iconography is replayed in *Jamón Jamón* (Bigas Luna, Spain, 1992), despite the claims of the advertising that announces it as 'a film where women eat men and men eat ham'. Predictably, it is the men who eat the women and the ham. Both Sylvia's boyfriends are crazy about sucking her tits. When she asks José Luis why he likes 'eating' them, he replies that 'I like . . . the way they taste', but he is unable to describe their flavour. However, his rival Raúl, Sylvia's true-love, is capable of putting his passion into discourse. With his head buried in her breasts he is able to apprehend the flavours that Sylvia had anticipated – 'Ham. Potato omelette . . . with onion . . . and garlic'. His taste is again questioned as a bewildered Sylvia wonders why he is going down on her. 'Because I want to eat you' is his direct response. The sexual violence implicit in this articulation of appetitive aggression is explicitly enacted in *Kika* (Pedro Almodóvar, Spain, 1993). The title character is raped by an escaped convict, the ordeal being initiated by his insertion of a mandarin segment into her sleeping body, which he then savours as a slice of the forbidden fruit he is about to consume. His rapacious appetite subjects Kika to a series of violations, objectifying her into meat and drink for his viciously heterosexual desire.

Like Water for Chocolate (Alfonso Arau, Mexico, 1992) offers a slightly different take on this figuration of sex in terms of food, translating sexual appetite into culinary experience. A sentimental love story, the film follows the unconsummated love of Tita and Pedro, prevented from marrying by Doña Elena's insistence that tradition precludes the youngest daughter from anything other than a dutiful servility to her mother. Frustrated by this intransigence, Pedro expediently accepts an offer of marriage to Rosaura, Tita's older sister, believing that it is the only way to secure proximity to the woman he loves. Unaware of the intricacy of his infidelity, Tita is thrown into an unendurable melancholia, lamenting the loss of her love and transposing the coldness inside onto the external world in the form of an endlessly enveloping quilt. Her pain is exacerbated by her mother's cruelty, who responds to her sadness by giving her the responsibility of preparing the wedding banquet. The night before the wedding, still labouring in the kitchen, she is unable to prevent her tears from falling into the cake batter. The liquid flavours the cake with essence of melancholy, and the effect on the wedding celebrations is dramatic. On eating the cake everyone undergoes a strange transformation, their mirth giving way to misery and a violent mourning for lost loves. Food operates as Tita's mode of expression, its emotional effectivity consisting in the ability to produce identification through internalization. Therefore, although the possibility of Tita and Pedro's love being sexually consummated is precluded by the policy of his marriage and the policing of her mother, Tita is able to turn their consumption of food into a divine communion, the tender morsels transubstantiating as they cross the borders of their bodies. The crucial ingredient in this exchange is mutuality, manifested in the return of the roses given to Tita by Pedro in the dish 'Quails in Rose-petal Sauce'. The camera tracks across the dinner table, displaying the beauty of the culinary *mise en scène* before a reverse angle shot pans up to frame Pedro's face as he takes his first mouthful of breast meat. His ecstatic expression is accompanied by idyllic non-diegetic music and augmented by the cut to Gertrudis' equally enraptured face. Eyeline matches connect the cuts to Doña Elena, Tita and finally Rosaura, who, unable to appreciate the flavour, merely plays with the food on her plate. The camera returns to Pedro, whose engorged lips proclaim that 'this is nectar of the gods'. A suspicious look is exchanged between Rosaura and her mother before Doña Elena damningly declares 'it's too salty', and her daughter excuses herself from the table with an upset stomach. The camera continues to frame orgasmic eating as the narration interjects:

> A strange kind of alchemy had occurred. Not only Tita's blood . . . but her whole being had . . . dissolved into the rose sauce . . . into the flesh of the quails . . . and into every aroma of the dish. She entered Pedro's body . . . voluptuous, fragrant, ardent and utterly sensual. They had discovered . . . a new way of communicating . . . in which Tita was the sender . . . Pedro the recipient . . . and Gertrudis the lucky one in whom . . . this sexual encounter was synthesized through the meal.[4]

Magical realism takes over as Gertrudis rushes to the wooden washroom and strips to shower, emitting rose-perfumed steam from her naked body. The scene is intercut with revolutionary bandits fighting government soldiers, and the scent of Gertrudis captivates the rebel leader who rides towards its source. Her heat climaxes with the washroom catching fire, Gertrudis running out into the arms of the oncoming man. The tender white flesh of the quails is too much for any man to resist, and their magically metonymical power transforms Gertudis into an equally enticing dish. White women's flesh becomes the favoured flavour, the rose-petal fragrance barely concealing the deathly desires of the heterosexual romance.

The ability of culinary creativity to engender excessive trans-formation is a major concern of the puritan sisters in *Babette's Feast* (Gabriel Axen, Denmark, 1987). They fear that the plans of the French woman who has lodged with them since fleeing the Commune to repay their hospitality with a proper French dinner border on the daemonic. The inventory of incredible ingredients to be supplied by her nephew leads the sisters to believe that they are witnessing preparations for a 'witches' sabbath'. Their anxiety is fuelled by the impropriety of sensual excess at an event held to commemorate and celebrate their father, a puritan preacher and their village's spiritual leader. They confide their concerns to their guests, agreeing in advance that no one shall think or speak of the food they eat and the wine they drink, thereby repressing in advance the possibility of being overcome by their repast. However, an additional, unexpected guest frustrates their taciturn tactics. The General, nephew of one of the faithful and once suitor to one of the sisters, is a welcome presence at their table. He is astounded by the splendour and sophistication of the dishes presented to him, lauding their quality to his silent companions. He recognizes the *caille en sarcophage*[5] as the distinctive creation of the female chef at the famous *Café Anglais* in Paris. He eulogizes:

> General Gallifet, who was our host for the evening . . . explained that this woman, this head chef . . . had the ability . . . to transform the dinner into a kind of love affair . . . A love that made no distinction . . . between bodily appetite and spiritual appetite. General Gallifet said that in the past . . . he had fought a duel for the love of a beautiful young woman. But now there was no woman in Paris . . . for whom he would shed his blood . . . except for this chef.

The point is not lost on the congregation, nor is the effect of Babette's cooking. The sisters fondly remember their lost loves, and the guests confess their trespasses, forgiving and blessing one another. In producing this state of sated spirituality, Babette's feast meets the words of the puritan pastor: 'righteousness and bliss shall kiss one another'. The food serves as a holy heterosexual sacrament, sweetening the melancholia of loss with the illusion of remembrance.

Communion enacted through consumption returns in the symmetrical structure of *Like Water for Chocolate*. Tita's tragic life is enlivened by the ellipsis that enables her niece Esperanza to marry despite the fact that Rosaura had wanted to follow the family tradition of sibling slavery. Her death also reopens the route of sexual consummation for Pedro and Tita. The wedding is much happier than its predecessor, largely because the stuffed chillies with nut sauce and pomegranate incite everyone into a fervour of sexual desire that demands instant gratification. The older couple take their time however, and, completely alone for the first time, they make love in a candle-lit barn. The deferred delirium is too much for Pedro who dies *in flagrante*. Tita, remembering her doctor's metaphor for Nirvana, decides to take it literally and to internalize inedibly magic matches that ignite her insides and free her to follow her love to the bliss of unification through annihilation (Freud, 1991, vol. 11, p. 329).

This end is perhaps the inevitable extreme of heterosexual fantasies of incorporation. Freud argues that when the pleasure principle is subsumed into the death instinct it is because the Nirvana's dissolving *jouissance* marks the end of desire, a return to the originary unity shattered by the violence of splitting. The closure of the psychoanalytic narrative occurs as the desire generated by identification and the corresponding melancholia guaranteed by incorporation are resolved through a deathly recombination. The repeated attempts of male heterosexuals to foreclose this end and to achieve unification through assimilating the parts of the self alienated in the other appear to be literalized in incorporative fantasies combining food and sex. The four bourgeois protagonists of *La Grande Bouffe* (Marco Ferreri, Italy, 1973) enter into an agreement to eat themselves to death, believing that this mode of excess will guarantee the success of ending in a blissful Nirvana. Marcello insists that this cannot be effected without sex, and decides to present three prostitutes as his contribution to the feast. However, the real sustenance is provided by Andrea, a school teacher co-opted into the gluttonous fraternity. Whilst the other women are literally sickened by the scene, Andrea revels in it, becoming the flavour of the moment. A plate of pasta is garnished with a paste inscribing her name, and her arse is used as a caste for an impressively voluptuous *tarte*. Andrea becomes the agent of the men's bliss, fucking and feeding them until they reach their ends. The last to go is Hugo, who is fed an enormous pink *blancmange* in the shape of Andrea's breasts. The woman as food, sex as death fantasy could not be clearer than in this film's pornographic imagery. But the metonymical linkage enacted within the film is nevertheless contained by the film's metaphorical status *as film* – it is always already a substitute for a referential reality ineluctably beyond its own diegesis. Actual transgression of the *metaphoricity* of eating the other instantly reveals the power relations immanent within this aggressively narcissistic fantasy – that aggrandizement of the male ego has as its condition the annihilation of the female other.

However, this does not preclude the possibility of a reverse fantasy in which the self is consumed by the other. Tennessee Williams' short story 'Desire and the Black Masseur' presents this as a narrative of atonement, the white man desiring subjection at the hands of his racial other. His pleasure is proportionate to the violence of his partner's blows, and culminates in the ecstasy of being eaten by him. After licking the bones clean, the black man ponders: 'Yes, it is perfect, . . . it is now completed!' (Williams, 1988, p. 211). The racialization of the cannibalistic other is, of course, a trope imported from the hysterical stereotypings of colonial discourse that translate desirable difference into fearful otherness. But Williams' text eschews such ambivalent transpositions, literalizing the white man's fantasy of being annihilated and assimilated by the Black Masseur. Such totemic atonement is enacted as an elaborate ritual of mourning in the textual transgressions of Jean Genet's *Funeral Rites*. The author's narrative voice champions becoming other ('blacker than the blacks') in order incorporate his lost lover (Genet, 1990, p. 180), the manoeuvre inevitably culminating in a consuming consummation:

> To eat a youngster shot on the barricades, to devour a young hero, is no easy thing. We all love the sun. My mouth is bloody. So are my fingers. I tore the flesh to shreds with my teeth. Corpses do not usually bleed. His did. (p. 12)

The image of the melancholic male homosexual as a figure of fear and disgust recurs in the anatomy of projection and displacement that characterizes heterosexuality's fascination with the fantasy of incorporation. The vampire is perhaps the most graphic incarnation of this preoccupation. For example, *Nosferatu the Vampyre* (Werner Herzog, Germany, 1979) presents vampirism as an uncontrollable desire that condemns the afflicted creature to be torn between its repression and its indulgence. The morbidity that characterizes the condition is directly inherited from late nineteenth-century discourses of sexuality. Their association of non-procreative practices and psycho-pathic proclivities is carefully encoded in the emergence of the new species of 'the homosexual' (Foucault, 1979, p. 43) and his representational relative 'the vampire'. The latter's deadly lust for blood does not differentiate between genders in its object choice, and thereby threatens to penetrate the borders of heterosexuality and the boundaries of the male body. Moreover, the terrible teeth that somatically symbolize the vampire's phallic power are merely organs in an all-consuming buccal orifice, an horrifically hermaphroditic *vagina dentata* that sucks the life and soul from the victims inserted into it. The possibility of becoming mere fodder to service such rapacious appetites motivates the homophobic panic mobilized in Herzog's portrayal of vampiric hospitality. In the *mise en scène* of the banqueting suite, the cornucopia of fruits and food furnished for the guest contrasts sharply with the emaciated presence of his host. The unpalatable pallidness of his appearance is reflected in the lifelessness of the food: chicken, green apples, white grapes – even the wine is insipidly clear. As Harker consumes the colourless cuisine, Nosferatu's fixed gaze upon him suggests that he is next on the food chain. Looking up to meet this lacerative look, Harker cuts through the bread to his thumb. Apparently concerned by the possibility of the wound infecting him with blood poisoning, the count offers to suck it for him. Harker's objection merely obviates the eventual engorgement, with the wan figure contemplating his hunger before acting on his desire. Harker's panic-stricken reaction is met with the enticement that 'you know its for the best', but the vampiric seducer resists taking it further. The protagonist's homophobic horror suggests that the fantasmatic figure is a projection of heterosexual masculinity's encrypted homosexual desires. They appear to return in the shape of the male vampire who threatens to devour the subject, to subject *him* to an incorporated existence within a dreadful tomb. The construction of the monstrous other as a morbid melancholic is also racially inflected, with Nosferatu's physicality reminiscent of the grotesque stereotype of Jewishness embodied by Max Schreck in the source film, *Nosferatu: A Symphony of Horror* (F. W. Murnau, Germany, 1922). The ghostly foreigner personifies the 'corpse buried in the other' that comes back to haunt the subject's own unspeakable history of incorporation that has encrypted a foreign body in the vaults of the self (Abraham, 1994, pp. 171–6). The phobia induced by the appearance of the phantom is a displacement of the denial that the body is already a residence of the living dead, the site of the internment of homosexual desire effected by the magic of incorporation. The reverse fantasy of being incorporated by the other is frequently imaged as an ambivalent combination of fear and desire, particularly in the commercialized cinematic productions that reinscribe the vampire narrative with heterosexual determinacy. A case in point is *Bram Stoker's Dracula* (Francis Ford Coppola, USA, 1992), which represses the novel's homoerotic subtext and resuscitates its conventional narrative of heterosexual romance. Harker's initial encounter with the vampire is completely desexualized – the cavernous castle dining room precludes proximity and the nearest Harker comes to being cut is when he is violently confronted with the end of Dracula's enormous sword. Instead the erotic threat to Harker emanates from three insatiable vampettes who appear to embody his normative fantasy of being consumed in group sex. Their oral attentions become increasingly furious and as one of them prepares to fellate him her fangs emerge to enact a fantastic castration. Fortunately Dracula intercedes and prohibits this engorgement, offering his minions the small compensation of sharing a succulent child. This uncanny inversion of the woman's relation to the infant, which features the former feeding on the latter rather than vice-versa, is repeated in Lucy's honeymoon tomb. After her alliance with Dracula has been consummated, Lucy's fiancés and former suitors resolve to remove her vampiric status before her virgin teeth taste their first blood. However, once in the crypt they discover that the coffin is uncovered and the body exhumed. Lucy's serpentine figure approaches Arthur, tempting him to 'come to me', but the bloodstained baby hanging by her breast attracts his more urgent attention. This travesty of traditional maternity assuages his conscience in assisting Dr Van Helsing to perform the annihilation of Lucy through staking and beheading. This dual strategy of penetration and castration enables the men to resolve their ambivalent relationship to the monstrous other, and to recuperate the acquired phallic power of the female vampire back into the homosocial order. This point is nicely illustrated by the graphic match that cuts from Lucy's severed head to a joint of rare red meat about to be enjoyed by Van Helsing's fraternity – men are reinstated as the eaters, women the eaten. However, Lucy had only ever operated as a object of exchange between men and, although Coppola's film does its best to obscure it, her vampiric seducer remains the over-riding threat to heterosexual masculinity. The exigencies of conventional closure ensures that the men inevitably overcome their fantasmatic adversary, reducing him, and the history of incorporation embodied by him, to dust. But we know that the specter of incorporated homosexuality is bound to come back to haunt its heterosexual hosts.[6]

The final offering in this selection of representations of incorporation is from Italo Calvino's *Under the Jaguar Sun,* served as an afterword to prevent melancholic male heterosexuals being put off their food:

> Meanwhile I understood: my mistake with Olivia was to consider myself eaten by her, whereas I should be myself (I always had been) the one who ate her. The most appetizingly flavoured human flesh belongs to the eater of human flesh. It was only by feeding ravenously on Olivia that I would cease being tasteless to her palate. (1993, p. 26)

This recipe has all the ingredients for a successful straight *consommé*.

Notes

1. Expressed in the language of the oldest – the oral – instinctual impulses, the judgement is: 'I should like to eat this,' or 'I should like to spit it out'; and, put more generally: 'I should like to take this into me and keep that out'. That is to say: 'It shall be inside me' or 'it shall be outside me'. . .The original pleasure-ego wants to introject into itself everything that is good and eject from itself everything that is bad. What is bad, what is alien to the ego and what is external are, to begin with, identical, (Freud, 1991, vol. 11, p. 439).
   All future references to volumes in the *Penguin Freud Library* will be referred to as 'Freud, 1991' followed by the volume number as above.

2. For a more expansive discussion of this point see Ellmann (1993: 29–33).

3. *Huevos* translates as both eggs and balls.
4. The subtitles differ on the commercially released video recording and the networked television presentation. I offer this as a synthetic translation of the original Spanish.
5. Quails again – obviously the sexiest flesh to be found.
6. For a further, and considerably more complex, discussion of spectrality and the uncanny, see Derrida, (1994).

References

Abraham, N. (1994) Notes on the phantom, in Abraham, N. and Torok, M. *The Shell and the Kernel*. Chicago: University of Chicago Press.

Abraham, N. and Torok, M. (1980) Introjection–incorporation: mourning *or* melancholia', in Lebovici and Widlöcher (eds), *Psychoanalysis in France*. New York: International Universities Press.

Abraham, N. and Torok, M. (1986) *The Wolfman's Magic Word: A Cryptonomy*. Minneapolis: University of Minnesota Press.

Abraham, N. and Torok, M. (1994) Mourning *or* melancholia: introjection *versus* incorporation, in *The Shell and the Kernel*. Chicago: University of Chicago Press.

Bataille, G. (1982) *Story of the Eye*. London: Penguin.

Butler, J. (1989) *Gender Trouble: Feminism and the Subversion of Identity*. London: Routledge.

Calvino, I. (1993) *Under the Jaguar Sun*. London: Vintage.

Derrida, J. (1986) *Fors:* The Anglish words of Nicholas Abraham and Maria Torok, in Abraham, N. and Torok, M. *The Wolfman's Magic Word: A Cryptonomy*. Minneapolis: University of Minnesota Press.

Derrida, J. (1994) *Specters of Marx*. London: Routledge.

Ellmann, M. (1993) *The Hunger Artists: Starving, Writing and Imprisonment*. London: Virago.

Ferenczi, S. (1980) *Final Contributions to the Problems and Methods of Psychoanalysis*. New York: Brunner & Mazel.

Foucault, M. (1979) *The History of Sexuality Volume 1: An Introduction*. London: Penguin.

Freud, S. (1991) Fetishism, in vol. 7: *On Sexuality*. London: Penguin, pp. 345–8.

Freud, S. (1991) *Three Essays on the Theory of Sexuality*, in vol. 7: *On Sexuality*. London: Penguin, pp. 33–170.

Freud, S. (1991) *Beyond the pleasure principle*, in vol 11: *On Metapsychology*. London: Penguin

Freud, S. (1991) *The Ego and the Id*, in vol. 11: *On Metapsychology*. London: Penguin, pp. 339–408.

Freud, S. (1991) Negation, in vol. 11: *On Metapsychology*. London: Penguin, pp. 435–42.

Freud, S. (1991) *Civilization and its Discontents*, in vol 12: *Civilization, Society and Religion*. London: Penguin, pp. 243–340.

Freud, S. (1991) The uncanny, in vol 14: *Art and Literature*, London: Penguin, pp. 335–76.

Genet, J. (1990) *Funeral Rites*. London: Faber and Faber.

Isaacs, S. (1952) The nature and function of fantasy in Rivière, J. (ed.) *Developments in Psychoanalysis*. London: Hogarth Press.

Klein, M. (1988) Weaning, in *Love,*

Guilt and Reparation and Other Works 1921–1945. London: Virago.

Lacan, J. (1989) The mirror stage, in *Écrits*. London: Routledge.

Lacan, J. (1993) *The Seminar of Jacques Lacan*. London: Routledge.

Torok, M. (1994) The illness of mourning and the fantasy of the exquisite corpse, in Abraham, N. *The Shell and the Kernel*. Chicago: University of Chicago Press.

Williams, T. (1988) *The Collected Stories of Tennessee Williams*. London: Picador.

Index